Teaching Woodwinds

A Method and Resource Handbook

Teaching Woodwinds

A Method and Resource Handbook

William Dietz, General Editor

Jerry Kirkbride
Hal Ott
Mark Weiger
Craig Whittaker

SCHIRMER
CENGAGE Learning™

Australia • Brazil • Japan • Korea • Mexico • Singapore • Spain • United Kingdom • United States

SCHIRMER
CENGAGE Learning™

**Teaching Woodwinds: A Method
and Resource Handbook**
William Dietz, General Editor
Jerry Kirkbride, Hal Ott, Mark Weiger,
Craig Whittaker

For product information and technology assistance, contact us at
Cengage Learning Customer & Sales Support, 1-800-354-9706
For permission to use material from this text or product,
submit all requests online at **cengage.com/permissions**
Further permissions questions can be emailed to
permissionrequest@cengage.com

Library of Congress Control Number: 97017928

ISBN-13: 978-0-02-864569-8

ISBN-10: 0-02-864569-3

Schirmer
25 Thomson Place
Boston MA 02210
USA

Cengage Learning is a leading provider of customized learning solutions with office locations around the globe, including Singapore, the United Kingdom, Australia, Mexico, Brazil, and Japan. Locate your local office at:
international.cengage.com/region

Cengage Learning products are represented in Canada by Nelson Education, Ltd.

For your course and learning solutions, visit **academic.cengage.com**

Purchase any of our products at your local college store or at our preferred online store **www.ichapters.com**

Printed in the United States of America
11 12 13 14 15 16 17 22 21 20 19 18

Contents

CONTRIBUTORS   ix

PREFACE   xi

PART 1   BASSOON

Chapter 1   Introduction   3
             History   4
             Assembly and Care of the Bassoon   7
             Care and Maintenance   10

Chapter 2   Fundamentals of Bassoon Playing   12
             Breathing   12
             Embouchure   13
             Tonguing   14
             Tone and Vibrato Production   19
             Posture and Hand Positions   21

Chapter 3   The Preparatory Octave   27
             Progressive Exercises in the Preparatory Octave   29
             The Fingering for B♭   31
             Tuning on the Bassoon   32
             Tunes in the Preparatory Octave   33
             The Remaining Notes in the Preparatory Octave   35
             Exercises for Chromatic Notes in the Preparatory Octave   35
             Tunes in the Chromatic Octave   37

Chapter 4   Bassoon Technique   40
             The Half-Hole Notes   40
             Exercises Using the Half Hole   44
             Tunes Using the Half Hole   46
             The Upper Register   47
             Exercises for the Upper Register   48
             The Secondary Break   49
             Exercises for the Secondary Break   49
             Tunes for the Upper Register   49
             Flicking Technique   51
             Exercises for Flicking Practice   55
             Tunes for Flicking Practice   56
             Completing the Second Octave   57
             Exercises in the Second Octave   57
             Tunes in the Second Octave   58

Chapter 5   The Extreme Ranges of the Bassoon   61

Chapter 6   Additional Information   65
    Guidelines for Choosing a Bassoon Student   65
    Choosing a Bassoon   67
    The Bocal   68
    The Reed   69
    Bassoon Supplies   73
    Methods and Study Materials   74
    The Importance of Chamber Music in a Student's Development   75
    *Some Recommended Works for Beginning
        a Wind Quintet Collection*   77
    Books, Journals, and Other Items of Interest   80
    Fingerings on the Bassoon   81

PART 2   CLARINET

Chapter 7   Introduction   91
    History   91
    Assembly of the Clarinet   94
    Care and Maintenance   97

Chapter 8   Fundamentals of Clarinet Playing   99
    Embouchure   99
    Posture and Position   100
    Finger and Hand Positions   101
    Breathing   105
    Tonguing   106

Chapter 9   Technique   110
    The Registers   110
    Learning the Chalumeau (Low) Register   111
    Tunes in the Chalumeau Register   116
    The Remaining Notes in the Chalumeau Register   117
    The Chromatic Scale   119
    Tunes in the Chromatic Chalumeau Register   119
    Learning the Throat Tones   122
    Learning the Clarion (Upper) Register   123
    Lower Break Exercises   124
    The Remaining Notes in the Clarion Register   125
    The Clarion Chromatic Scale   127
    Tunes in the Clarion Register   127
    The Altissimo Register   131
    The Fourth-Finger Keys   133
    Chromatic and Alternate Fingerings   136
    Tuning and Intonation of the Clarinet   140

Chapter 10   Reeds   143
    Choosing Reeds   143
    Reed Placement   144
    Common Reed Problems   144
    Care of Reeds   144

Chapter 11   Additional Information   146
    Choosing a Clarinet   146
    The Mouthpiece   148

Methods and Etudes   148
Selected Repertoire for Clarinet   149
Other Works for Clarinet   151
Selected Works for Clarinet Alone   152
Key Numbers Chart   153
Fingering Chart   153

PART 3   FLUTE

Chapter 12   Introduction   159
History   159
Assembly and Alignment   161
Care and Maintenance   163

Chapter 13   Fundamentals of Flute Playing   166
Breathing   166
Embouchure   167
Tone Production   169
Tonguing   171
Position and Balance   173
Dynamics and Intonation   177
Vibrato   178
Performing on Other Members of the Flute Family   180

Chapter 14   Additional Information   182
Selecting an Instrument   182
Fingerings   183
Exercises and Tunes   194
Literature and Methods   222
Flute Resources   235

PART 4   OBOE

Chapter 15   Introduction   243
History   243
Assembly   244
Care and Maintenance   245
Hand Position   248
Posture   250

Chapter 16   Fundamentals   259
Breathing   259
The Primary Octave   260
Embouchure   266
Articulation   269

Chapter 17   Techniques   271
The Half Hole   271
The Octave Keys   276
Pivoting   281
Alternate Fingerings   281
Tuning   285
Fingering Charts   287

Chapter 18   Reeds   300
            Evaluating Reeds   300
            Troubleshooting Chart   304
            Oboe Reed, Cane, and Tool Suppliers   306

Chapter 19   Selected Repertoire and Materials   311
            Solo Repertoire   311
            Chamber Music   314
            Standard Methods for Oboe   315
            Reference Books   317

Chapter 20   Guidelines   319
            Guidelines for Choosing an Instrument and a Player   319
            Giving Your Oboe a Checkup   321
            Outline of Concepts from the Introductory to the Advanced   322

Chapter 21   Additional Information   326
            Selected Oboe Repertoire   326
            Collections   333

PART 5   SAXOPHONE

Chapter 22   Introduction   341
            The Saxophone Family   341
            Assembly   342
            Care and Maintenance   343

Chapter 23   Fundamentals of Saxophone Playing   344
            Breathing   344
            Playing Position   345
            Embouchure   346
            Tonguing   347

Chapter 24   Progressive Exercises   349
            Tuning on the Saxophone   357

Chapter 25   Additional Information   368
            Guidelines for Choosing a Saxophone Student   368
            Choosing a Saxophone   368
            The Mouthpiece   369
            The Reed   369
            Caring for the Reed   370
            Vibrato   370
            Saxophone Supplies   372
            Selected Methods and Materials   372
            Selected and Representative Works   373
            Troubleshooting Guide for the Saxophone   374

INDEX   381

Contributors

William Dietz has studied at West Virginia University and the University of Washington and received the Doctorate of Music in Bassoon Performance from Florida State University, where he studied with William Winstead. He is currently Professor of Music (bassoon and wind chamber music) at the University of Arizona School of Music and Dance, where he has been on faculty since 1983. He is a member of the Arizona Wind Quintet, a faculty ensemble at the University of Arizona.

William Dietz has served as principal bassoonist with various orchestras, including the Orquesta Sinfonica Nacional de Costa Rica, the Flagstaff Festival of the Arts Orchestra, and the Desert Foothills Festival Orchestra. He is currently a member of the Tucson Symphony Orchestra. As a recitalist and chamber musician he has performed throughout the United States, Canada, Mexico, Central and South America, and in Europe. He has premiered several works at the annual conferences of the International Double Reed Society, and in 1994 he released a compact disk of new works for the bassoon.

Dr. Dietz has been a regular contributor to such professional publications as *The Instrumentalist, Dialogue in Music Education, The Double Reed, Bandworld Magazine,* and the *National Association of College Wind and Percussion Instructors Journal.* In addition, he is the editor of *BassooNews,* a newsletter generated by the University of Arizona School of Music and Dance addressing items of interest to bassoonists. He is a consultant to the Prestini Reed Corporation and editor and owner of White Oak Press, a music publishing company devoted to the publication of multiple bassoon music.

As a continuing member of the world-famous Dorian Wind Quintet since 1970, **Jerry Kirkbride** has toured extensively in the United States, Canada, Mexico, and Europe, as well as in India, Pakistan, and the Middle East. Before joining the Dorian, he was principal clarinetist with the Metropolitan Opera National Company and was a creative associate at the Center of the Creative and Performing Arts at the State University of New York at Buffalo. Apart from his quintet work, he has performed in numerous chamber music concerts in the United States and Europe.

After graduating from the University of Southern California, where he studied with Mitchell Lurie, Mr. Kirkbride was awarded a Fulbright Grant to continue his studies in Rome, where he worked with such artists as Nadia Boulanger, Efrem Kurtz, and Franco Ferrara. Mr. Kirkbride edits and arranges for International Music Company and has recorded for Vox, Columbia, CRI, Deutsche Grammophon, New World, and Summit Records. He has been Professor of Clarinet at the University of Arizona since 1987 and is currently principal clarinetist of the Arizona Opera and clarinetist with the Arizona Wind Quintet. He has performed annually at the Desert Music Fest in Carefree/Cave Creek, Arizona, since the inception of the festival in 1992.

Hal Ott is Professor of Music at Central Washington University, where he teaches flute and music history and performs with the Central Wind Quintet. He is currently principal flute with the Yakima Symphony Orchestra. He has been a member of the Peoria Symphony Orchestra, Peoria Civic Opera Orchestra, and All-Northwest Bach Festival Orchestra and has served as a faculty member at both the Columbia Flute Festival and the Icicle Creek Flute Festival. He holds a BME degree from Bradley University, an MM degree from the University of Illinois, and a DM from Florida State University. He has presented clinics, adjudicated, and performed on both the flute and the Baroque flute throughout the United States, Europe, and the People's Republic of China; he has also performed on National Public Radio on numerous occasions. He was a finalist in the Erwin Bodkey Competition sponsored by the Cambridge Society for Early Music, and he has performed and premiered several works at numerous National Flute Association conventions. Dr. Ott has published articles in *Flute Talk* and *The National Flutist Quarterly*. His CD, *Flute for Thought*, features music by twentieth-century American composers.

Mark Weiger has given performances throughout the United States, Canada, England, France, and Italy, presented two Carnegie Hall recitals, been a finalist in nine international competitions, and was Second Prize winner in the New York International Oboe Competition. He earned his degrees at the New England Conservatory of Music and the Julliard School. He has been principal oboist with the Kansas City Chamber Orchestra and the Illinois Symphony and Chamber Orchestra. Previously on the faculty at the University of Missouri at Kansas City, Mr. Weiger holds the post of Associate Professor of Oboe at the University of Iowa. In 1996 he was chosen to be the first oboist to serve as an American Artistic Ambassador for the U.S. Information Agency. He has been principal oboist of the Great Music West Festival (Wyoming/Utah), New Hampshire Music Festival, Yellow Barn Festival (Vermont), Ensemble da Camera (Iowa), and Britt Festival (Oregon), and has served as vice president of the Midwest Double Reed Society. His writings have been published in the *IDRS Journal*, the *MDRS Journal*, and the *Band Director's Guide*. He can be heard on the Crystal, CRS, Green Mountain, and Albany Records labels.

Craig Whittaker is an Associate Professor of Music at the University of North Carolina at Greensboro, where he teaches saxophone and serves as coordinator of jazz studies. Dr. Whittaker holds degrees in saxophone performance from the State University of New York at Potsdam, Northern Illinois University, and the University of Arizona. An active performer in both Classical and jazz styles, he has performed in North America and Europe and has presented workshops in several countries. His recordings with the UNC-Greensboro Percussion Ensemble and Spectrum Jazz Quintet have received critical acclaim and his compositions have been aired on American Public Radio. Dr. Whittaker serves as director of the southeast region of the North American Saxophone Alliance and president of the North Carolina unit of the International Association of Jazz Educators. He has published several articles in professional journals and was the recipient of the "Outstanding Classical Soloist" award from *DownBeat* magazine in 1984. He is a Yamaha Artist.

Preface

The materials presented in this volume offer a method and resource handbook for music education students. Thi hands-on experience is critical to understanding the principles of each instrument, therefore each section includes exercises and playing examples intended to provide a cursory study of each instrument. The music presented in each section attempts to follow a logical progression of challenges focusing on introducing each note and then incorporating it into the technique of the player. The playing materials are not intended to result in an advanced performance level, but rather to provide a practical experience that will encompass a conservative playing register and cover all basic techniques.

As the student learns to adjust intonation it is often helpful to provide a fixed pitch level by supplying a simple keyboard accompaniment. Selected tunes from each section have been supplied with chord symbols. An approach that works well is to play the melody with the group in unison (with bassoon an octave higher) in the right hand and supply a very simple chordal accompaniment in the left. Even playing along in unison without an accompaniment will help keep the group on track. (Remember that with the clarinet and saxophone the chord symbols are at concert pitch, while the instrumental part is transposed.) The tunes in each section have been chosen from a variety of sources. Many are melodies music education students may recognize from their general music education methods and materials classes.

Although many students are able to reach a very respectable playing level in the instrumental techniques class, the main objective is to produce teachers who will be able to recall the fundamentals of playing when called upon to do so and to direct their students to materials to assist them in their development. Toward this goal, more extended resource materials in each section are presented for reference when and if the need for them arises during the course of one's teaching career. The text can be filed away at the end of the instrument classes, to be drawn out again when the need arises for the resource material contained in the volume.

Acknowledgments

It is impossible to acknowledge the numerous people involved in assisting in a collaborative project such as this. Many friends, family, and colleagues have assisted the various contributors of this volume through their gifts of advice, support, proofreading, and other tasks too numerous to mention. The support systems of the various contributors are best acknowledged directly by the contributors themselves, and I add my sincere appreciation to their collective unsung yet vital roles in the completion of this book.

There are, however, a number of people who have assisted in the general creation of the book and who were instrumental either in its genesis or its completion.

Dr. James O'Brien, Professor of Music at the University of Arizona, deserves special thanks for suggesting that the original manuscript might be worthy of publication, as does Professor Gary Cook, Director of the School of Music at the University of Arizona, who lent his strong support to the project from its inception.

Special thanks also to Scott Connuck, a music teacher and English as a Second Language specialist in Nogales, Arizona, who suggested many of the tunes that make up an important portion of the book, and to Dr. Marilyn Sommer, Director of the School of Music at Henderson State University, who made many thoughtful suggestions for the first drafts of the book.

I would like to thank Valerie Gawenda Bugh for her fine illustrations, which compliment this book, and for her enthusiasm for and patience with the project. I would also like to thank the various people who contributed photographs from their private and public collections, especially Professor Gerald Corey and Mr. Chip Owen of the Fox Instrument Company.

Much gratitude to the staff at Schirmer Books, especially Jonathan Wiener for his meticulous attention to my questions, and Jane Andrassi for her good humor and professionalism, and to both for their patience, support, and dedication to a quality product.

Finally, much appreciation and admiration to the outstanding team of contributors: Hal Ott, Jerry Kirkbride, Mark Weiger, and Craig Whittaker, whose expertise and tireless work coupled with their interest in music education have led to the completion of this volume.

–William Dietz

PART 1

Bassoon

WILLIAM DIETZ

CHAPTER 1

Introduction

The bassoon is a double reed instrument that serves as the bass and tenor voice of the woodwind choir. Its range is from BB♭ to about e².

Example 1.1. The range of the bassoon

Bassoons are generally constructed from seasoned maple, but other woods such as grenadilla and rosewood have been used. Bassoons have also been constructed of ebonite, a hard rubber material, and plastics. Modern bassoons have approximately twenty-four keys and are assembled from five parts: the crook or bocal, the tenor or wing joint, the boot or butt, the bass or long joint, and the bell joint.[1] With all the keys and holes closed, the bassoon becomes a long tube extending from the tip of the bocal to the end of the bell. This tube is bent double on itself, placing the keys and holes in a close arrangement that enables the fingers and thumbs to close the holes and operate the numerous keys.

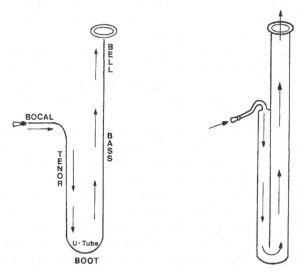

Figure 1.1. The bend of the tube

If the bassoon were unbent and stretched out to its entire length, it would be nearly nine feet long (254 centimeters). The bore of the bassoon is conical, that is, it gradually increases in diameter. The flare of the conical bore extends from 4 millimeters at the bocal tip to 39 millimeters at the end of the bell.[2]

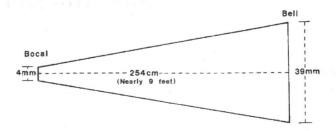

Figure 1.2. The conical flare of the bassoon

To produce an instrument of good quality, the machining of the bore and tone holes must be very precise. Final tuning and voicing is done by hand and requires considerable time and skill. The bocal is a crucial element and needs to be carefully matched to each instrument. Because of these factors, in part, bassoons are considerably more expensive than the other wind instruments.[3]

History

The early history of the bassoon is not nearly as clear as that of the other woodwinds. Few early instruments survive, and it is not possible to be certain when and where these were made.[4] Lyndesay Langwill, the author of *The Bassoon and the Contrabassoon*, tells us, "The origin of the bassoon is still shrouded in mystery. Even the country of its origin is uncertain."[5]

The two most important predecessors of the bassoon are the bass pommer and the dulcian. The bass pommer, sometimes called the bombard, is the largest member of the shawm family, which developed in Europe throughout the Middle Ages. Although it had the distinctive S-shaped bocal and double reed, it was constructed from a single straight tube and was thus somewhat awkward to hold and play.

The dulcian, on the other hand, was constructed by boring two parallel channels through a single block of wood and connecting them with a type of U-tube, thus achieving the necessary length of tubing by being bent over on itself as the bassoon is. It also had the distinctive S-crook, used a double reed, and had a conical bore.[6]

According to William Heckel, the author of *The Bassoon*, characteristics of these two early instruments can be found in the modern bassoon. The pitch and range of the bass pommer were incorporated into the bassoon, while the dulcian's contributions included the U-shaped bend to the conical tube, which made the tone color softer and more flexible. Both the pommer and the dulcian, although essentially distinct, have been shown by comparative testing of existing specimens to have somewhat similar tone quality and therefore may be regarded as parents of the modern bassoon.[7]

By approximately the time of the Baroque era, an instrument that was clearly the forerunner of the modern bassoon had evolved and came to have eleven lateral holes, three of them covered by keys. This Baroque-period bassoon, unlike the one-piece dulcian, was jointed. This important advancement enabled instrument makers to place the tone holes and control the flare of the bore more precisely, resulting in a more refined tone and

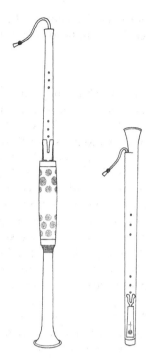

Figure 1.3. The bass pommer and the dulcian

a more accurate tuning. This jointed instrument, which probably originated in France, became to the Baroque era what the pommer and the dulcian had been to the Renaissance.[8]

In the next few decades the bassoon's efficiency was increased by the addition of more keys and by extending the range. Later refinements included the stabilization of certain notes and a further extension of the range. Soon the bassoon was becoming well established in the minds of composers and hence in the European orchestra. While the earliest use of the instrument was as a strengthening element to the bass line, gradually it began to assume a more independent and eventually an indispensable role in the orchestra. A pair of bassoons was to become the regular complement to the Classical orchestra.[9]

The bassoon of the late 1700s and early 1800s had a softness and beauty of tone but could be played easily only in a limited number of keys. As long as the bassoon was used merely for accompaniment or filling in, this served well enough, but as composers began to use the bassoon more soloistically, a more even voicing and smoother technique in all keys were required. Bassoonists called upon instrument makers to remove the major defects in sound and fingerings. Instrument makers recognized that the body of the bassoon needed to be reconstructed to achieve these advances. Major structural changes were begun by Carl Almenrader (1786–1843), joined later by J. A. Heckel (1812–77). Almenrader and Heckel vastly improved the key-work of the instrument and completely changed the bore. These technical changes improved many aspects of the bassoon, but changed the sound considerably. Further experiments and improvements permitting more exact gradations of the bore became possible only after new tools were developed. Eventually this led to the return of the sweetness of sound, which had been lost.[10] These improvements were affected largely by William Heckel. The Heckel Bassoon Company is recognized as one of the foremost makers of bassoons today. The standard fingering system of the bassoon is known as the Heckel system (also called the German system).

THE FRENCH BASSOON

Throughout the development of the bassoon, attempts have been made to simplify its fingerings. Even the famous instrument maker Theobald Boehm ventured, without much success, to reorganize the key system.[11] The only other surviving system today is the Buffet system, commonly referred to as the French system. The French bassoon has several distinct differences from the German (Heckel) bassoon in both sound and appearance. The tone is described as more subtle and vocal by its supporters, and nasal and less centered by its detractors. High-range playing is considered to be easier on the French bassoon. The keywork is quite different from the Heckel system and is generally considered to be simpler while providing fewer optional fingerings.[12] Although players of the French bassoon can be found in French-speaking parts of Europe and Canada and scattered throughout pockets in Latin America, for a time it was feared that preference for the German system might lead to the eventual extinction of the instrument. During the 1970s and 1980s, however, a renewed interest by all bassoonists in the French bassoon has reestablished its place in contemporary bassoon playing. Some of the world's greatest bassoonists today continue to be players of the French bassoon.

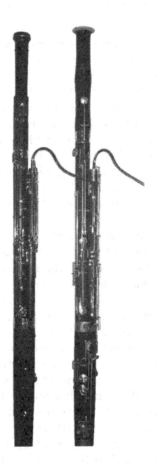

Figure 1.4. French bassoon (left) and German bassoon (right). Photo courtesy Gerald Corey

THE CONTRABASSOON

The contrabassoon or double bassoon is the true bottom of the woodwind section, sounding an octave below the bassoon. Some contrabassoons are equipped with extra tubing to extend the range down one half step lower to AAA (subcontra A), the lowest pitch found on most pianos.

The contrabassoon is a transposing instrument, sounding one octave lower than written. Although the fingering system is almost identical to that of the bassoon, the contrabassoon's size and slower response time make complicated technical passages difficult. The extreme registers are also problematic. Long sustained passages in the lowest register require continual replenishing of air and can be very fatiguing for the player, while the uppermost octave usually requires special fingerings to solve the many response and tuning problems. The best use of the contrabassoon (aside from the occasional solo passage) is as a reinforcement for the bassoon section.

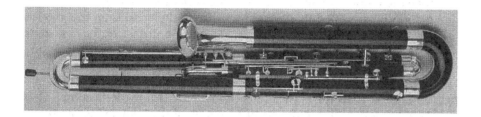

Figure 1.5. The contrabassoon. Photo courtesy of Fox Products Corporation

Assembly and Care of the Bassoon

The five parts of the bassoon are the bocal or crook, the tenor or wing joint, the boot or butt, the bass or long joint, and the bell.

Figure 1.6. The parts of the bassoon. L. to r.: bocal, tenor joint, boot, bass joint, bell

To assemble the bassoon, take the boot and locate the low E key (also called the pancake key). Make sure this key is facing you and that the two holes of the bore (the smaller will be to your right) are on top. On the bottom you will find the metal cap that protects the U-tube.

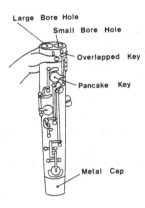

Figure 1.7. Orientation of the boot

Take the tenor joint and orient it so the cork or string tenon is pointing down and the small pad that closes the hole on the bocal is on top. Notice that the tenor joint has a concave side; the keyless surface of the bass joint will eventually fit snugly up against this concave surface. Locate the whisper key, the bottommost of the keys operated with the left thumb. Depressing it operates the pad that extends above the tenor joint. The whisper key faces toward the body and is "home base" for the left thumb.

Place the tenor joint in the small bore hole of the boot, being careful as you adjust the joint not to bind the single phalange key that extends from the bottom of the joint. This phalange key fits over a metal key on the boot that is operated by the pancake key. Now line up by eye the concave curve of the tenor joint with the curve of the large bore hole in the boot.

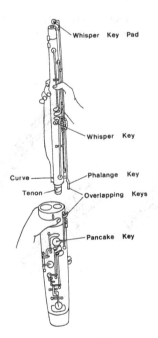

Figure 1.8. Placing the tenor joint

Take the bass joint and orient it so the larger end is at the top. Locate the surface area that has no keys. This segment of the bass joint will fit snugly up against the concave curve in the tenor joint. You may want to place the boot with its metal guarded bottom on the floor to help you gain leverage as you assemble your bassoon.

When the bass joint is in line with the tenor joint you should see a constellation of keys coming together. All of these keys are operated by the left thumb. Some bassoons have a locking mechanism to hold the tenor and bass joints together. If your bassoon has this mechanism, lock it now.

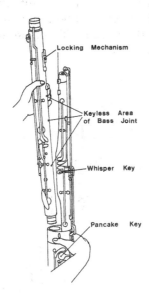

Figure 1.9. Placing the bass joint

Now take the bell and slip it over the large bored hole in the bass joint, being careful not to bind the single overlapping key.

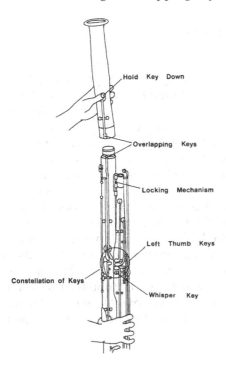

Figure 1.10. Placing the bell

Because the bocal is fragile and can be easily dented or bent, it is usually not inserted until the player is seated. As you insert the bocal be careful not to depress the whisper key, as this will often cause the bocal to tear the whisper key pad. The bocal should be adjusted by placing the hand at the arched curve (its strongest point). Never adjust the bocal by forcing or by applying pressure at the reed end, as this may bind and twist it. This is especially true if the fit of the bocal's cork into the tenor joint is tight. When the bassoon is properly assembled both the whisper key and the pancake key when *individually* depressed will operate the key that closes the pin-sized hole on the bocal.

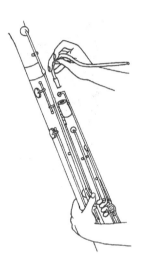

Figure 1.11. Inserting the bocal

Care and Maintenance

DAILY CARE

The bassoon is fairly easy to care for. After playing, the bocal should be removed and excess saliva should be blown out. The bocal should then be placed safely in the case. Next, remove the bell and the bass joint. They do not require swabbing because they do not receive any moisture. The tenor joint and the boot must be swabbed before being put away. The U-tube in the boot collects most of the moisture from saliva and condensation and must be dumped out before being swabbed. Always dump the moisture out of the smaller of the two holes. This side of the boot is lined with a protective material. The large-bored side of the boot is unlined and should never get wet. Air should be blown into tone holes to clear moisture. Finally, the boot should be swabbed with a specially weighted pull-through swab or with the long "fuzzy"-type swab that is often found in the cover of the case. This swab should have a linen cloth cover, which makes the swab more absorbent and prevents bits of material from the fuzz being lost in the boot as you swab. Do not force the swab or make repeated hard contact with the interior of the U-tube, as this can dent or even (over a period of time) rupture the U-tube.

The tenor joint also requires swabbing and blowing out of tone holes. The smaller of the pull-through swabs is fed into the larger of the two ends and is pulled through briskly two or three times to remove as much moisture as possible. Be sure to unfurl and unknot the swab completely before attempting to pull it through to prevent it from becoming caught or wedged in the rather narrow bore.

LONG-TERM MAINTENANCE

Long-term maintenance should include the following:

1. Dust under the keys with a clean, narrow paintbrush (about one inch in width) a few times a month.
2. Dust the inside of the bore of the bass joint and the bell.
3. Gently and carefully clean each tone hole with a pipe cleaner. Take care not to accidentally remove the tape that sometimes is added to tone holes for tuning or voicing.
4. Apply oil to the metal contact points a few times a year. Use light instrument key oil or clock oil. (A good brand is Nye's Clock Oil.)
5. Scrub out the bocal with a special bocal brush about every three months. Use liquid soap to feed the brush into the large end. Proceed gently and carefully. Run cold water through afterward to clear debris and rinse the soap out.
6. Clean the cork or string tenons and apply fresh petrolatum or cork grease as needed.

In addition, it is helpful to have instruments played by a bassoonist every year to be sure that they are working well. Repairs such as pad changes and key adjustments should be done by a reputable technician. Major maintenance such as an overhaul should be done in the factory of manufacture.

Notes

1. William Waterhouse, "Bassoon," in *The New Grove Dictionary of Music and Musicians*, ed. Stanley Sadie (London: Macmillan, 1980), 2:264, 265.
2. Ibid., 264.
3. Ibid.
4. Ibid., 268.
5. Lyndesay Langwill, *The Bassoon and Contrabassoon* (New York: Norton, 1965), 7.
6. William Hermann Heckel, *The Bassoon* (Old Greenwich, CT: Jack Spratt Woodwind Shop, 1950), 4.
7. Ibid.
8. Ibid., 10; Langwill, *The Bassoon and Contrabassoon*, 28; Waterhouse, "Bassoon," *New Grove Dictionary* 2:270.
9. Heckel, *The Bassoon,* 10; Waterhouse, "Bassoon," *New Grove Dictionary* 2:276.
10. Heckel, *The Bassoon,* 10, 13.
11. Langwill, *The Bassoon and Contrabassoon*, 19.
12. Waterhouse, "Bassoon," *New Grove Dictionary* 2:264.

CHAPTER 2

Fundamentals of Bassoon Playing

Breathing

Proper breathing on the bassoon, as on all wind instruments, is a component of playing that must be discussed with and taught to the beginner. This is because breathing in the manner that is correct for wind playing does not occur naturally but requires a considerable alteration from normal, life-supporting breathing.

The most obvious difference between normal and altered breathing is that normal breathing occurs without thought. Altered breathing requires thought at the outset, although after much practice, it should also occur without thought. This altered mode of breathing should become a natural function that engages automatically when playing a wind instrument.

A further comparison of the two modes of breathing reveals more specific differences. During normal breathing the inhalation is slow and relaxed and the exhalation is usually fairly rapid. The reverse is true of altered breathing, which is characterized by a fast inhalation, while the exhalation is slower and metered out. In addition, during altered breathing both the inhalation and exhalation are more thorough, with the lungs being more completely filled and emptied than during normal breathing.

It is during the slower, metered-out exhalation of altered breathing that the subject commonly referred to as *support* should be checked. The abdominal muscles and especially the diaphragm must be used to help slow the exhalation. The diaphragm will firm up with the inhalation and slowly relax with the exhalation.

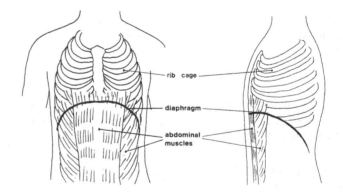

Figure 2.1. Locating the diaphragm and abdominal muscles

Since the slowed exhalation is an abnormal process, the student should practice it each day for a few minutes before beginning to blow through the instrument. The teacher should encourage the student to fill the lungs to capacity, while checking to be sure the shoulders do not rise, causing unnecessary tension. To insure a complete inhalation, the student should imagine filling the lungs from the bottom to the top, as if one were pouring water into a bottle. The entire process of correct and full inhalation, followed by slow, complete exhalation, should be practiced by the student and examined by the teacher at each lesson, without the instrument. By timing the rate of exhalation a student can usually increase lung power and improve control in a few weeks. A helpful exercise is the following:

1. Inhale completely and rapidly.
2. Lock support (sometimes called suspension): feel the diaphragm and abdominal muscles contract.
3. Exhale slowly as you count 1, 2, 3, etc. Gradually increase the count goal.

When the instrument is added, allow the student plenty of time to breathe before beginning to play—at least a full beat at a slow tempo. Constantly remind the student to take a full breath.

Once the technique of breathing and blowing is in place, a discussion of the use of the airstream is important. As the student develops musically, an ability to produce a well-connected, linear musical line becomes a vital part of phrasing ability. This concept is discussed below in the tonguing section of this chapter.

Embouchure

The term *embouchure*, as it pertains to wind playing, refers to the formation of the mouth while playing the instrument. As in all discussions of basic elements, there exist several schools of thought concerning embouchure formation on the bassoon. The two most commonly used bassoon embouchures are often referred to as the *smile* and the *whistle* embouchures. These names roughly describe the mouth's appearance as one forms the embouchure and are most easily defined by the position of the "corners" of the mouth. The smile embouchure pulls the corners of the mouth tight as in an exaggerated smile, while the whistle embouchure draws the corners to a central focal point in the center of the mouth (as if one were saying an exaggerated "whom" with a great deal of emphasis on the *m*).

Figure 2.2. The smile (hard cushion) and whistle (soft cushion) embouchures

Most bassoonists prefer the "whistle" embouchure as it is usually easier to play at the proper pitch level and with a centered but open sound. In addition, it is less fatiguing for sustained playing owing to the "bunching" of the lips in the center of the embouchure, providing a soft cushion between the teeth and the reed. The amount of lip that is tucked into the cushion varies from player to player and depends somewhat on the size of the player's lips. Care must be taken that not too much lip (primarily the bottom lip) be rolled in, since this may muffle the tone. A workable strategy for finding a proper lip placement is to curl the lips into the cushion so the fleshy part completely disappears from the outside of the embouchure, then to slowly pull the lips out as the chin is pulled down and flat. This usually will set the lips in a comfortable position. The skin covering the chin is smooth and tight and the jaw has a firm look to it. The lower jaw is set in a normal bite, without pulling it back or pushing it forward.

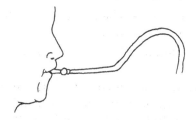

Figure 2.3. Side view of the proper embouchure (chin is pulled down and is flat)

When the student is comfortable with the feel of the embouchure and can reconstruct it easily, a discussion of the *oropharyngeal cavity*—the position inside the mouth and throat as one plays a wind instrument—is important. The goal on all wind instruments, and particularly the bassoon, is to maintain an open mouth and throat position while playing. The bassoon tone is very sensitive to this positioning. In addition, more advanced players will often make adjustments in pitch and timbre by minute variations of the cavity. The student, even at this early stage, should be made aware of the cavity and practice adjusting it as he plays. An analogy that often helps the student to locate the area of adjustment is simply to suggest imagining a golf ball in the mouth as one plays. The throat position can be further relaxed by suggesting the student think "ahh" while playing. These changes in the oropharyngeal cavity often immediately improve the tone of a young bassoonist and also serve to drop the pitch level considerably.

Tonguing

The tongue is always used to initiate a sound while playing the bassoon. Beginning a note without the tongue does not allow the player to control the release moment of the tone or to regulate the attack. An advanced player may choose various areas of the tongue to facilitate different types of articulation tasks such as tonguing in extreme registers or for producing accents. For beginners, however, it is important to learn one proper, simple technique that will serve for almost all tonguing operations. Variations in this basic tongue position on the reed can be learned later as the student advances in all areas of playing.

CONTACT POINTS OF THE TONGUE AND REED

When discussing tonguing, two simple but important points should be covered: (1) precisely which part of the tongue is used, and (2) exactly where the tongue touches the reed. Although there is some diversity in standard tongue placement among bassoonists, most use the upper surface of the tongue about four to six millimeters back from the tip. This area is touched to the bottom blade of the reed at the center, about one to three millimeters back from the edge of the aperture of the reed.

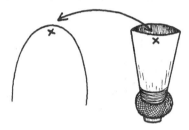

Figure 2.4. The contact points of the tongue (top surface) and the reed (bottom blade)

Figure 2.5. Top view of contact points

Since the entire articulation process is hidden from view inside the mouth, it is not always obvious when a problem in tongue placement occurs. A trained ear can sometimes hear a faulty tongue placement and adjust it, but often a problem may go without detection until it becomes a habit, when of course it is much more difficult to remedy. For this reason a seemingly inordinate amount of time should be spent describing and checking students' tongue placement during their first few months of study. After students seem comfortable with the tongue position they can be made an active participant in the learning process by the following methods:

1. Have students describe the placement as if they were teaching it to another bassoonist.
2. Ask the student to point out on the reed and the tongue the areas that make contact.
3. Have the student draw a diagram of the tongue and the reed and place an X on each to indicate the proper areas of contact.

COMMON ERRORS OF TONGUE PLACEMENT

Some common errors of tongue placement include:

1. Using the very edge of the tongue (Fig. 2.6)
2. Tonguing into the opening or onto the front edge of the reed (Fig. 2.7)
3. Touching the reed too far back on the tongue (Fig. 2.8)

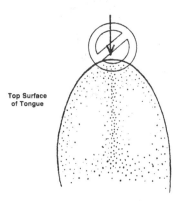

Figure 2.6. Tonguing error 1: using the edge of the tongue

Using the front edge of the tongue is a common tonguing error characterized by the student's inability to initiate a note without a hard attack. Often a slight distortion in the tone at the release moment is heard. In addition, because the tongue is higher in the mouth than it would be if tonguing correctly, a correct open mouth cavity is more difficult to achieve. This may ultimately affect the tone quality, robbing it of some lower partials. This error of tongue placement also usually requires the student to place the tongue incorrectly on the front edge of the reed.

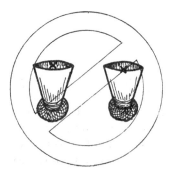

Figure 2.7. Tonguing error 2: tonguing into the opening or onto the front edge of the reed

Tonguing onto the front edge, or even worse, into the opening of the reed, may create a garbled initial tone and may make it difficult to tongue rapidly.

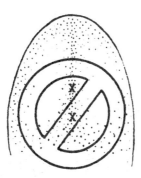

Figure 2.8. Tonguing error 3: touching the reed too far back on the tongue

Touching the reed too far back on the tongue is a common error with students who have switched to the bassoon from the saxophone. The aural clue for the teacher that this error is occurring is a dull, inarticulate, or muddy beginning of each note. Although many bassoonists use this approach to a certain degree to facilitate legato tonguing, especially in the low register, the young bassoonist should take care not to allow it to become the normal mode of tonguing.

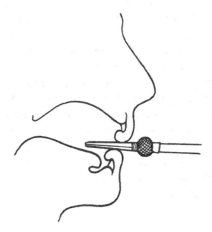

Figure 2.9. The reed extending beyond the tip of the tongue

Occasionally a student will have difficulty finding the proper contact between tongue and reed because the reed may extend naturally into the mouth beyond the contact point on the tongue. To remedy this situation, the teacher should be certain that the reed is not too far into the mouth, then help the student to experiment with an arched tongue position. By drawing the tongue back a bit, pointing it, and raising it slightly in the back, the student should be able to find the proper placement easily and quickly.

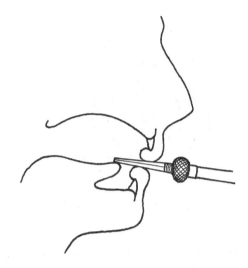

Figure 2.10. Locating the contact point by arching and pointing the tongue

COORDINATING THE TONGUE WITH THE AIR PRESSURE

A good tonguing technique is tied inextricably to proper exhalation. Once the teacher feels that the student is secure with the concepts of tonguing, a discussion of the mechanics of the air release is important. A mental picture of the operation of the air is helpful at this point. Imagine that the air is controlled by two valves, the main valve and the smaller articulation valve. The main valve is located inside the lungs and diaphragm and once turned on remains on, keeping the pressure constant, ready, and set in place behind the tongue. The tongue serves as the smaller control valve and regulates the amount of air that will pass into the reed. The student should understand that the large valve is not turned on and off between notes but rather is left on, keeping the pressure steady and continuous, while the small valve does the work of allocating when and how much air is used. Compare this operation to a garden hose. The water pressure is turned on at the source (lung pressure) while the tongue corresponds to the nozzle end of the hose, adjusting the flow of the water.

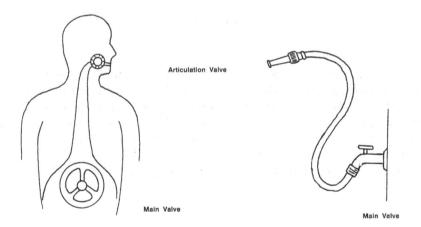

Figure 2.11. The two valves

Tonguing can be practiced without the bassoon by having the student practice tonguing behind the front teeth. As the student practices maintaining the air pressure and connection between the "notes," the teacher can listen for a letdown in the air pressure, which would transfer to the instrument as hard attacks and the inability to play a legato phrase.

Tonguing is a basic technique that should be carefully taught to the beginning bassoon student. Method books may supply many pages of exercises for tonguing practice but do not usually provide an explanation of the mechanics of the tonguing process. This may cause problems, since nearly any material, if practiced with proper tongue placement, will improve one's tonguing, while even a well-paced tonguing tutor will not improve one's tonguing if the basic technique is incorrect.

As in all basic elements of wind playing, advanced players master many more than a single method of application. They then apply the technique that best fits the passage they must play. The development of these advanced tonguing techniques will be greatly assisted if the student has first learned a strong basic technique.

Tone and Vibrato Production

TONE PRODUCTION

Above all the other elements that make up the totality of a bassoonist, tone is probably the most individual characteristic because it is based in large part on the subjective issue of personal taste. Furthermore, tone is in many ways dependent on the formation of many other elements of playing, such as breathing, tonguing, embouchure, reed style, and vibrato, and differences in concepts of these fundamentals can strongly affect tone. Most bassoonists recognize an inherent weakness in the bassoon tone to carry over an accompaniment of any volume, due in part to the register of the bassoon but also to its characteristic tone quality. In addition, it is quite a challenge to demonstrate a relatively even quality through all the registers of the bassoon.

The bassoon's rich, diverse history and the various national schools of playing provide a wide spectrum of acceptable sounds, and therefore the role of the teacher who is not a bassoonist is perhaps to help students develop discerning and critical ears and to guide them in formulating a personal concept of characteristic tone. Development of the student's ear should primarily be accomplished through listening. It is important to include listening assignments early in the student's development because the actual physical changes in the body that must be accomplished in order to achieve a good tone, such as an open throat position and steady airstream, may make little sense to the young student who has no concept of a beautiful sound. The listening process provides the student with a model to strive for. The maturing bassoonist should continually listen to live as well as recorded performances. This component of study should not be confined to listening only to bassoonists but should extend to artists on other instruments as well, providing a learning experience in regard not only to tonal production but also to phrasing, vibrato, and other nuances.

VIBRATO PRODUCTION

Once a student has progressed to the stage where a good tone can be produced consistently, the issue of vibrato production should be considered.

Vibrato is a technique used by vocalists and instrumentalists to expand the expressive possibilities of their sound. There is some discussion among bassoonists as to how vibrato is produced, where and how it should be used, and indeed as to what elements even define vibrato. Most bassoonists consider vibrato to be concerned with small, controlled changes in the pitch and intensity (dynamics) of a note. Various schools of thought arise when considering how these changes are produced. The standard American school of playing maintains that vibrato is produced by the diaphragm. Vibrato production that involves jaw movement is discouraged by the mainstream of bassoonists.

The characteristic bassoon vibrato ranges from four to seven pulses per second. Recent research on the subject indicates that the large, slow-moving diaphragm muscle alone is not capable of producing a vibrato at the most rapid end of this range. Many bassoonists believe that the vocal cords play an important role in vibrato production, especially as the frequency of pulses increases. This type of vibrato is still referred to as the "diaphragm vibrato," and indeed control of the diaphragm is necessary for its production. But the vocal cords allow for a faster fluctuation in pitch and intensity (higher number of pulses per second).

Pitch fluctuation is discussed in terms of the distance from the true pitch. The various schools of vibrato production subscribe to one of the choices shown in Figure 2.12. Although most bassoonists choose to pulse slightly above and below the true pitch, all three styles of vibrato have their proponents. Of main importance in any vibrato is that the pitch must not stray so far from the true pitch that poor tuning results.

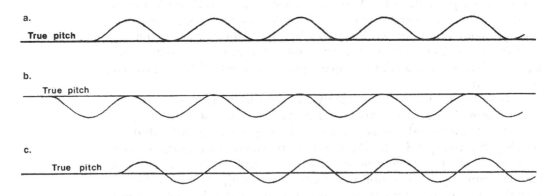

Figure 2.12. Vibrato choices: (a) pulsing from the true pitch to slightly above it; (b) pulsing from the true pitch to slightly below it; (c) pulsing from the true pitch to slightly above and below it

In learning vibrato it is helpful to reserve a portion of one's practice time exclusively for vibrato practice as distinct from finger technique. Any note in the midrange, such as middle C, works well. The student should couple this vibrato practice with listening to recordings and live performances of bassoonists, singers, violinists, and other musicians in order to train the ear to model appropriate, classically oriented vibrato use in performance. Eventually the development of a personal style of vibrato will become a part of the bassoonists' artistic sensibility—natural and ingrained into their playing.

EXERCISES AND TOOLS FOR LEARNING VIBRATO

METRONOME USE It is helpful to use a metronome set at quarter note equals
60, which provides a gauge of one click per second. The student should first
practice without the bassoon by panting at one pulse per click of the
metronome. Once the concept of moving the air in this manner is in place,
the technique should be transferred to the bassoon and the number of
pulses per second should gradually be increased. Remember that the pulses
should be minute changes in both pitch and volume. Often a sufficient pitch
change will occur when the student concentrates on the volume change.

At four or five pulses per second it becomes difficult and tiring to continue to use only the diaphragm. The vibrato begins to sound forced and
unnatural. It is at this stage that the listening assignments become important. If all goes as planned, the ear will automatically shift the vibrating
mechanism to include the vocal cords, and the sound of the vibrato should
become more unaffected and less mechanical. Getting past this point can be
facilitated by aspirating a "hahaha" syllable while playing. Eventually the
faster vibrato will "lock in" and become embodied into one's playing.

THE RECORDER AS A TOOL FOR VIBRATO PRODUCTION Students who have an unusually difficult time with vibrato production can be encouraged to learn the
technique on a recorder. The recorder's simplicity of tone production and fingerings, as well as the absence of a reed occupying the vocal cavity, facilitates
vibrato production. After the technique is mastered it can then be transferred
to the bassoon.

SEPARATING THE MECHANICS FROM THE USAGE

The purpose of vibrato exercises is, of course, to locate and develop the
mechanism for producing it. But vibrato is primarily an artistic tool, and its
use should vary depending on the character and range of the music. Artistic
playing does not require that every note receive vibrato. Indeed, it is important that the student be able to play without vibrato. Since the best use of
vibrato emulates that of singers, students who sing often have less difficulty
placing the mechanism for vibrato production and using it in a natural manner. Also, students who change to the bassoon from the flute usually can
transfer their vibrato skills directly to the bassoon. Clarinetists who move to
the bassoon usually have no preconceived ideas about vibrato production,
but saxophonists must be warned against producing vibrato on the bassoon
with jaw or lip adjustments, which is the accepted technique on the saxophone but is generally considered poor technique on the bassoon.

Posture and Hand Positions

MODES OF SUSPENSION

The two most popular methods of suspension for the bassoon are the neck
strap and the seat strap. Other methods include the shoulder harness and
the spike; although each of these latter two methods has some validity, neither is used widely.

THE SEAT STRAP VERSUS THE NECK STRAP

Both the seat strap and the neck strap have advantages and disadvantages.
The seat strap, although the more commonly used of the two methods, is

of course unsuitable for performing or practicing in a standing position. The main advantage of the seat strap over the neck strap is that it eliminates the substantial weight (approximately 6.5 pounds) that the latter suspends from the neck. This considerable weight (especially for a young student) impedes efficient posture and can cause a beginner to slump, hampering efficient breathing. The main disadvantage of the seat strap (if not corrected by the teacher) is that it often places the major portion of the bassoon's weight on the left hand and consequently the left wrist and arm of the bassoonist.[1]

During the first lessons, as the teacher shows the proper holding position to the student, special attention should be paid to adjusting the bassoon so that an inordinate amount of the bassoon's weight does not fall on the left hand. The lessening of the weight from the left hand is essential to eliminating tension while the student is developing technique. Bassoon students who have switched over from the saxophone are especially prone to placing the major weight of the bassoon on the left hand. The hands should be used as little as possible to actually support the bassoon. Often a great deal of the weight of the instrument will fall on the phalanx of the left index finger, the finger that executes the important half-hole technique. To execute this technique with ease, the index finger must be free from supporting the weight of the bassoon.[2]

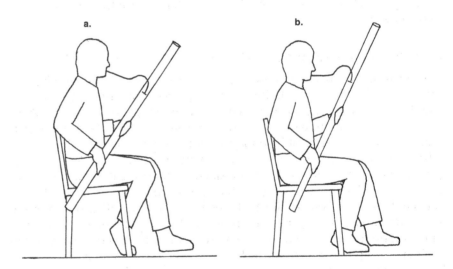

Figure 2.13. Extreme angle (a) may cause too much weight to fall on the left wrist. Compare with correct balance (b).

When the bassoon is held in a more vertical position (that is, a position in which it approaches a perpendicular angle to the floor), a great deal of the weight is shifted from the left hand to the seat strap. To gain a vertical position one can slide the bassoon's boot forward toward the knee so the bassoon's contact point with the leg is at midthigh. This helps achieve the near-vertical position but often places the bassoon at arm's length from the bassoonist, which may cause tension in the neck and arms as the bassoonist reaches out for the reed and instrument.

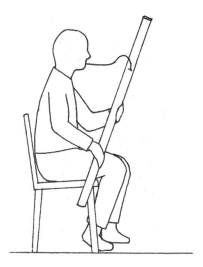

Figure 2.14. The bassoon held with boot too far forward on the thigh, causing arms to be overextended

Another method that bassoonists can use to reach the vertical, thereby lessening the weight from the left hand, is to raise the right foot with a footrest, such as guitarists use. This places the bassoon nearer the vertical position without pulling it away from the bassoonist.

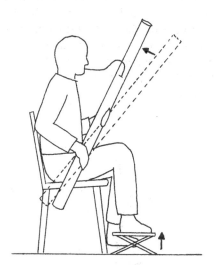

Figure 2.15. Reaching the vertical with the help of a footrest

A correct position for holding the bassoon would strike the balance point in which the fingers have the greatest freedom to work without being hampered by balancing the instrument or unnecessarily supporting its weight.[3]

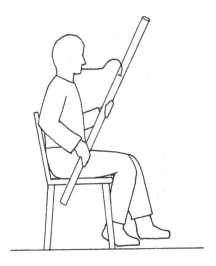

Figure 2.16. The correct balance

THE NECK STRAP AND HANDREST

In comparison to the seat strap, the neck strap seems to be better designed for balance. This device allows the bassoonist to eliminate some of the weight from the left hand by applying pressure with the right hand against the boot of the bassoon. The contact point of the neck strap to the bassoon serves as a type of fulcrum, and slight pressure from the right hand serves to counteract the weight on the left hand. With this action of applying pressure, the handrest becomes important. Many practitioners of the neck strap find that the handrest is essential, since the right thumb must be free for manipulating the four keys on the back of the boot joint. Without the handrest the thumb has to hold the instrument as well as work the keys.[4] With the handrest in place, counterpressure applied by the palm of the right hand to the handrest relieves pressure from the left hand as the bassoon is raised toward the vertical.

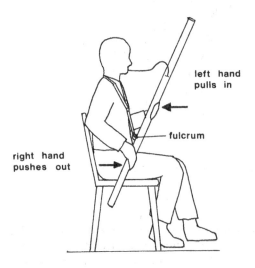

left hand
pulls in

fulcrum

right hand
pushes out

Figure 2.17. The neck strap

Some practitioners of the seat strap use the handrest, which in these cases seems to serve more as an aid in helping the player locate the holes and keys than as an aid in positioning the bassoon.[5]

There is much discussion among bassoonists as to the effectiveness of the handrest. Some accomplished bassoonists feel that the handrest helps to maintain an arch in the right hand, allowing for greater facility. Others feel that the thumb should ideally float freely above the thumb keys, ready for use, and that the handrest detracts from ease of finger and thumb movement.[6] For those who opt for the neck strap as their mode of suspension, the handrest would appear to be an essential element in this arrangement, while for those who use the seat strap the handrest would be optional.

POSITIONS OF THE HANDS

Both hands should be held in a natural position with the wrists as straight as possible. While holding the left wrist straight is not too difficult, the right wrist cannot be absolutely straight without raising the elbow of the right arm. Therefore a compromise position must be found that allows the right wrist to be as straight as possible without raising the elbow uncomfortably high. The straight wrist position allows free finger movement without undue stress. A simple exercise of wiggling the fingers of both hands with the wrists bent and then repeating the exercise with the wrist straight demonstrates the strain put on the wrists when they are bent.

Special attention should be drawn to the placement of the left index finger. This finger performs the important half-hole technique, which requires proper finger placement. It is important that the index finger be arched and placed on the first hole well above the top joint on the fleshy tip of the finger. The other fingers of the left hand can be set either flat or poised on their tips depending on the comfort of the bassoonist. The young bassoonist with small hands and fingertips may have difficulty covering the second and third holes of the left hand completely with fingertips; adjusting the placement of the fingers with a flatter position will provide a larger fleshy area to cover the holes.

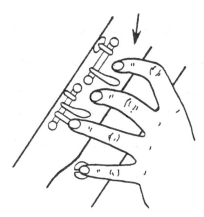

Figure 2.18. The arched position of the left-hand index finger

Beginning students often feel the need to rest the right thumb on the instrument. As they develop their technique, they will discover that the thumbs seldom get the opportunity to rest. For the beginning stages it is helpful to have a place to rest the right thumb that will not cause an unnatural hand position. A comfortable place that does not interfere with a good hand position is above the B♭ key, positioned lightly against the bassoon.

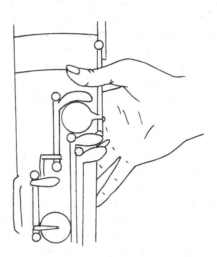

Figure 2.19. The right thumb at rest

SUMMARY

The seat strap is the preferable mode of suspension, particularly for the young student. Care should be taken by the teacher to insure that the student finds a comfortable position that does not allow too much weight to fall on the left hand. When the seat strap is used, the handrest is a matter of personal choice; many bassoonists, however, find that it is an absolute necessity when a neck strap is used.

Notes

1. Werner Seltmann and Gunter Angershofer, *Fagott-Schule*, 6 vols. (Mainz: Schott, 1977), 1:73.
2. Taken from an interview with Sol Shoenbach, 28 May 1987, Philadelphia, Pennsylvania.
3. Everett Timm, *The Woodwinds*, 2d ed. (Boston: Allyn and Bacon, 1971), 78.
4. William Spencer, *The Art of Bassoon Playing*, 4th ed. (Evanston, IL: Summy-Birchard, 1958), 22.
5. Frederick Westphal, *Guide to Teaching Woodwinds*, 4th ed. (Dubuque, IA: Brown, 1985), 218.
6. William Polisi, "Basic Steps in Teaching Bassoon," *The Instrumentalist* 28 (1973): 61.

CHAPTER 3
The Preparatory Octave

The natural notes from F to f constitute the basic octave on the bassoon. Learn these notes in descending order by starting at the top with f (called "open" f) and adding one finger at a time. Remember that the whisper key must be depressed for all these notes and that, as a general rule, the jaw drops as the notes descend to assist with response and tuning. When these notes are well memorized they can be used as a foundation for learning the notes of the next octave.

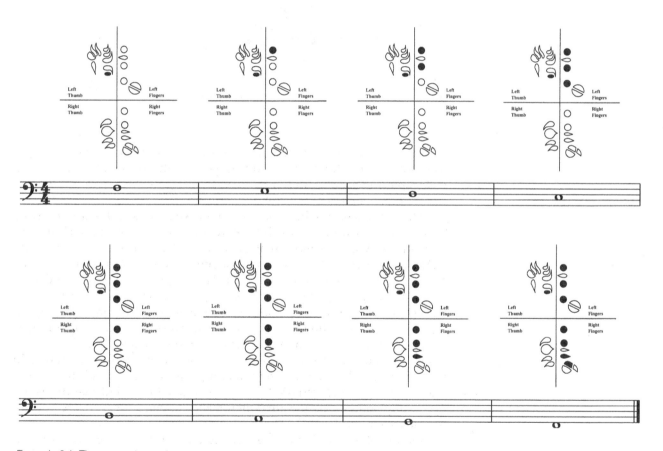

Example 3.1. The preparatory octave

By starting at the top and working down, you will know immediately if a hole is not completely covered, allowing air to escape. As you proceed downward, if a note does not respond well, backtrack and remove one finger at a time until a stable note is found; then continue to the bottom of the passage. When you have a more comfortable feel for the geography of the bassoon and a sense of when a hole is completely covered, try to start at the bottom of the scale and work to the top. This is generally more difficult, since it requires a complete covering of every hole before the low F will speak. If the low F does not speak easily, you must guess which hole is not covered completely. Check carefully the spread of the left hand.

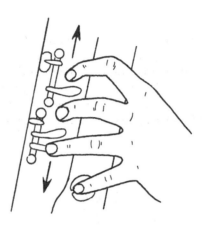

Figure 3.1. The left-hand spread from index finger to ring finger

Open f and the e immediately below it are quite sensitive to proper reed adjustment and embouchure support. Both notes will drop about a half step lower than written if the reed is too lightly trimmed or if there is not enough firmness in the embouchure.

Many notes on the bassoon have a weakness of stability and must be "placed" into their proper pitch level by the assistance of embouchure and air support. Also remember that because the bassoon has this "flexibility factor," a proper pitch can often be obtained from an incorrect fingering. Young students often argue that if the correct pitch can be obtained with the wrong fingering, then that fingering is acceptable. They must be convinced that proper technique in itself is a goal of instrumental playing. In order to progress to difficult music a student must know the proper fingering and the correct way of getting from one note to another. The student often is not advanced enough to hear the sometimes minute differences in pitch or timbre that an incorrect fingering may cause. Remind the student that a scale can be played on the piano with one finger, but that this is not necessarily good technique and will not allow a person to advance beyond the most elementary level.

On the other hand, an advanced student may know several different fingerings for each note on the bassoon. These secondary fingerings become an important component of bassoon playing and provide options in fingering patterns, in pitch variation, and in timbre. A student who has securely learned the primary fingerings should be encouraged to begin to study the many standard optional fingerings. An excellent and complete guide to these fingerings is *Essentials of Bassoon Technique* by Lewis Hugh Cooper and Howard Toplansky.

Progressive Exercises in the Preparatory Octave

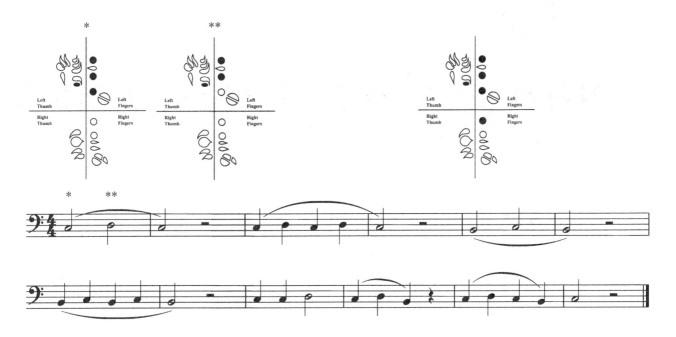

Exercise 3.1. Introducing C, D, and B

Exercise 3.2. Introducing E

Exercise 3.3. Introducing F

Exercise 3.4. Introducing A (Weissenborn)

Exercise 3.5. Introducing G (Weissenborn)

Exercise 3.6. Working down to F

The Fingering for B♭

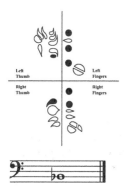

Example 3.2. B♭

B♭ is easily found by first fingering A, then adding the B♭ key. Remember that if the right thumb needs to rest, it should be placed just above the B♭ key. This will insure that the hand stays in good position. You will find as you learn more notes and begin playing more complicated music that the right thumb will have little time to rest, and you will feel less of a need to place it for instrument stability.

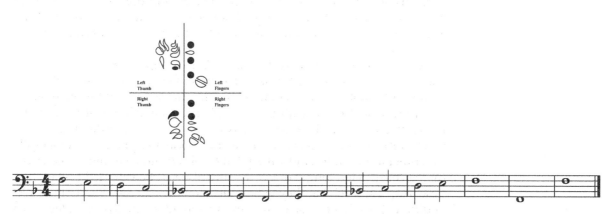

Exercise 3.7. The F major scale

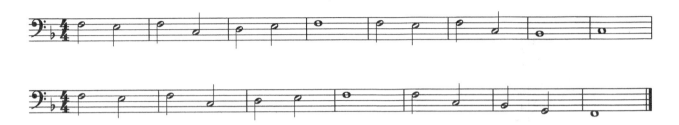

Exercise 3.8. Returning to open F

Exercise 3.9. Stressing B♭ (Weissenborn)

Tuning on the Bassoon

The following familiar tunes use the notes learned thus far. A simple piano accompaniment, which may be fashioned with the given chord symbols, will establish a pitch base on which the tuning tendencies on the bassoon can be experienced, providing an opportunity to learn the various techniques used for pitch adjustment.

Two types of tuning must be dealt with when playing the bassoon: (1) pitch level tuning, and (2) internal tuning.

Pitch level tuning has to do with the general level at which the instrument is required to play. Despite the efforts of many musicians to establish A = 440 as a standard pitch level, this level may vary somewhat from ensemble to ensemble and from piano to piano. The bassoon has virtually no tuning slide aside from the bocal. This can be adjusted only a very small amount before the hole on the whisper key is no longer covered by the pad. In any case, this small adjustment on such a large instrument leaves little flexibility in pitch level for the bassoonist. In addition, some bassoonists believe that ideally the bocal should not be pulled out at all, since this creates a gap in the conical bore that may affect the response or tuning of individual notes.

Considering all of these factors, it is clear that the bassoonist must attempt to "preset" the instrument to match the required pitch level or risk an uncomfortable playing situation. Setting the pitch level for the bassoon has a great deal to do with the "setup": the combination of instrument, bocal, and reed. While a young bassoonist may have little choice as to which instrument to play, the reed and bocal may be more practically experimented with to adjust the pitch level. Within a certain range, reeds can be constructed longer or shorter and also can be trimmed to flatten or raise the pitch level that they will produce on the bassoon. Similarly, bocals of different lengths can be chosen to assist in adjusting the pitch level of a bassoon. More specifics about the reed and bocal, and how they affect the pitch, can be found in chapter 6.

The second type of tuning, *internal tuning,* concerns the "fine tuning" of specific notes. Even when the pitch level of the instrument is satisfactory, certain notes may lie unusually sharp or flat on the instrument and will need to be "favored" to sound in tune. These out-of-tune notes differ from instrument to instrument, requiring that the bassoonist get to know the particular instrument well. Internal tuning is accomplished by using the following methods individually or in combinations:

1. *Lip and jaw pressure.* Firming the lips or closing the jaws will raise the pitch slightly, while relaxing the muscles around the lips and dropping the jaw will lower the pitch.

2. *Shape of oropharyngeal cavity.* An open mouth and throat position (as in pronouncing the vowel sound *aah*) will drop the pitch, while a more closed position (vowel sound *ee*) will raise it.

3. *Amount of reed taken into the mouth.* Slightly sliding a bit of reed into the mouth will raise the pitch, whereas playing more on the tip will slightly lower it.

4. *Velocity of air.* Speeding the airstream will raise the pitch, and slowing it will drop it.

These methods—used singly and, more commonly, in combination—provide a margin of tuning adjustment that is absolutely vital for playing well in tune.

Tunes in the Preparatory Octave

Mary Had a Little Lamb

French Tune

Twinkle, Twinkle, Little Star

Hudson River Steamboat

Joy to the World

The Remaining Notes in the Preparatory Octave

Each of the remaining notes in the preparatory octave is best taken from the note that lies one half step below it. Finger the natural note, then add the required key(s) to find the raised half step.

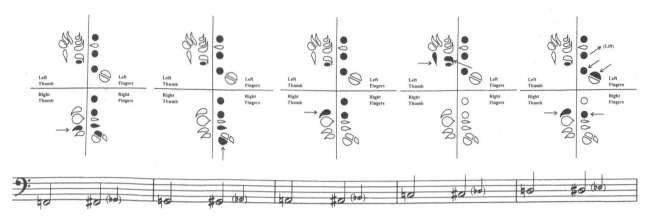

Example 3.3. Finding the remaining notes in the preparatory octave

Exercises for Chromatic Notes in the Preparatory Octave

Exercise 3.10. Reviewing B♭

Exercise 3.11. Introducing E♭

Exercise 3.12. Introducing A♭

Exercise 3.13. Introducing F♯

Exercise 3.14. Introducing D♭

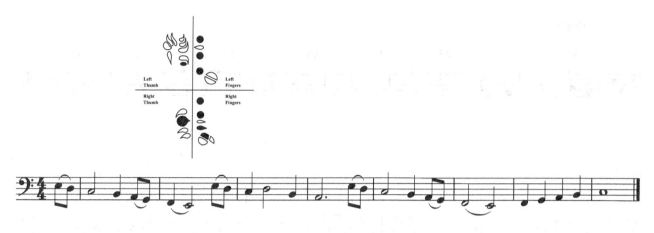

Exercise 3.15. Down to E

Exercise 3.16. Building a chromatic scale

Tunes in the Chromatic Octave

The Scale Song

The Bells

Hot Cross Buns

Mi Gallo

Leaves

Emil Schmiedl

Deck the Halls

Habañera

Bizet

Bsn. I

Bsn. II
(piano)

CHAPTER 4

Bassoon Technique

The Half-Hole Notes

An essential skill on the bassoon is the half-hole technique. A clear understanding of the procedure and a methodology for introducing it to the student are important considerations for the bassoon teacher.

DEFINITION OF THE HALF HOLE

For three notes on the bassoon, the octave is produced by venting the instrument with the index finger of the left hand. The resulting group of notes is commonly referred to as the "half-hole notes." These notes, f♯, g, and a♭, serve as a bridge between the lower register and the upper register, the notes of which are produced by venting with the whisper key.

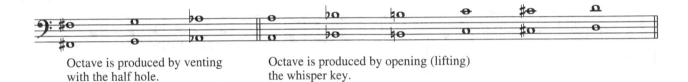

Octave is produced by venting with the half hole.

Octave is produced by opening (lifting) the whisper key.

Example 4.1. The half-hole notes and upper-register notes

The left index finger produces the half hole by partially opening the top hole in the tenor joint. Although this seems a somewhat crude method of venting the bassoon, attempts by instrument makers to add a key for executing this technique, as is done on the oboe, have not met with a great deal of acceptance by bassoonists. This may be because a keyed half hole does not allow for any variation in the size of the opening for the different notes—a matter of utmost importance in mastery of the half-hole technique.

POSITION

Although bassoonists may disagree as to the best position of the fingers on the holes of the bassoon, most agree that the left index finger should be placed well toward the fleshy tip (see Fig. 4.1) and that the finger should be arched (see Fig. 4.2). The sensitive tip of the index finger allows for a precise control of the opening of the half hole, enabling the bassoonist to offer various gradations of the aperture.

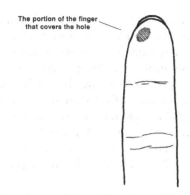

Figure 4.1. The placement of the left index finger

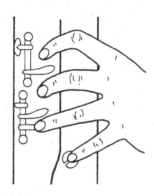

Figure 4.2. The arch of the left index finger

FINGERINGS AND SIZE OF THE HALF HOLE: THE EFFECT ON RESPONSE AND INTONATION

The notes f♯, g, and a♭ are essentially fingered as they are in the lower octave but are vented by uncovering a portion of the left index finger. The very term "half hole" is somewhat of a misnomer, since actually uncovering the hole halfway may not always produce the best results. In fact, each of the notes requires a slightly different-sized opening. For example, f♯ requires a larger opening than g or a♭; otherwise it has a tendency to growl or produce a pitch that vacillates between the two octaves. The a♭, in contrast, will not respond well unless the opening is quite small. The optimum size for g falls somewhere between the size for f♯ and a♭, and once the bassoonist has found the most successful aperture for the g half hole, the other two notes can be gauged against this standard. In most cases, a general error for the finger position of all three notes is an opening that is too large. If the opening is too great, the pitch will tend to be high and the response of the note may lack clarity, especially when one attempts to slur to these pitches.

The three half-hole notes should be thought of as a group with two common features in their fingerings: (1) use of the half hole, and (2) whisper key depressed.

It is important to remember that, when the passage permits, the whisper key should be closed (depressed) when the half hole is used. Just as a too-open half hole can affect the pitch and response adversely, failure to depress the whisper key will create the same problems. These two errors of finger technique, if committed together, tend to exacerbate the pitch and response problems. This is especially true at the softest dynamic levels, since the response may be more difficult and the pitch on these characteristically sharp notes tends to be higher still when one is playing softly or tapering a phrase. Therefore the teacher should take care to insure that the student is aware of the effects of the whisper key and half hole on the pitch and response of these notes.

Most bassoonists find that in playing g, the "resonance" (low Eb) key is also necessary to lower the pitch and to help the timbre of the note match more closely the timbre of the other notes in this register. The use of this resonance key usually does not correct the f♯ and ab's tendency to sharpness, but rather makes the pitch and timbre problem more pronounced. This varies considerably from instrument to instrument, however, and each bassoonist must ultimately decide this issue independently.

APPROACHES TO TEACHING THE HALF HOLE

In introducing the half-hole notes, a mirror is a helpful tool in assisting the student to gauge the size of the opening. An effective technique for learning to judge the proper size of the aperture involves approaching each of these notes from the octave below in a slurred passage.

Example 4.2. Exercise for learning correct half-hole size

After the lower note is articulated, the index finger should roll down and slightly to the bassoonist's left until the upper octave speaks clearly. The student should observe in the mirror how far the hole is uncovered. The slight pull of the index finger to the left as it rolls downward and open serves to uncover the hole in the direction of the angle that it is placed on the bassoon (see Fig. 4.3). The egg-shaped hole does not lie squarely on the bassoon, but is angled slightly to the bassoonist's left (see Fig. 4.4). In addition it is drilled into the instrument at a sharp downward angle (see Fig. 4.5).

Figure 4.3. Half-hole position of the left index finger. The finger rolls down and pulls slightly to the left following the direction of the angle of the hole.

Figure 4.4. The angle of the egg-shaped hole on the tenor joint

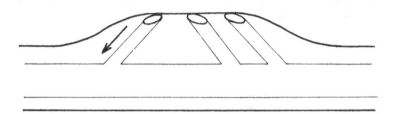

Figure 4.5. The angle of the first hole through the bassoon

The action of the finger is best described as a rolling motion. The finger should not slide as the hole is opened, nor should it ever leave the surface of the bassoon. The student should practice the exercise shown in Example 4.2, concentrating on keeping the throat position constant while passing from the lower note to the upper. Constricting the throat may lead to bad tuning and poor tone quality.

This simple approach is best for introducing the half-hole notes, but a better test of how the student controls the size of the opening occurs when one approaches the half-hole notes from the open f. Since the fingers are not in place while playing the f, there is no foundation on which to locate the correct half-hole setting.

Larger   "Normal"   Smaller

Example 4.3. Slurring to the half-hole notes

In playing the intervals in Example 4.3, the slur from f to the above notes often results in the accidental production of one of the upper partials of the harmonic series of these pitches, a situation that bassoonists commonly refer to as "cracking the note." The student who practices these slurred exercises will discover the size of the half-hole opening that produces the cleanest response. If the size for the g half hole is to be considered "normal," then one must aim for a slightly smaller opening for a♭ and a slightly larger size for f♯. Remember that the pressure on the whisper key must remain constant.

The passages should be practiced as slurred intervals. This is much more difficult to execute properly, since there is no moment of silence as the tongue touches the reed to mask the change.

OTHER NOTES USING THE HALF HOLE

In addition to the notes that lie immediately over the break of the bassoon, there are two other notes found in the upper register of the bassoon that require the half hole for best results. These notes, g¹ and a♭¹, as with the lower set of half-hole notes, require the whisper key whenever possible, since pitch and particularly response are greatly affected if it is not included as a regular part of the fingering.

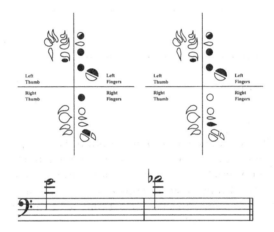

Example 4.4. Fingerings for g¹ and a♭¹

The following rule of thumb is important for consistent and clear artic- ulation of all half-hole notes: *only one* venting technique should be used at a time. If the half hole is open, the whisper key should be closed (depressed). If the whisper key is open it is not necessary to vent with the half hole as well.

Exercises Using the Half Hole

Exercise 4.1. Roll open to G (* indicates half hole)

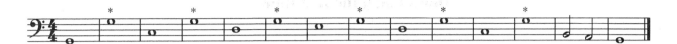

Exercise 4.2. Returning to G (∗ indicates half hole)

Exercise 4.3. Finding F♯ (∗ indicates half hole)

Exercise 4.4 The G-major scale (∗ indicates half hole)

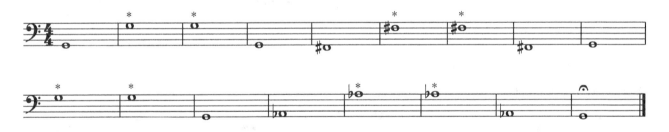

Exercise 4.5. Mixing them up (∗ indicates half hole)

Exercise 4.6. Extending the chromatic scale

Tunes Using the Half Hole

O Come, All Ye Faithful

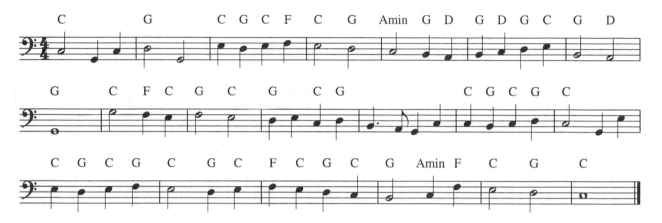

Row, Row, Row Your Boat

Mary Had a Little Lamb

My Country 'Tis of Thee

The Streets of Laredo

The Upper Register

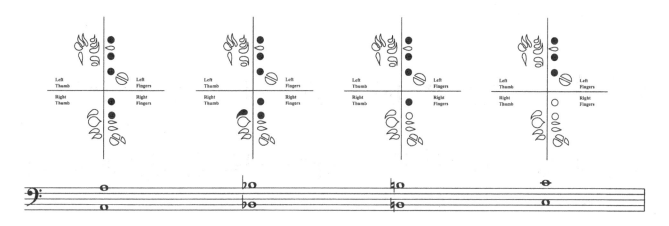

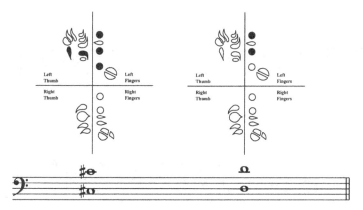

Example 4.5. Fingerings for the upper register

The upper-register notes a–d¹ are fingered exactly as their counterparts in the low register, with the slight alteration that the whisper key is not depressed. The release of the whisper key opens the tiny hole on the bocal button. Remember, these notes are not vented with the half hole. The notes in this register require a slightly firmer embouchure and an airstream of faster velocity than the notes of the lower register. Practice the notes by approaching them from the lower octave. Simply release the whisper key and tongue. (Do not attempt to slur to these notes, as this requires a special technique called flicking, which is dealt with in the next section.)

Exercises for the Upper Register

Exercise 4.7. Lift thumb, tongue, increase air speed

Exercise 4.8. Another octave jump

Exercise 4.9. Study in C Major

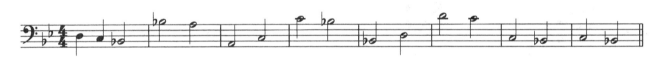

Exercise 4.10. Mixing them up

Exercise 4.11. More octaves

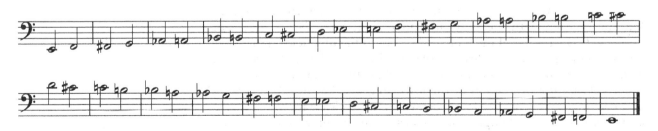

Exercise 4.12. Extending the chromatic scale

The Secondary Break

Passing from the half-hole notes to notes in the upper register requires careful attention to fingerings. Remember that the high range notes (a–d[1]) do not use a half hole, but are vented by releasing the whisper key. At the moment the whisper key is raised, the half hole should be completely closed by an upward rolling motion of the left index finger.

Exercises for the Secondary Break

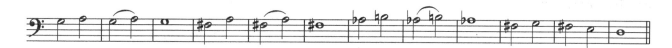

Exercise 4.13. The secondary break

Exercise 4.14. Slow and careful

Tunes for the Upper Register

Lightly Row

d - whisper key down
u - whisper key up

Joseph Dearest, Joseph Mild   Traditional German Carol

d - whisper key down
u - whisper key up

Music Alone Shall Live

We Shall Overcome

Simple Gifts

Shaker Hymn

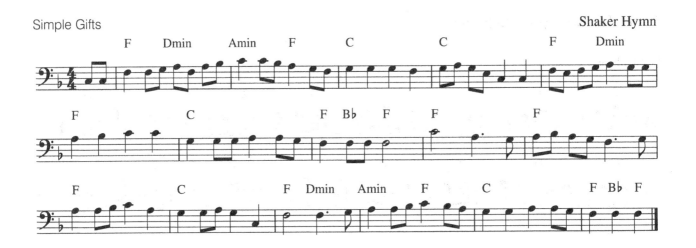

De Colores (Duo)

(continued)

Flicking Technique

There are several uses for the "flicker" keys of the bassoon. The most important has to do with the technique necessary to slur properly from one register of the bassoon to another. This technique, commonly referred to as "flicking," is distinct from other woodwind techniques and is often neglected in the training of young bassoonists owing to a lack of clear understanding as to when and why the technique is necessary and how it is executed.

Low   Middle or Half   High
            Hole

Example 4.6. Divisions of the bassoon registers

By dividing the affected range of the bassoon into three parts, one can begin to see when it is necessary to "flick." For the purpose of this explanation only, the term *low register* is used here to define the notes from F through f (the notes lower than this are only rarely required to slur more than an octave and will not be considered in this discussion).

The *middle* or *half-hole register*, as discussed in the first part of this chapter, consists of a group of three notes (f♯, g, a♭) occurring immediately over the break of the bassoon. Because they are vented by using the half hole, they do not generally need to be flicked to obtain a clear response.

The *high register* is here defined as the notes from a through d¹. The fingerings of the notes above d¹ have their own distinct fingerings that are not related to the lower octave and therefore usually are not problematic in a slurred passage.

Flicking should take place when a note in the low register is slurred to a note in the high register. Hence there is an actual difference in finger technique between the execution of the two measures in Example 4.7.

Flicking Optional   Flicking Required

Example 4.7. A tongued and slurred comparison

Inexperienced students will often execute both of these octaves without flicking, instead forcing the slur in the second measure by biting slightly or blowing harder. The outcome of these approaches is that often the timing of the response of the upper note is left somewhat to chance. The flicking technique, when executed correctly, enables the bassoonist to be in absolute control of the instant of response of the upper note.

Many bassoonists recommend flicking even when a leap from the low register to the high register is not slurred, as the technique insures a quick, sure response. This may be especially helpful in passages that contain rapid notes passing from low to high register, but in general the impact of one's tongue against the reed is a sufficient stimulus to sound the upper note.

1 . . 2 . . 3 . . 4

Example 4.8. A flicking exercise

The flicking exercise shown in Example 4.8. may be practiced as follows:

Count 1. Play the low note normally, with the whisper key depressed.

Count 2. Lift the left thumb from whisper key into position over the proper flicker key. The low note continues to sound. If the note jumps up the octave prematurely, one of the following factors may be responsible:

    1. The velocity of the airstream is too rapid.
    2. The jaw is too tight.
    3. The throat is closed.
    4. The fingers are not tightly seated over the tone holes, causing a leak to occur.
    5. The reed accidentally touches the tongue.

Count 3. Lightly tap the flicker key (do not hold it down as one would an octave key). Increase the air velocity, keep the throat open and the shoulders relaxed, and firm up lips and focus them around the reed. The flicker key should be approached by the thumb directly, or stroked with a slightly downward motion, rather than the commonly used upward movement, which continues the action of the thumb ascending past the flicker key. This upward motion pulls the thumb farther away from the home base of the whisper key.

Count 4. Return the thumb to its position above the whisper key and repeat.

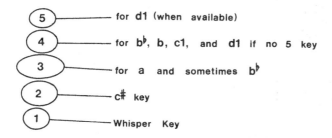

Figure 4.6. The "flicker" keys: left thumb keys of the tenor joint

A good test for deciding which key to use for bb requires one to play that note with the various flicker keys depressed (as one would an octave key on the oboe or saxophone) and compare the tuning resulting from the use of each key. Choose the key that gives the truest pitch.

Many teachers begin the study of flicking by using only the no. 4 key for all passages; only later, as the student gains a more secure knowledge of the geography of the instrument, will they point out that certain notes respond better and are better in tune with optional flicker keys. Other teachers introduce all the flicker keys simultaneously from the beginning of the study of flicking. Each approach has validity.

Slurring to c#¹ presents a particular technical problem if one uses as a primary fingering for that note the position shown in Example 4.9.

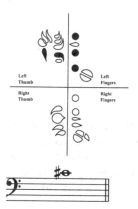

Example 4.9. A common fingering for c#¹

It would be impossible to flick to this fingering because the thumb is already occupied with the c♯ key. A special fingering for slurring to c♯¹, which does not require flicking, is then required.

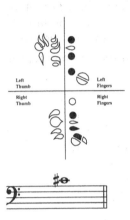

Example 4.10. A slur fingering for c♯¹

ADDITIONAL INFORMATION

When flicking in actual performance, remember that the secret to success requires the thumb to leave the whisper key early. In the exercise given in Example 4.8 (p. 52), the thumb leaves the whisper key halfway through the duration of the note. In actual performance, long note values would not require positioning the thumb this early, but for rapid passages the thumb often must leave the whisper key immediately after the lower tone has been articulated.

Flicking is necessary not only for octaves, but also for any other interval that must be slurred from the low register to the high. Thus Example 4.11 would be executed exactly as the above octave passage but with the additional change of fingering at the instant of the flick.

Example 4.11. Flicking other intervals

FLICKING DESCENDING INTERVALS

Some secondary, more advanced technical situations where flicking might be called for would include downward slurs from notes above what we have defined here as the "high" range (see Ex. 4.12). Often the note in the "high" range will not speak clearly or immediately; if the appropriate flicker key is struck at the moment of desired response, however, a smooth and seamless slur should result.

Example 4.12. Flicking to the "high" register when approached from above

Another situation that may require the use of a flicker key is shown in Example 4.13. Individual notes in this range of the bassoon (particularly the notes a and b♭) often require assistance in speaking clearly, especially at a soft dynamic level. Tapping the flicker key at the moment of desired response makes a clear attack possible. Some bassoons have a serious problem with response on these notes. A check should be made of the pin-sized hole in the bocal to insure that it is not closed with dirt or other debris. The small holes that are vented by the flicker keys should also be checked. Additional causes for this problem may concern the strength of the reed (usually too stiff) or a poor match between bocal and bassoon.

Example 4.13. Initiating a note in the "problem" register

Flicking is an important procedure that is difficult to incorporate into an already developed bassoon technique. If flicking is taught from the very beginning stages of study, it becomes a natural part of one's approach to playing. A competent bassoonist needs to feel at ease with this skill, as it makes possible a refined approach to bassoon playing.

Exercises for Flicking Practice

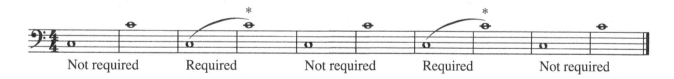

Exercise 4.14. Flicking . . . (ARE YOU ALL THUMBS?)

Exercise 4.15. More fun with flicking

Exercise 4.16. My friend Flicker (Weissenborn)

Exercise 4.17. Now try this! (Weissenborn)
* flick

Tunes for Flicking Practice

Little Annie Rooney

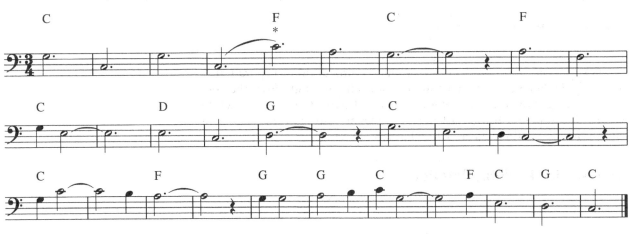

Scarborough Fair   English Folk Song

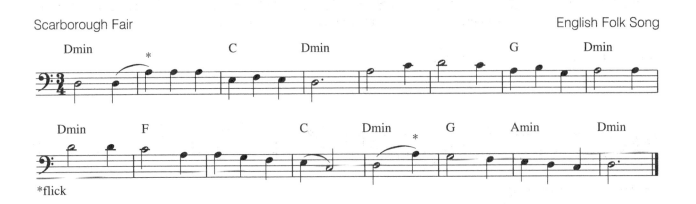

*flick

My Bonnie Lies over the Ocean

Completing the Second Octave

THE ADDITION OF E♭, E, AND F

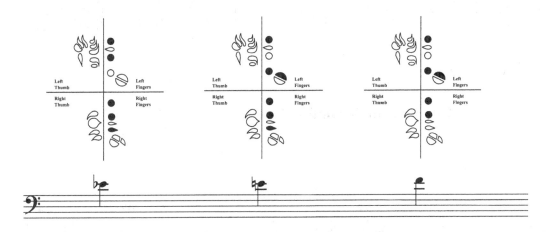

Example 4.18. Introducing e♭¹, e♮¹, and f♮¹

Exercises in the Second Octave

Exercise 4.19. F major descending

Exercise 4.20. D and above

Exercise 4.21. Octave practice. *Play slowly and tune carefully*

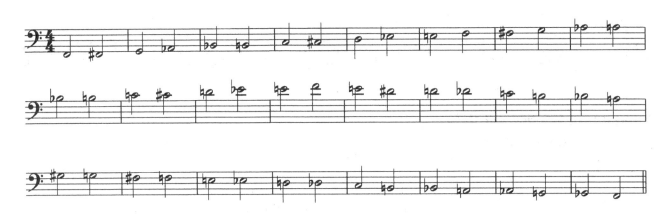

Exercise 4.22. Two-octave chromatic scale

Tunes in the Second Octave

Joy to the World

Johnny Has Gone for a Soldier

Early American

Spring Has Come

Japanese Folk Song

Dos y Dos

Mexican Folk Song

Chester for Four Bassons

William Billings

*flick

If only two bassoons are available, play I & IV. If only three, play I, II, IV.

CHAPTER 5

The Extreme Ranges
of the Bassoon

Both the extreme lower and upper registers of the bassoon present special problems for bassoonists. Young bassoonists are often taught the lowest notes early in their training, but the highest octave is often neglected and becomes a no-man's-land for many bassoon students.

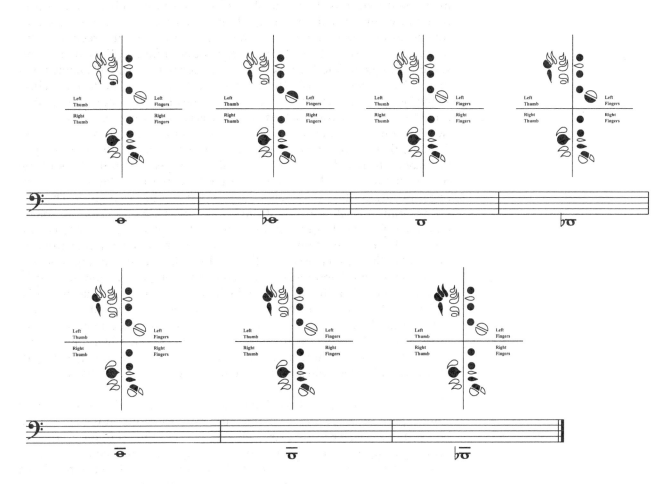

Example 5.1. The lowest register of the bassoon

Two major factors affect the production of the lowest notes of the bassoon: (1) the condition of the instrument, especially the seal of the pads; and (2) the type of scrape or trim of the bassoon reed.

If the young bassoonist is having difficulty producing the lowest tones, the instrument should be checked for leaks by testing each joint individually. A vacuum test can be easily done by an instrument technician, and pad adjustment or replacement may be called for. Another common problem is faulty assembly of the bassoon. Since producing the lowest notes requires the thumb to leave the whisper key and depress the keys on the bass joint, the pancake key takes over the responsibility of closing the hole on the bocal. If the pancake key, when depressed alone (i.e., without the whisper key), will not firmly close the pin-sized hole on the bocal, some adjustment needs to be made in the assembly of the instrument. Simply rotating the tenor joint a bit counterclockwise will usually solve the problem. If no positioning of the tenor joint can be found to close the pad to the bocal hole successfully, some adjustment needs to be made to the key mechanism by a technician.

The trim of the bassoon reed (see chapter 6) is also important to the successful production of the lowest notes of the bassoon. If we recognize that the bassoon actually can serve as two different instruments, it is easier to understand the problem of reed adjustment. Initially we have a bass-voiced instrument that must have the ability to play softly, with control, and in tune in the lowest register. Of equal importance, though, is the bassoon's role as an expressive tenor instrument. Unfortunately, the reed style for maximum success of these two voices is quite different. Bassoonists constantly struggle to find the mix of reed characteristics that will enable them to do all of the various tasks the bassoon is called upon to perform. If a bassoonist is playing primarily in one voice or the other, it is often wise to find a reed style that favors that particular voice. For example, many professional second bassoonists use a specialized scrape and reed dimensions to facilitate their work. The bassoon reed that works best in the lowest register may be trimmed a bit lighter overall, but especially in the back of the reed near the collar. This will enable the bassoonist to play with ease of response and control. It also aids in playing flatter in this register. The bassoon is built in such a way that the lowest notes are often sharp in pitch, and open placement of the embouchure and oropharyngeal cavity is critical to adjusting the tuning (see chapter 3 for hints on internal tuning). Reeds of a slightly increased length will also help with the tuning problem.

In symphonic band music, the second bassoon part is often more technically difficult than the first part, which often lies in a comfortable middle register and does not extend into the more complicated highest register. Notwithstanding the problems that may arise involving students' egos and sense of their "territory" with chair placement, it is often helpful to assign the weaker player the upper part and let the more advanced player negotiate the technical difficulties and sensitive tuning of the second bassoon part.

The notes beginning with e♭^{1} have no relationship in fingering to their counterparts an octave lower. In fact, the main difficulty in producing the notes of this register is the extremely complicated fingering for each note. Moving a half step is not usually the simple operation of changing a single finger. Dexterity is a major advantage for bassoonists as they begin to learn the notes in this range. Fingerings in this register are often incorrectly or incompletely learned by the young bassoonist, and these faulty positions can often create subtle problems of response and tuning. A further complication arises with the use of the tenor clef. No iron-clad rule states when the range of a bassoon part requires a switch to tenor clef; the choice is arbitrary and is left to the discretion of the composer or copyist. The student must be prepared to recognize notes in the highest octave in either clef (and occasionally in treble clef as well). Therefore the student must simultaneously learn the most complicated fingerings on the bassoon and alternative notation for each note. It can be a very stressful time for the bassoonist who struggles with this "double whammy." The process of learning tenor clef is similar to learning a new language, and young bassoonists need to be reassured that over time it will become almost second nature to them.

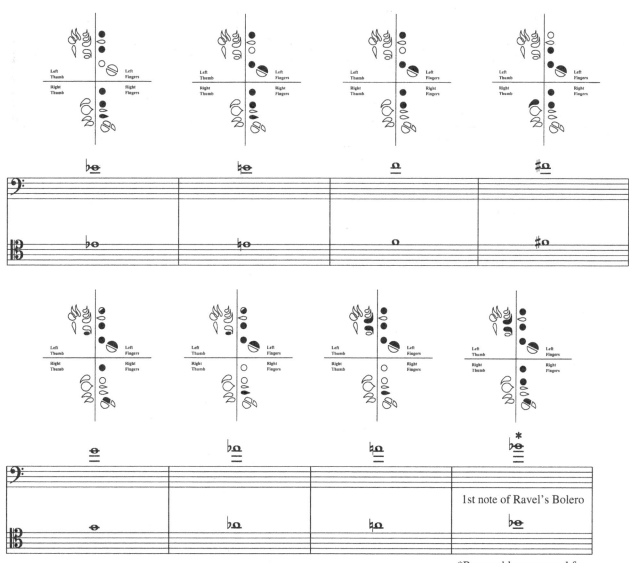

1st note of Ravel's Bolero

*Reasonable range goal for high school bassoonist.

(continued)

Example 5.2. The highest octave of the bassoon

Example 5.2. (*continued*)

Beginning of extreme high register.

1st note of Stravinsky's Rite of Spring.

CHAPTER 6

Additional Information

Guidelines for Choosing a Bassoon Student

To state any hard and fast rules governing the selection of a prospective bassoon student would ultimately be unfair to students and music teachers alike. Nevertheless, general guidelines can help the teacher gauge the likelihood of a student's success with the bassoon. A teacher must gather and evaluate data and weigh the chances for success.

WHY IS THE SELECTION PROCESS IMPORTANT?

Choosing an individual for bassoon study is a matter of some consequence. Because a school district may own only one bassoon, which is an expensive instrument, the teacher does not have the luxury of starting a large number of students on the bassoon with hopes that one or two will "take" to the instrument. The teacher cannot afford to squander that valuable bassoon on an uninterested or less than qualified student—not if one hopes eventually to have a bassoonist contributing to the band or orchestra program.

The choice of this individual, if made wisely and with careful consideration of the skills necessary for success as a bassoonist, is a vital first step in the selection process.

WHEN TO BEGIN

Although not always the case, bassoon students are often transferred from another instrument and therefore have a previous background in music. This procedure generally works well because these students already have learned to read music* and have a basic understanding of rhythm and meter. They should, through transference of these basic skilss to the bassoon, be able to progress rapidly through the beginning stages. In addition, because such students are a few years older, they are generally more mature, have developed practice habits, and have gained some finger coordination and strength.

It is not usually a good investment of a teacher's time or resources to transfer someone to the bassoon who is nearing high school graduation. The change is best made when enough years remain to enable the student to contribute to the band or orchestra program. Generally, that time will be after only two or three years of study on the student's first instrument.

The instrument to transfer from is usually a matter of little consequence, although the transfer is usually made from another woodwind, since there are often an excess number of flute, clarinet, and saxophone students. It is important, of course, to transfer a student who is having relative success with the first instrument. Experience has shown that a poor clarinetist or

---

* Learning to read bass clef is usually a fairly simple matter. At first, students should simply relate the note in its position on the staff with a fingering and not be concerned with its new name. Eventually, they will learn to identify the symbol for each note with its proper bass clef (and later tenor clef) name.

saxophonist will also usually make a poor bassoonist. Understandably, music teachers are often hesitant to sacrifice their best clarinet or flute player for bassoon study. Nevertheless, prospective bassoon students should have achieved some level of real success on their first instrument. It goes without saying that successful bassoon students are often intelligent and hard working, with a mature attitude—as are successful students on any instrument.

THE STUDENT'S ENTHUSIASM

In addition to the above stated attributes, bassoon students must also have perseverance, as the rewards in playing this challenging instrument are not immediate. It is a tremendous benefit toward success if students are excited and enthusiastic about bassoon study. This enthusiasm will help carry them through the arduous early stages; indeed, minor obstacles can often be overcome if students have a strong desire to play the bassoon. In addition, many bassoonists are somewhat extroverted. This is an important character trait, since the bassoon student will not be a member of a large section, but rather will often be the only one playing a particular part. The outgoing youngster will often be more suited to this solo function.

PHYSICAL CONSIDERATIONS

A student's stature should not be the deciding factor in whether he or she is a good candidate for bassoon study, although a student who finds the bassoon extremely cumbersome to assemble, carry, or hold may become discouraged. Hand size is not especially critical unless the hand is extraordinarily small. Dexterity, strength, and especially finger independence are more crucial considerations.

FACIAL BUILD AND THE EMBOUCHURE

Some aspects of the student's facial build that may lead to problems in embouchure development include a pronounced underbite and protruding or unusually large teeth that make forming and holding the embouchure difficult or uncomfortable. Because the lips must cushion the teeth from the reed, a combination of very large teeth and thin lips may make holding the embouchure a difficult and painful task.

A PHILOSOPHY FOR BASSOON STUDY

The instrumental teacher who conveys the idea that the double reed instruments are reserved only for those who are exceptionally interested and serious may have more success in attracting the most qualified students. It is a wise strategy for the instrumental teacher to insist that bassoon students study privately. The bassoonist's unique problems, such as reed and instrument adjustments, are best dealt with by a specialist. In addition, private study should continue the year round, and not only during the concert band season. Requiring private study is warranted because the bassoon is usually owned by the school and lent to the student bassoonist. It is not unreasonable for the band or orchestra director to insist that this expensive equipment be used correctly and to its maximum efficiency for the eventual benefit of the entire ensemble.

There are, of course, no guarantees that following these guidelines will produce a fine bassoon player, but it is worth the instrumental teacher's time and trouble to give this matter careful consideration.

Choosing a Bassoon

As a band director, you may be faced with the challenge of purchasing a bassoon. Your choice of instruments is quite important, since the expense of a bassoon does not allow for much trial and error. Because even an inexpensive instrument involves the expenditure of thousands of dollars, you may have to live with your choice for quite a long time.

The bassoon models listed below are well-known brands commonly found in the United States. The prices are constantly rising and, in the case of the European instruments, are tied to fluctuating exchange rates.

Model

Fox
Fox Products Corporation
6110 S. State Road 5
P.O. 347
South Whitley, IN 46787
(219) 723-4888

Heckel
(available only directly from German factory)
Biebrich, Germany

Kroner
(made in Europe, available from)
Custom Music Co.
1930 Hilton
Ferndale, MI 48220
(800) 521-6380
(313) 546-4135

Puchner
(made in Germany, available from)
Custom Music Company
1930 Hilton
Ferndale, MI 48220
(313) 546-4135
(800) 521-6380

Schreiber
(made in Germany, available from)
Boosey and Hawkes
Buffet Crampon, Inc.
1925 Enterprise Court
Libertyville, IL 60048
(847) 816-2500

Moosmann
(made in Germany, available from)
Miller Marketing
2002 Renaissance Blvd.
Suite #140
King of Prussia, PA 19406
1-800-323-3216
Fax: (610) 278-5029

Yamaha
(made in Japan, available from)
Yamaha Corp. of America
3445 E. Paris Avenue S.E.
P.O. Box 899
Grand Rapids, MI 49512
(616) 940-4900

Instrument Vendors

Wichita Band Instument Co.
2525 E. Douglas
Wichita, KS 67211
1-800-835-3006
(316) 684-0291
Fax: (316) 684-6858

Woodwind and Brasswind
19880 State Line Road
South Bend, IN 46637
1-800-348-5003

Others

The Bocal

Besides an instrument in good repair, a bassoonist's setup should include a good reed and a bocal that is suited to the instrument. The bocal is often the weak link in this arrangement.

The bocal affects the overall pitch level, the internal tuning, the response, and the tone quality. In addition, some bocals may play a particular range with more ease than others. For example, some professional bassoonists keep a "high range bocal" especially for works such as *Bolero* and *The Rite of Spring*.

A bocal may work well on one instrument and poorly on another. Therefore, although there are some general guidelines, it comes down to trial and error to find the best bocal for each instrument.

Bocals are usually marked with a number and a letter. The number (0, 1, 2, 3, or 4) indicates the length of the bocal, zero being the shortest length and four the longest. If your bassoon students are playing consistently sharp in all registers, perhaps a longer (higher numbered) bocal will help correct the problem. A normal-length bocal is a #2, which is equivalent to a #3 in the Fox model (the Fox bocals are one number higher for equivalent length). No bocal will make the bassoon play perfectly in tune. Every instrument has some out-of-tune notes, which need to be favored. In addition, the bassoon has a natural tendency to sharpness in the lowest register. A student must learn to compensate for this internally rather than just use a longer bocal. The letters on the bocal usually indicate a model number or identify the thickness or type of metal. A standard Heckel bocal is the #2CC; an equivalent-length, top-quality Fox bocal is the #3CVC.

A good-quality bocal may considerably improve the tone and response of an average bassoon. The cost is substantial but often worth the investment when compared with the price of a new instrument. Purchasing a new bocal is a fairly inexpensive method of upgrading existing equipment.

The Reed

No matter how skilled a performer may become or how good the instrument, the bassoonist is constantly at the mercy of the reed. Even the finest reed is short-lived, and a bassoonist will need a constant supply of new ones for practice and performing. Many commercial, mass-produced reeds are not of good quality. Others are well made but lack the final adjustments that could make them responsive to a specific instrument. Furthermore, synthetic reeds (usually plastic) should be avoided except perhaps at the very youngest ages; these reeds generally do not cultivate good playing habits or a concept of good tone. The ideal situation is to find a reputable bassoonist to teach your bassoon students. Generally a teacher will supply students with reeds until they progress to the point where they are able to make their own. If this is not possible, sometimes contacts can be made with out-of-town players and teachers who are willing to sell reeds. Advanced students can be encouraged by their private teachers to make their own reeds. Reed making is a time-consuming and challenging art. Only extremely serious students will find this aspect of the bassoon worth their time and trouble, and they will need guidance from an experienced reed maker. In cases where this is not possible, the texts *Bassoon Reed-making: A Basic Technique* by Christopher Weait and *Bassoon Reed Making* by Popkin and Glickman are helpful (full references to these books may be found near the end of this chapter).

While custom-made reeds are ideal, some factory-made reeds are quite good and can be "doctored" by the bassoon student who has the right tools and a little know-how. Basic reed tools include a reed knife, a mandrel, a plaque, a reamer, and a pair of needle-nose pliers.

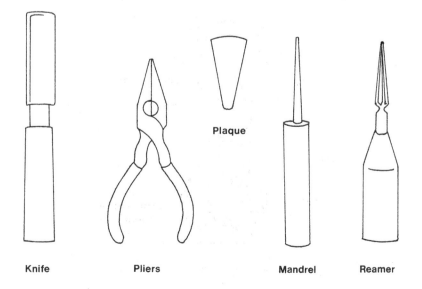

Plaque

Knife   Pliers   Mandrel   Reamer

Figure 6.1. The basic reed tools

The *mandrel* is used to hold the reed while trimming. Insert it firmly into the bocal end of the reed. The *plaque* is inserted between the blades of the reed and provides a solid surface on which to scrape the blades. The *knife* is used to remove cane from the lay of the reed. The *reamer* is used to enlarge the reed opening for the bocal if the fit is too tight (the bocal should fit in the reed about five-sixteenths of an inch). *Pliers* are used to tighten loose wires and to adjust the aperture of the reed by applying gentle pressure to the wires.

A reed may need to be doctored if it is difficult for the student to produce a tone with ease. Purchased reeds are often unfinished and thus too stiff. They may require a viselike embouchure to produce a controlled sound, and attacks may be difficult and percussive, because the basic scrape, though proportionally correct, may be too heavy. These reeds can often be made immediately better by *lightly* scraping or sanding cane from the entire surface of the blades (use 400-gauge waterproof sandpaper). Simply remove an even layer of cane overall. This procedure alone will often improve a reed substantially. Sometimes a reed will stiffen up as it is broken in and will require this overall scraping several times before stabilizing.

A reed may need further scraping from specific areas if it does not blow freely and if the "crow" is not easily obtained. (The crow is the multiphonic sound of mixed high and low tones that bassoonists use to quickly test a reed's balance.)

Before discussing further adjustments to reeds, it will be helpful first to identify the various parts of the reed and the different areas of the lay (the surface of the blades).

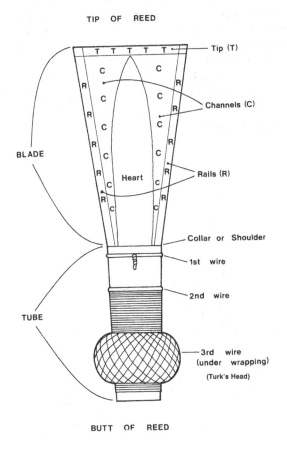

Figure 6.2. The bassoon reed

In very general terms, the reed is thin at the tip and becomes gradually thicker toward the collar. From side to side, the reed is thickest at the heart and gradually thins to the edges of the blades as it passes from the heart to the channels and finally to the very narrow rail areas.

When working on the reed, be sure it is wet before beginning to scrape the blades. Reaming out the reed, though, is best done when the reed is dry. This prevents shredding the wood inside the tube of the reed. Cane from the lay should be taken off in small amounts, constantly checking by blowing after every several scrapes. Cane should be taken off smoothly, and "dug-out" areas should not appear. Checking the reed by shining a light through it is helpful. The blades should be trimmed symmetrically, with the left and right sides of each blade matching. Ideally all four "halves" of the blades should be identical.

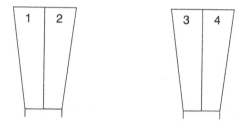

Figure 6.3. Trimming the blades symmetrically

MAKING MINOR ADJUSTMENTS TO FACTORY-MADE REEDS

If a reed will not produce an easy attack, it may be necessary to thin out the tip and define the "arch." Areas of different thickness on bassoon reeds should always occur gradually. The arch should therefore be subtle and gradual in its formation. The tip (area T) sometimes needs major thinning, and this is done by a process called "chipping." Take the knife and work only on the tip. Count the strokes and then do the same to the other side. Now use the knife and sandpaper and gently blend this area into the arch. As a guide, shine the light through the reed to view the formation of the scrape.

Figure 6.4. Chipping the tip and forming the arch

Difficulty in producing low notes may require that wood be taken from the area highlighted in Figure 6.5. This will also flatten the pitch of a reed.

Figure 6.5. Locating the trimming area for low note response

Difficulty in producing a clear articulation without a "growl" in the register 𝄢 can be averted by using the flicker key at the moment of articulation (see chapter 4). In addition, opening small "windows" on the reed by extra thinning to the shown areas (as in Fig. 6.6) will often make the response clearer.

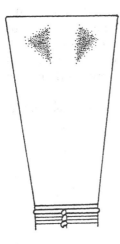

Figure 6.6. Trimming area for clearer response of problem register

The pliers can be used to adjust the aperture of the reed. A normal aperture should be approximately one-sixteenth of an inch from blade to blade in the center of the tip. A smaller aperture may not allow sufficient air to pass through the reed, while a larger aperture may tire the embouchure and make control difficult. Both the first and second wires are manipulated to make most adjustments of the aperture. To open an aperture, gently squeeze the first wire at the sides of the reed along the seams, then apply slight pressure on the second wire from the perpendicular direction. To close the aperture, do the reverse procedure. Sometimes two pairs of pliers are used and the gentle pressure is applied simultaneously.

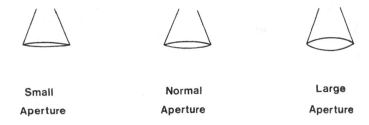

Small   **Normal**   **Large**

Aperture   **Aperture**   **Aperture**

Figure 6.7. Various apertures of the reed

Bassoon Supplies

The following is a partial listing of sources for bassoon supplies: reed tools, cane for reed making, good-quality finished reeds, method books, bocals, music for the bassoon, and other materials not usually carried by a neighborhood music store. Write or call and ask for a current price list.

Vendor

Berdon
P.O. Box 483
Hobart, WA 98025
(425) 392-1866
Fax: (425) 392-8130

Charles Double Reed Co.
30 Pleasant Street
P.O. Box 2610
Conway, NH 03818
1-800-REED-TIP (733-3847)

Christlieb Products
3311 Scadlock Lane
Sherman Oaks, CA 91403
(818) 783-6554

Chudnow Woodwinds
5 Manchester Court
Napa, CA 94558
(1-800) 780-4340

Forrests Music
1849 University Avenue
Berkeley, CA 94703
(1-800) 322-OBOE

Jack Spratt Woodwind Shop
11 Park Ave, P.O. Box 277
Old Greenwich, CT 06870
(1-800) 626-9277

Jones Double Reed Products
Box 3888
Spokane, WA 99220-3888
509-326-1529
Fax: 509-326-5482

Edmund Neilson Woodwind Products
61 E. Park Blvd.
Villa Park, IL 60181
(630) 833-5676

Peter Angelo
P.O. Box 4005
Greenwich, CT 06830
(203) 661-2571

Prestini Reed Corporation
P.O. Box 2296
351 E. Patagonia Highway
Nogales, AZ 85628-2296
(520) 287-4931

Vigder's Bassoon Supplies
9540 Telegraph Rd., #19
Ventura, California 93004-1715
(805) 647-1070

Others

Methods and Study Materials

The most important and universally recognized bassoon method is the *Practical Method for Bassoon* by Julius Weissenborn. Weissenborn (1837–88) also wrote several pedagogical works for bassoon and piano and a set of bassoon trios. The Weissenborn method is not suitable for beginning players unless they have studied music previously. The method proceeds rapidly and assumes a general knowledge of music fundamentals. If a student is a true beginner, a suggested course of study is the *Elementary Method for Bassoon* published by Rubank. Rubank also publishes an *Intermediate Method* and an *Advanced Method*, but a student should begin the standard course of study in the Weissenborn method as soon as is possible. Two other sets of important studies for the bassoon are the Scale Studies Op. 24, and the Concert Studies Op. 26 by Ludwig Milde. These more advanced works are commonly introduced to suppliment the Weissenborn when the student begins to learn tenor clef.

The following list of solo works for bassoon contains pieces which are generally pedagogical in nature and are suitable for young bassoonists.

STUDY PIECES

ELEMENTARY AND INTERMEDIATE WORKS

BENSON, WARREN. *Song and Dance.* Boosey and Hawkes.

BENOY, A. W., AND A. BRYCE. *First Pieces for Bassoon.* Oxford.

BEST, ARTHUR. *Little Elephant.* Belwin.

————. *Grandfather's Waltz.* Belwin.

COCKSHOTT, G. *Three Pieces on Appalachian Folk Tunes.* Novello.

COHEN, SOL B. *Song of the Troubadour.* Belwin.

DEARNLEY, C. H. *Eight Easy Pieces by Classical Composers.* Chester.

HERFURTH, C. P. *Classical Album of Early Grade Pieces for Cello.*

THOMAS PAINE. *Scherzo.* Belwin.

WEISSENBORN, JULIUS. *Two Pieces.* International.

MORE CHALLENGING WORKS FOR STUDENT BASSOONISTS

GALLIARD, J. E. *Six Sonatas.* International.

MOZART, W. A. *Concerto for Bassoon* (3d mvt.). International.

PHILLIPS, B. *Concert Piece.* Carl Fischer.

SENAILLÉ, J. B. *Allegro Spiritoso.* Southern.

TELEMANN, G. P. *Sonata in F Minor.* International.

WEISSENBORN, J. *Capriccio.* International.

The Importance of Chamber Music in a Student's Development

Chamber music is generally defined as a small ensemble that does not require a conductor and in which no two parts play in unison throughout. Because each part is covered by only one player, independence and leadership among the participants are fostered, making the chamber music experience an important component in a young musician's training. Being solely responsible for one's part is a new experience for many young players whose primary training has been as a participant in a large ensemble, an environment where many players in a section cover each part, or where parts are often doubled or tripled among different sections of the ensemble.

The intimate nature and clear texture that small ensembles provide allow problems of intonation and ensemble to be more easily identified and corrected than in larger groups. This exposure particularly encourages attention to tone quality development and to the concept of blend. In addition, for instruments such as the bassoon and oboe the chamber music experience offers an opportunity to be easily heard and to be challenged by parts that are often more demanding than those found in larger ensemble works.

The most standard type of chamber ensemble for winds, and that for which a substantial body of literature exists, is the woodwind quintet (more properly called the wind quintet since its instrumentation—flute, oboe, clarinet, bassoon and horn—is not exclusively woodwind). This instrumentation has been used to extraordinary success by such composers as Franz Danzi (1763–1826) (nine quintets), Anton Reicha (1770–1863) (twenty-four quintets), Paul Hindemith, Carl Nielson, Samuel Barber, and others. The medium has many important works and is also favored with a number of recognized masterworks. While much of the wind quintet literature is extremely difficult and would be most suitable for advanced students and professionals, there are a number of works that are particularly well suited to a younger, less experienced group and that would provide an excellent introduction into the chamber music experience. (See following section on recommended works.)

Because there are usually a limited number of bassoons and oboes in a large ensemble, it is difficult to form many wind quintets made of the standard instrumentation. In order to involve as many of the large ensemble members as possible in *some* sort of chamber ensemble, it is necessary to organize other combinations of instruments. Many publishing companies offer a training division of small ensemble music with practical groupings such as multiple clarinet, flute, and saxophone. Some works offer optional parts that allow for flexible instrumentation, depending on the resources available (such as bass clarinet substituting for bassoon, flute for oboe, and saxophone for horn). Many of these works are quite simple arrangements, but are attractive and serve well for young musicians who are just beginning to understand the fundamentals of ensemble playing. A music director with some skill in arranging may find a challenge in arranging works for the very specific resources of his own ensembles. Of special note is a rich repertoire of saxophone quartet literature made up of the standard instrumentation of soprano, alto, tenor, and baritone saxophone. Many of these works, like the wind quintet literature, are best left to advanced students or professionals.

Chamber ensembles are most successful when they are coached regularly, requiring a significant time commitment from the music director. Often the youngest groups can be coached occasionally by more advanced players (which serves as a learning experience for both the ensemble and the coach) and even the most inexperienced ensemble can benefit occasionally from a rehearsal without a formal coach.

The investment of time in chamber music practice and performance reaps obvious rewards, as the students develop independence, more critical listening skills in regard to tuning, blend, and ensemble playing, and personal discipline. These resulting improvements will quickly find their way into all musical situations from solo playing to large ensemble playing. A yearly chamber music concert and participation in local solo and ensemble competitions can provide the necessary motivation to generate enthusiasm and love of chamber-music playing. In addition to the aforementioned musical rewards of small-ensemble playing, chamber music can provide a source of great diversion and entertainment for students as they enjoy both the music and the camaraderie of fellow musicians.

A few helpful resource books handy for reference or that you may want to investigate at your local library are listed below. Included are only volumes that provide a graded listing of works.

Ensemble Music for Winds and Percussion: A Catalogue
George N. Heller
MENC
1201 16th St. N.W., Washington, DC 20036
Library of Congress Catalogue number: 72-114403

Works in this volume are graded from easiest (I) to most difficult (V). There are extensive chamber listings of works (clarinet trio, flute quartet, etc.) of same-instrument ensembles. The book is divided into sections such as ensembles for woodwinds and ensembles for mixed woodwinds and also brass and percussion ensemble works.

Catalogue of Chamber Music for Woodwind Instruments
Roy Houser
Da Capo Press, 1973
227 West 17th St., New York, NY 10011

This volume is organized by number of players beginning with trios. The works of each grouping are then listed alphabetically by composers so that the various combinations available for each grouping are mixed together. Although the works are not graded in a traditional sense, each grouping has a section titled "training pieces," which might be of special interest to a band director.

A Teacher's Guide to the Literature of Woodwind Instruments
Mary Rasmussen and Donald Mattran
Brass and Woodwind Quarterly
Box 111, Curham, NH

This volume contains only works for woodwinds (with exception of horn, which is included in the wind quintet section). Listings are given of same-instrument ensembles as well as mixed duos, trios, quartets, and quintets. There is also a listing of solo works for each instrument. Works are ranked on a "grade school to college level" scale. There is helpful commentary on the recommended works.

Selective Music Lists
Compiled cooperatively by MENC, American String Teachers Association, National Association of College Wind and Percussion Teachers (NACWAPI)
MENC, 1979
1201 18th St. N.W., Washington, DC 20036
Library of Congress Catalogue number: 79-64091

This volume is geared to solo and ensemble competitions, and has solo works for every instrument as well as ensembles of various instrumentation. The works are graded on a 1–6 scale, and the publisher is provided.

Some Recommended Works for Beginning a Wind Quintet Collection

QUINTETS

The following works are very accessible for a high school level wind quintet. All are published with a score.

AGAY, DENES. *Five Easy Dances for Woodwind Quintet*. Presser.
> This delightful work includes a polka, tango, bolero, waltz, and rhumba. A flutist with a well-developed high register and good leadership qualities helps to make for a successful performance of this work.

LIADOV, ANATOL (ANATOLY LYADOV). *Eight Russian Folk Songs*. Western International Music Co.
> An interesting and stimulating works for a young quintet with a very Russian character. The oboe part is written rather low, creating some response and tuning challenges for the young player.

MUCZYNSKI, ROBERT. *Movements*. Shawnee Press.
> This interesting, challenging work is composed of five short movements. (f,s,f,s,f) In addition to the challenge of the controlled, sustain playing found in the two slow movements, the three fast movements offer challenges for rhythmic precision, syncopation, and some mixed meter. The piece also requires a wide range of dynamics, attention to tone color, blend, and phrasing.

WASHBURN, ROBERT. *Quintet for Winds*. Oxford University Press.

This work is in three movements and requires a strong flute player with good technique, a good high register, and the ability to lead the ensemble. It is in many ways a more difficult work than the *Suite* by Washburn, containing some difficult technical passages, mixed meter, and challenging bassoon and horn parts.

WASHBURN, ROBERT. *Suite for Woodwind Quintet*. Elkan-Vogel.

Also in three movements. The *Suite* is enjoyable and fairly easy for all instruments, and provides solo opportunities for all the instruments.

Music Vendors

Byron Hoyt
Sheet Music Sevice
2525 16th St.
San Francisco, CA 94103
(415) 431-8055

Eble Music Co.
P.O. Box 2570
Iowa City, IA 52244-2570
(319) 338-0313

Kendor Music Inc.
Main and Grove Street
P.O. Box 278
Delevan, N.Y. 14042
(716) 492-1254
(Graded woodwind ensemble music collection)

Music Mart
3301 Carlisle Blvd. NE
Albuquerque, NM 87110
1-800-545-6204
(505) 889-9777

Joseph Patelson Music House
160 W. 56th Street
New York, NY 10010
(212) 757-5587
Fax: 212-246-5633

Pepper of Los Angeles
P.O. Box 550
Gardena, CA 90247
1-800-345-6296

Portland Music
125 NW 5th Ave.
Portland, OR 97209
1-800-876-9777

T.I.S. Music Shop
1302 E. 3rd Street
P.O. Box 1998
Bloomington, IN   47402
1-800-421-8132

Trevco Music
P.O. Box 4
Tallevast, Fl 34270
(813) 758-7277
(extensive collection of solo and ensemble music for double reeds)

Volkwein Brothers Inc.
138 Industry Dr.
Pittsburgh, PA 15212
(412) 788-5900

Others

SELECTED AND REPRESENTATIVE WORKS

The bassoon is a versatile instrument, and although the number of works for solo bassoon is small compared to those for the flute or the violin, there are a number of important solo works. In addition, the bassoon is a remarkable chamber instrument. Its irreplaceable voice and range are found not only in the wind quintet but also in other types of chamber music groupings. The following is an annotated list of a few important works for the bassoon in the solo and chamber idioms. There are many excellent recordings, but there is no substitute for a live performance. Students are encouraged to attend a bassoon recital if possible.

FRANÇOIS DEVIENNE. QUARTET OP. 73, NO. 1, FOR BASSOON AND STRINGS Devienne (1759–1803) was a French flutist, bassoonist, and prolific composer whose output includes several symphonies, concertos for bassoon, and much chamber music. He published an important method for the flute in 1795. In addition to three quartets for bassoon and strings, Devienne also wrote a set of duos for two bassoons.

PAUL HINDEMITH. SONATA FOR BASSOON Paul Hindemith (1895–1963) was a German composer, teacher, conductor, and violist. A prolific composer, he was dedicated to teaching as well as writing "practical music." In addition to the Sonata for Bassoon, written in 1939, he wrote a sonata for nearly every instrument. Another important wind work is his *Kleine Kammermusik* for wind quintet.

W. A. MOZART. CONCERTO FOR BASSOON AND ORCHESTRA, K. 191 Over the course of his short life, Mozart (1756–91) composed in nearly every medium, including opera, symphony, concerto, and chamber music. The Bassoon Concerto was written in 1774, when Mozart was only eighteen years old, for the amateur bassoonist Thaddaus von Durnitz. There is evidence that Mozart may have written three other concertos for von Durnitz, but they have been lost. Mozart wrote another important work for the bassoon, the Sonata for Bassoon and Cello, K. 292.

CAMILLE SAINT-SAËNS. SONATA FOR BASSOON OP. 168   Saint-Saëns (1835–1921), a French composer, pianist, organist, and writer, influenced an entire generation of composers with his mastery of the art of composition and his technical virtuosity at the keyboard. The Bassoon Sonata was composed in the year of his death and is one of the last pieces he composed. He also composed sonatas for oboe and clarinet.

ALEXANDRE TANSMAN. SONATINE FOR BASSOON AND PIANO   Tansman (1897–1985) was a French composer, conductor, and pianist of Polish origin. He was influenced by Chopin, Stravinsky, and Ravel and composed in nearly every style of his day, including tonal, atonal, polytonal, and serial music. He also wrote a flute sonata.

ANTONIO VIVALDI. CONCERTOS FOR BASSOON (VARIOUS)   The Italian composer Antonio Vivaldi (1678–1741) was extraordinarily prolific and wrote thirty-eight concertos for the bassoon. In addition, his six sonatas for cello have become a standard part of the bassoon repertoire. The bassoon concertos were apparently written for the orphaned or abandoned girls who were his music students at the Pio Ospedale della Pietà (Little Hospice of Mercy) in Venice.

CARL MARIA VON WEBER. ANDANTE AND HUNGARIAN RONDO FOR BASSOON AND ORCHESTRA; CONCERTO FOR BASSOON AND ORCHESTRA   With the exception of the Mozart Concerto, these two works for bassoon and orchestra are probably the most popular and commonly performed pieces for the bassoon. Weber (1786–1826) was German and is best known for his Romantic operas.

SAMUEL BARBER. *SUMMER MUSIC* OP. 31, FOR WOODWIND QUINTET   The American composer Samuel Barber (1910–81) was a professor of composition at the Curtis Institute of Music in Philadelphia. *Summer Music* was written in 1956 for the Chamber Music Society of Detroit.

IGOR STRAVINSKY. OCTET   Stravinsky (1882–1971) wrote the Octet in 1922 during his neoclassical period. The unusual instrumentation (flute, clarinet, two bassoons, trumpet in C, trumpet in A, trombone, and bass trombone) is reported by Stravinsky to have come to him in a dream. The bassoon parts are virtuosic and central to the work.

Books, Journals, and Other Items of Interest

Some public school music programs provide a sufficient budget to allow the director to build a small library of solo pieces and étude books for each instrument. In addition, if finances permit, it is often helpful to have a few texts pertaining to each instrument on hand. The following texts would provide an interested bassoon student materials for further study.

JOPPIG, GUNTHER. *The Oboe and the Bassoon.* London: Batsford, 1988.

LANGWILL, LYNDESAY. *The Bassoon and Contrabassoon.* New York: Norton, 1965.

These two books contain detailed histories of the bassoon and its evolution. They also contain information about famous players and important works for the instrument.

POPKIN, MARK, AND LOREN GLICKMAN. *Bassoon Reed Making*. Evanston, IL: Instrumentalist, 1969.

WEAIT, CHRISTOPHER. *Bassoon Reed-making: A Basic Technique*. New York: McGinnis and Marx, 1980.

These are useful texts for students as they learn reed making.

COOPER, HUGH, AND HOWARD TOPLANSKY. *Essentials of Bassoon Technique*. Union, NJ: H. Toplansky, 1968.

A complete guide to primary, optional, and trill fingerings.

THE INTERNATIONAL DOUBLE REED SOCIETY

The International Double Reed Society supports research, teaching, and performance of the double reed instruments. The organization, which discounts student memberships, publishes a journal with articles on various aspects of bassoon and oboe. An annual convention features many performances and lectures, occasions to try out new instruments, and opportunities to purchase all double reed–related equipment and music. The International Double Reed Society maintains a list service for its members.

For information, write to the International Double Reed Society, 626 Lakeshore Drive, Monroe, LA 71203-4032.

THE GLICKMAN-POPKIN BASSOON CAMP

The Glickman-Popkin Bassoon Camp, a week of concentrated study (especially in reed making) each summer, includes famous guest artists, instrument repairmen, and music and supply store representatives. Contact Mark Popkin, 740 Arbor Rd., Winston-Salem, NC 27104-2210.

Fingerings on the Bassoon

Many notes on the bassoon can be fingered in several different ways. Advanced bassoonists use these alternate fingerings to facilitate difficult passages. Some fingerings can give a sharper or flatter pitch center and can assist the bassoonist in tuning. Furthermore, because a particular fingering may produce a pitch with special qualities, such as darker or brighter timbre, a bassoonist may choose a fingering option that takes advantage of this distinctive feature, making the choice of fingering another tool in the bassoonist's artistic kit. An excellent and thorough source of most bassoon fingering possibilities can be found in *Essentials of Bassoon Technique* by Hugh Cooper and Howard Toplansky.

For a beginning bassoonist it is essential first to learn a set of correct primary fingerings. Once these are mastered, the student should gradually begin to learn many of the helpful alternate fingerings. Several published fingering charts for the bassoon contain errors or present secondary or trill fingerings in place of primary fingerings. The following fingering chart presents one primary fingering for each note. In most cases the fingering given is the same as the first choice in *Essentials of Bassoon Technique*.

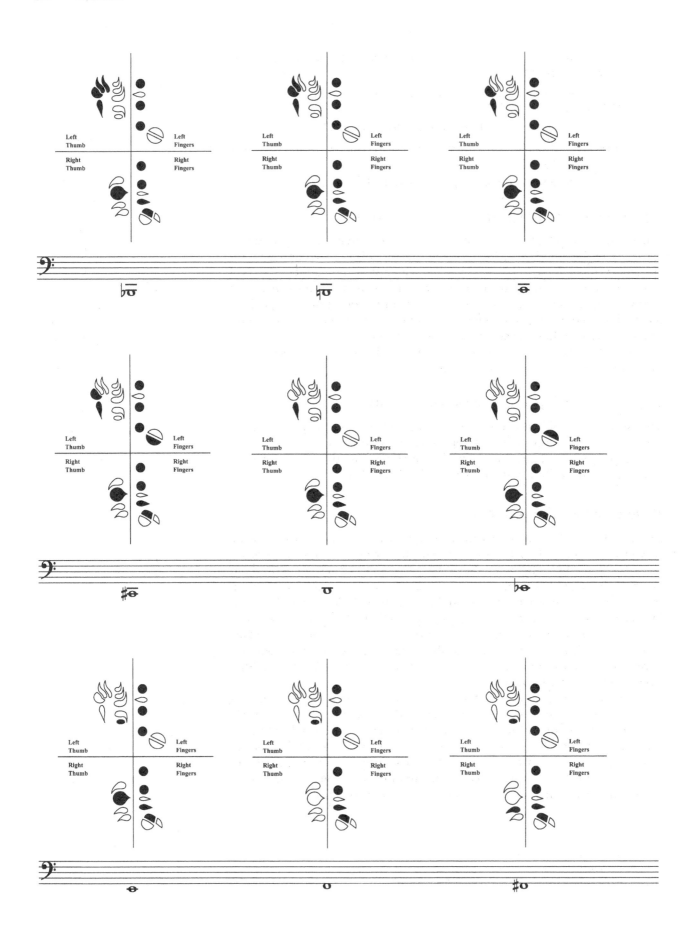

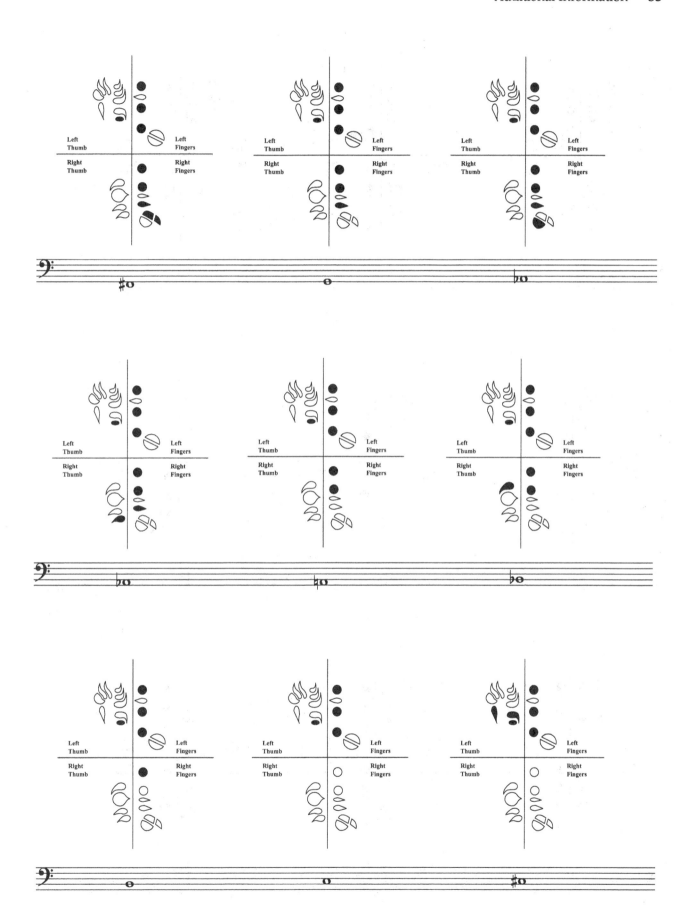

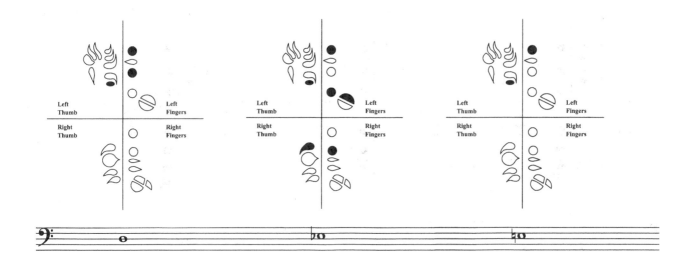

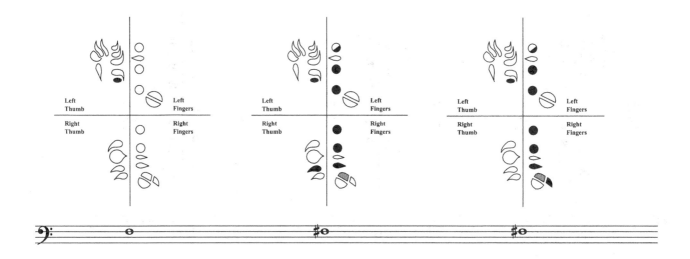

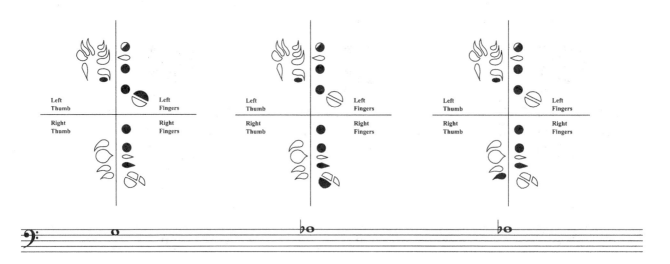

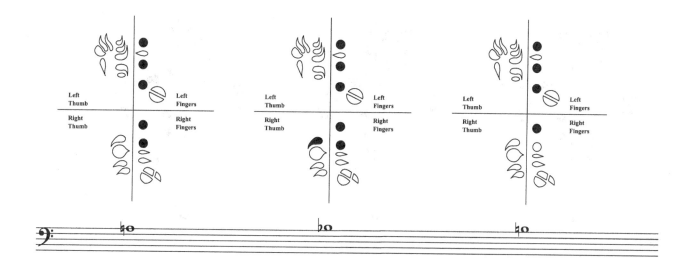

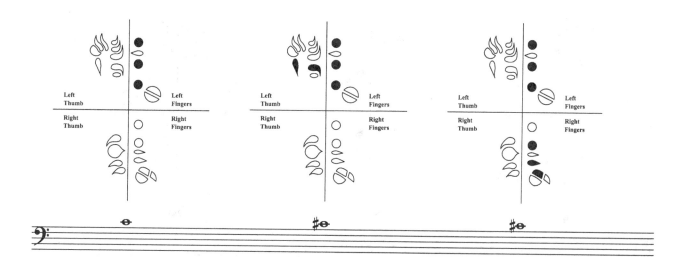

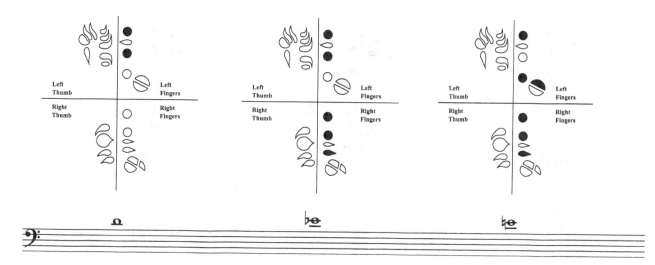

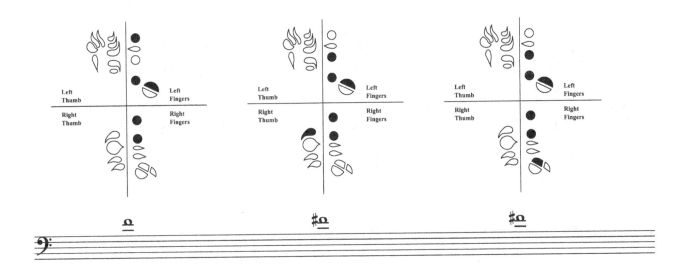

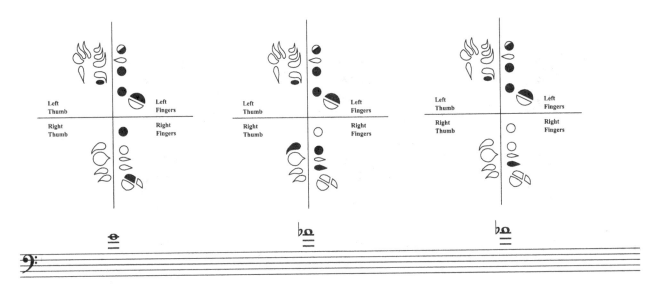

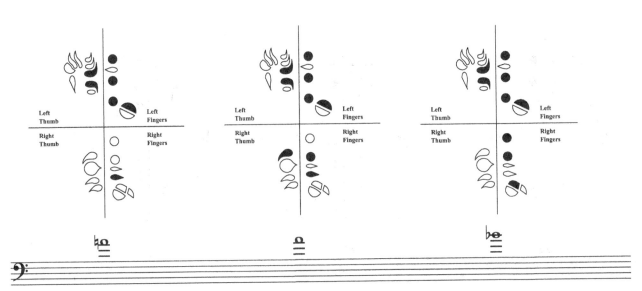

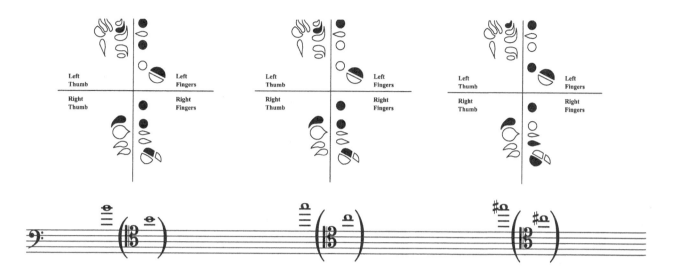

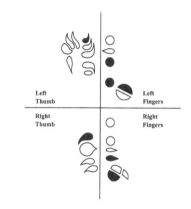

PART 2

Clarinet

JERRY KIRKBRIDE

CHAPTER 7

Introduction

The clarinet is a single reed woodwind instrument with a cylindrical bore. The B♭ clarinet is the most commonly used clarinet and the one on which beginners start. It is about 60 centimeters (23.6 inches) long and has a range of more than three octaves. The clarinet is most often made from grenadilla wood. Some are also made of plastic and metal. Plastic clarinets are made for the beginning student and for outdoor use. The metal clarinet is made exclusively for outdoor performance.

Example 7.1. The range of the clarinet

The clarinet family in order from the highest- to the lowest-pitched instruments consists of the following:

D clarinet

E♭ clarinet

B♭ clarinet

A clarinet

Alto clarinet in E♭

Bass clarinet in B♭

Contra-alto clarinet in E♭

Contrabass clarinet in B♭

All of these clarinets function the same from instrument to instrument. The fingering remains basically the same from one to the other, although the spread of the fingers differs with the size of the particular clarinet. Because of the varying mouthpiece and reed size, there must be some embouchure adjustment from instrument to instrument.

History

The invention of the clarinet around 1700 is credited to the Nuremberg instrument maker Johann Christian Denner. The first known reference to Denner and the clarinet was made by J. S. Doppelmeyer in his *Historische Nachricht von den Nurburgischen Mathematicis und Künstlern* in 1730: "At the beginning of the present century he [Denner] invented a new sort of pipe, the so-called Clarinette, to the great satisfaction of music lovers."

The predecessor of the clarinet was the chalumeau, a peasant pipe with a single reed attached to a tapered mouthpiece. The word *chalumeau* derives from the Latin *calamus*, a small reed, or from the Greek *calane*, a reed pipe. The chalumeau had no barrel or bell and was much shorter than the modern clarinet. The instrument usually had seven holes, and its range was an octave plus one note (from f to g^1). It did not overblow into the upper register.

Denner's new instrument, the clarinet, had a bell and a wider bore and was longer than the chalumeau. The barrel and the mouthpiece were made in one piece. This instrument had eight holes and two keys placed at the upper end exactly opposite each other, one on the front to be played by the index finger and producing $b\flat^1$, and one on the back played by the thumb and producing a^1. By using both keys at the same time, a very poor-sounding $b\natural^1$ was produced. The thumb key also served as the speaker (register) key, allowing the clarinet to overblow a twelfth. This made it possible to play from f to d^3.

Denner and his sons continued to experiment with and improve their clarinet. The upper register was difficult to obtain and produced an imperfect scale. By placing the thumb hole higher and narrowing it, they changed the notes the first two keys played, creating the basic arrangement of the modern clarinet: the index finger key by itself played a^1 and the two keys together produced $b\flat^1$. They also inserted a small metal sleeve into the speaker key hole, penetrating almost to the center of the bore, improving the $b\flat^1$ and preventing the collection of water in that tone hole.

This improvement created a serious problem: $b\natural^1$ could be played only by lipping down the c^2, with very poor results. Around 1740 Denner's son Jacob is generally credited with solving this problem by lengthening the clarinet, adding a bell at the bottom for resonance, and adding a key to be played by the fourth finger or thumb of the right hand. This key covered a hole added near the bottom of the lower joint that produced a low e and, by adding the register key, b^1, a twelfth higher. This improvement allowed the clarinet to play a complete range of almost three octaves, from low e to c^3.

The clarinet continued to have problems chromatically. Half steps produced by fork fingerings often did not speak well, and some notes were basically unobtainable. Several instrument makers worked on this problem, and a five-key clarinet appeared around 1760. Two new keys had been added on the lower joint of the instrument, producing $g\sharp/d\sharp^2$ and $f\sharp/c\sharp^2$.

Music written for the clarinet began to appear by the middle of the eighteenth century. Vivaldi composed three concerti grossi that included two clarinets in C and two oboes. Handel wrote an overture for two clarinets in D and corno di caccia in 1748. Johann Christian Bach used the clarinet during the 1760s in the wind symphonies he wrote for outdoor concerts in Vauxhall Gardens.

The earliest clarinet concertos were written by Johann Melchior Molter for the three-key clarinet in D. Carl Philipp Emanuel Bach wrote six sonatas for clarinet, bassoon, and harpsichord. These works emphasized the upper register of the clarinet, with little use of the chalumeau (lower) range.

The clarinet was continually being improved by means of experiments in the size of the bore, the diameter, the taper, and the undercutting of the tone holes. This changed the character of the clarinet and resulted in works using both registers freely. Many of these concertos, by such composers as Karl Stamitz, Ernst Eichner, and Georg Fux, were written for the members of the Mannheim Orchestra, which began using two clarinets around 1760.

The Viennese clarinet virtuoso Anton Stadler, working with the instrument maker T. Lotz, lengthened the clarinet, extending the range down to a low c. It was for this clarinet, called the "basset clarinet," that Mozart wrote the original version of his great concerto, K.622. There is evidence that the Quintet for Clarinet and Strings was also written for Stadler's basset clarinet.

During this time, the clarinetist needed to possess a set of clarinets in several different keys, most often in C, B♭, and A. Each clarinet had its own sound character and would play more fluently in its home key and closely related keys. This was due in part because the pads used on these clarinets were made of felt and did not close the holes as tightly as modern-day pads. This encouraged the players to use the clarinet that would use the least number of keys in a performance.

Sometime around 1791, Jean Xavier Lefèvre, a clarinet virtuoso from Paris, added a sixth key, producing c♯^{1}/g♯^{2}. This was done simultaneously by several other instrument makers as well. Moreover, several clarinetists and instrument makers were experimenting with a variety of keys. When Spohr wrote his Clarinet Concerto No. 1 for Johann Simon Hermstedt, he requested that the soloist use a clarinet with thirteen keys. Heinrich Baermann, for whom Weber wrote his concertos, had a ten-keyed instrument.

Iwan Müller, a Parisian born in Russia, introduced a newly designed thirteen-key clarinet in 1812. His method of making the clarinet was revolutionary: the tone holes were all countersucks as opposed to being built up above the tone hole, and he used pads made of leather filled with wool held in a hollow cup. This not only insured the covering of the hole but also improved the acoustic result. Müller claimed that this clarinet, in B♭, could play in any key with equal ease.

In 1812 Müller attempted to have his new instrument adopted as the officially accepted clarinet by the Paris Conservatoire. However, the members of the committee rejected his instrument because they felt that each clarinet had its own musical character and sound and this should be preserved. This clearly contradicted the practice of most composers to write for the clarinet that played most easily in the key of their work, regardless of the character of their music.

Although Müller had to close down his instrument shop in Paris as a result of this rejection, he toured England, Holland, and Germany with his new instrument, establishing it as the finest clarinet yet produced. He continued to experiment with new keys and made use of the ring key system. Moreover, he was the first to abandon the use of cord to hold the reed on the mouthpiece, using a metal ligature similar to those in use today.

The final major change in the development of the clarinet was a combination of work by three people. Theobald Boehm revolutionized the flute by designing a completely new key system for that instrument. He added a series of ring keys that circled the finger holes and, when depressed, covered an additional hole at a distance from the finger hole. Hyacinthe Klosé suggested to the instrument maker Louis Buffet that a clarinet could be made using this so-called Boehm system. Working together, they produced a clarinet with seventeen keys and six rings that controlled twenty-four tone holes. The Klosé-Buffet clarinet, presented at the Paris exhibition in 1839, is essentially the instrument used today in most of the world, including the United States.

Müller's clarinet served as the basis for two other important fingering systems, one made by Albert of Brussels, the other made by Oskar Oehler, an instrument maker from Berlin. Albert's clarinet system, also called the "simple-system," first appeared around the 1850s and had models with thirteen keys and with fourteen keys. The fourteen-key model was used by the great English clarinetist Henry Lazarus and was very popular in England and Belgium well into the twentieth century. Over several years during the first part of the twentieth century, Oehler added some of the Boehm system advantages to Müller's instrument. As well, he made other improvements involving the shape and position of the keys and worked on perfecting the general mechanism of the clarinet. This "Oehler" system clarinet is the instrument used in Germany today. Clarinetists and instrument makers have made many other experiments but the Boehm and the Oehler system clarinets remain the basis for these experiments and are the instruments used by clarinetists around the world.

Assembly of the Clarinet

The five parts of the clarinet are the mouthpiece, the barrel, the upper joint, the lower joint, and the bell. Before assembling the clarinet, check to see that all the corks have enough cork grease on them to slide easily into their counterparts. If the corks are dry or sticky, take a small amount of cork grease and spread it around the cork with your finger. As the clarinet is being assembled, the reed should be placed in the player's mouth or in a glass of water to moisten it. Water makes the reed supple so it can vibrate freely.

The most efficient way to assemble the upper and lower joints of the clarinet with the idea of preventing mechanical problems is probably too difficult for young students to manage because their hands are too small. Nevertheless, I will describe this procedure and then give an alternative for younger students to use until they are able to master the first procedure.

Begin assembling the clarinet by placing the lower joint in the right hand with the rings and holes facing upward and the top of the joint facing away from the body. Position the right thumb over the keypad located just below key #17. Rest the palm of the hand over the keypad directly below. Extend the fingers to the other side of the joint, resting them on the single keypad located there. Be careful not to put pressure on any of the key mechanisms or connecting rods. This grip helps set the pads and prevents the bending of any of the rods or key mechanisms, which can result in the pads not covering and the keys getting out of adjustment. An alternative for younger students is to grip the lower joint with the thumb positioned below the thumb rest and the fingers grasping the body of the instrument over the key rings.

Take the upper joint into the palm of the left hand with the rings and holes facing upward. Place the ring finger on the lowest ring, which, when depressed, raises the bridge key extending over the cork on the bottom end of that joint. Insert the upper-joint tenon into the lower joint in a twisting motion until the joints are flush together and the upper bridge key is exactly lined up with the lower bridge key. Always use a twisting motion. Do not push them together.

Now cradle the two joints in the palm of the right hand with the thumb rest against the right thumb. Take the bell with the left hand and twist it onto the bottom of the lower joint until the two pieces are flush together.

To continue the assembly, take the three assembled pieces with the left hand around the upper joint, again being careful not to bend any key mechanism. Take the barrel in the right hand and twist the wider end of the barrel onto the upper joint's top tenon until the two pieces are flush together and the labels are lined up. Be careful to put the left hand around the upper joint. If the left hand goes around the lower joint, the alignment

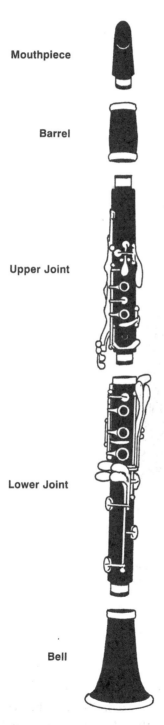

Mouthpiece

Barrel

Upper Joint

Lower Joint

Bell

Figure 7.1. The five parts of the clarinet

of the bridge keys will be disturbed and there is a risk of bending keys in the area between the upper and lower joints.

To complete the assembly, take the assembled parts with the left hand around the upper joint. With the right hand, take the mouthpiece without the reed, ligature, or cap and twist it into the top of the barrel, lining up the hole in the mouthpiece with the register key on the back of the clarinet.

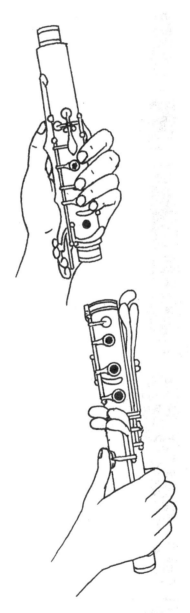

Figure 7.2. Hand position for assembling the clarinet

PLACEMENT OF THE REED AND LIGATURE

The ligature holds the reed in place on the mouthpiece. The widest part of the ligature is the bottom, and the screws are always on the right side. Some ligatures are made with the screws on the reed side of the mouthpiece and some with the screws on the opposite side.

To attach the reed to the mouthpiece, place the moistened reed on the mouthpiece with the flat side of the reed resting on the flatbed of the mouthpiece and the thin part of the reed pointing toward the tip of the mouthpiece. Line up the tip of the reed with the tip of the mouthpiece with just a hint of the mouthpiece visible over the tip of the reed. Hold the bottom of the reed in place with the left thumb and take the ligature in the right hand with the wide end of the ligature on the bottom. Slide the ligature over the top of the mouthpiece, being careful not to damage the reed. The ligature should be moved down onto the mouthpiece and over the reed until the top of the ligature sits just below the line on the mouthpiece. If there is a problem moving the ligature low enough on the mouthpiece, loosen the screws until the ligature is able to rest below the line on the mouthpiece. When the ligature is in place, tighten the bottom screw securely. The top screw should be tightened securely, then loosened one turn back. This allows the reed more freedom to vibrate but keeps the reed in place on the mouthpiece.

Care and Maintenance

DAILY CARE

The day-to-day care of the clarinet is important. After playing, the collected saliva and condensation inside the clarinet must be cleaned with a clarinet swab. A clarinet swab is generally made of cloth, often cotton or linen, with a long string with a weight attached at the end. There are many types of swabs, but they all fit this general description.

The clarinet should be cleaned out each time it is put away. To clean out the clarinet, take it apart and put it in the case. With the exception of the mouthpiece, take each piece of the clarinet one at a time, put the weighted end of the swab through each piece and slowly pull the swab through it. Be especially careful with the upper joint to pull the swab slowly so it does not get caught on the register key vent inside. As the swab is pulled through, wipe the joints dry. Blow air through the tone holes to clear any moisture. If there is a great deal of moisture in any tone hole, take a piece of ungummed cigarette paper and place it under the pad to soak up the excess condensation.

To clean the mouthpiece, remove the ligature and reed. Take the cloth end of the swab and twist it so it can be fed through the mouthpiece. Gently swab back and forth with the cloth, absorbing the collected moisture. Do not feed the weight through the mouthpiece, as you risk chipping the end of the mouthpiece. If the drawstring is continually passed over the end of the mouthpiece, it will gradually reface the mouthpiece as the string slowly wears away the tip of the mouthpiece.

Often while one is playing the clarinet, condensation will build up in one of the tone holes, usually under the pad of either the $c\sharp^1/g\sharp^2$ or the $e\flat^1/b\flat^2$ key or somewhere else in the upper joint. This will cause a fuzzy tone on these notes or a squeak. When this happens, try to blow the water out of the hole. If the problem persists, again take a piece of ungummed cigarette paper and soak up the water. If this does not solve the problem, take the clarinet apart and pick up the upper joint with the left hand. Close the tone holes with the left fingers and stop up the end of the joint with the palm of the right hand. Hold open the key above the hole where the water problem is located and blow in and out through the top of the upper joint. Any water lurking in the tone hole will either be blown out the tone hole or drawn into the inside of the upper joint. To pick up any condensation drawn inside, run the swab through the joint once again.

To avoid excess water in the clarinet during performance, it is wise to swab the clarinet out between movements of a piece or during long periods of rest. The clarinetist should always have a swab and a piece of cigarette paper within reach during performances.

LONG-TERM MAINTENANCE

Long-term maintenance should include the following:

1. Dust carefully under the keys with a clean, narrow paintbrush a few times each month.

2. Gently clean out each tone hole with a pipe cleaner. Dirt from the fingers builds up in the tone holes and will eventually affect intonation. Do not disturb any tape added to the tone holes for tuning purposes. The player's hands should be washed before playing the clarinet to help avoid this problem.

3. Apply oil to the metal contact points every month or so. Use a drop of light key oil on each metal contact, being careful not to let it get onto any of the pads.

4. Keep the corks greased. The fit of the joints will vary with the humidity. When the weather is humid, the corks expand; the fit becomes tighter and may require cork grease on a more regular basis. When the weather is dry, the corks shrink and the fit becomes looser. In this case, be careful not to put too much cork grease on the corks, as they might come apart during a performance. Keep the corks greased so there is a firm fit between the joints without any risk of the parts becoming stuck together.

CHAPTER 8

Fundamentals of Clarinet Playing

Embouchure

There are two basic embouchures for playing the clarinet: single lip and double lip. The embouchure used by most clarinetists, the single lip, is easier to teach, to learn, and to use. Thus I will limit my discussion of the clarinet embouchure to the single-lip approach.

Although there are different approaches to forming the single-lip clarinet embouchure, I prefer the one that can be described in terms of "smiling." The corners of the mouth are pulled back, stretching the red part of the lower lip, which is then curled over the lower teeth. Do not put too much lip into the mouth. The edge of the red of the lower lip should be in view. Put the mouthpiece into the mouth with the reed over the lower lip, place the upper teeth down on the top of the mouthpiece about three quarters of an inch from the tip, and close the upper lip around the mouthpiece to make the embouchure airtight. With the mouthpiece in the mouth and the corners of the mouth stretching as in a smile, pull down with the point of the chin so the chin is set firmly against the teeth and gums inside. This pulls the lower lip down and away from the reed and allows it to vibrate freely. The embouchure should be firmly set with no flabbiness in the lips or chin.

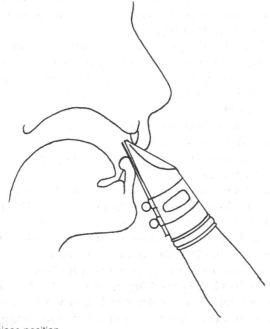

Figure 8.1. Mouthpiece position

A good way to demonstrate this is to have the student form the clarinet embouchure with a straw. Have the student take the straw and draw in while closing the open end of the straw with a finger. This re-creates the feeling of the embouchure at work.

The most difficult part of learning the clarinet embouchure is determining the pressure against the reed and mouthpiece, or the "bite," when the mouth is closed. It is important that the mouthpiece sit in the mouth firmly enough to inhibit any movement as the clarinet is played. It is equally important that the pressure against the reed is not so much that it hinders the reed from vibrating freely.

To check if the mouthpiece is set properly in the mouth, the instructor should take hold of the barrel as the student is playing and turn it left and right to see how much the mouthpiece moves. If the mouthpiece moves with little resistance, the embouchure must be firmed up by pulling the corners of the mouth out more to stretch the lower lip, by closing the "bite" more, or by both methods. If, instead, the mouthpiece will not move at all and the tone sounds pinched, have the student relax the "bite" a little until the tone sounds freer.

It is important that the student learn from the outset that the embouchure is used only to attach the clarinet to the player. It is often overused by students in their effort to play each note. This is a concept that should be discouraged from the beginning. The embouchure should be set solidly. The only movements should occur to help in leaps from the upper to the lower register and for minor intonation adjustments. Both of these techniques are somewhat advanced and probably should not be mentioned at first.

Posture and Position

The proper posture for playing the clarinet in a seated position is to have the upper body in an upright position. The shoulders and arms should be in a natural position, with no tension created by pointing the elbows out or moving the arms forward. Hold the head in an upright position so the face points directly forward. Bring the clarinet to the mouth in a comfortable and natural way without leaning forward to meet it.

To help students find the proper position, have them sit in a chair without the clarinet and rest their hands naturally on their legs. Then have them raise their arms and hands as if they were going to be placing them on the clarinet. This will give them the feeling of the proper and natural position for playing the clarinet.

Hold the trunk of the body erect and do not bend over in any way. This places the lungs in their most efficient position for the maximum air intake. If the trunk is bent forward, the lungs become cramped and cannot be filled to their maximum capacity.

Once the clarinet is placed in the student's mouth, the angle of the clarinet should be about forty-five degrees from the body. This places the bell of the clarinet near the knees of a person of average height.

The bell should not be held between the knees. This creates a rigid, inflexible posture and muffles the sound in the extreme low register. The sound of the low f and e can easily get lost in the folds of clothing. This position also builds the bad habit of picking up the weight of the instrument by the knees. This becomes a particular problem when the performer plays standing up and suddenly must compensate for the weight previously picked up by the knees.

Figure 8.2. Posture when playing the clarinet in a seated position

Finger and Hand Positions

To play the clarinet, take the lower joint of the instrument in the right hand so the thumb rest rests on the top side of the right thumb at the first joint. This places the first, second, and third fingers over the rings and holes of the lower joint and leaves the little finger to play the four keys at the bottom of the instrument.

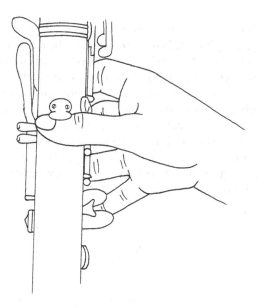

Figure 8.3. Correct position for the right thumb

Put the left hand over the upper joint with the left thumb in position to cover the ring and hole and to push the register key under the clarinet. This places the first, second, and third fingers over the rings and holes of the upper joint and leaves the little finger to play the four keys at the side.

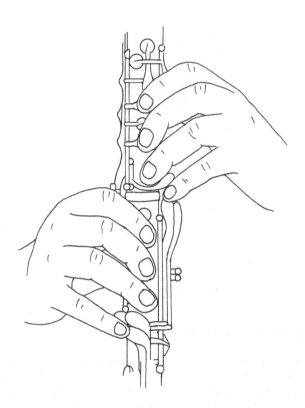

Figure 8.4. Proper position for the fingers

It is important to learn the correct hand position from the beginning. This avoids learning bad habits that become difficult to change in later years. Both hands should be held in a natural position over the rings and holes. To demonstrate this, have the student, without the clarinet, allow the hands to hang freely at his or her sides, forming their natural curved position. Then slowly have the student raise the hands as if to be placed onto the clarinet. This is the proper amount of finger curvature.

When placed on the clarinet in their proper and natural position, the fingers should line up comfortably with the appropriate holes and rings. To close a hole, the student should use more of the fingertip as opposed to the flat part of the finger.

Figure 8.5. Correct finger position

The fingers should never be more than an inch away from the keys and rings when they are not actually covering a hole and ring or pushing down a key. The fingers should not be so close that they affect the sound or intonation of another note being played.

Common errors in hand and finger position include the following:

1. Picking up the weight of the clarinet with the fingers when they are placed down.

2. Placing the thumb rest too far back on the thumb to compensate for the weight of the instrument.

3. Flattening out the fingers as they close the rings and cover the holes.

4. Pushing down too hard with the fingers, identifiable by the white around the tip of the finger created by too much pressure. This is often especially true at louder dynamics.

5. Raising the fingers too far above the clarinet when they aren't playing a note.

WEIGHT COMPENSATION

Because the weight of the clarinet is placed entirely on the right thumb, beginning students will find various ways of compensating for this weight. Students will often compensate for the weight of the clarinet by picking up the weight of the instrument as they put their fingers down. One clue that they are doing this is a shifting movement of the clarinet as the student raises and lowers the fingers. Another is the telltale white fingers resulting from squeezing with the fingers. Usually the student is not even aware of doing this. To correct this, have the student slowly play an F major scale down from f^1, paying particular attention to finger movement and making sure he or she does not pick up any weight of the clarinet from note to note.

Another way the student will compensate for the weight of the clarinet on the thumb is to place the thumb rest too far back on the thumb. This results in the fingers of the right hand being too cramped and out of position. Make sure the thumb rest is placed in the proper position around the first joint on the thumb.

Beginning students may also use the embouchure to "hold" the clarinet, biting on the mouthpiece to pick up some of the weight of the instrument. This can be discovered and fixed during the general process of working on the embouchure.

There are two ways to help the student support the clarinet's weight: have the student either rest the bell of the clarinet on the knee, if he or she is tall enough, or use a neck strap. The first solution can be used whenever the weight becomes temporarily painful or uncomfortable. As with any other physical toning, it is best to build up the muscles little by little. Too much weight for too long a time will tear down the muscles instead of building them up. A student who is practicing in periods of thirty minutes should be able to get through the practice period without any such problems. The use of a neck strap is becoming increasingly common. As stated above under "Posture and Position," do not hold the clarinet between the knees to solve the weight problem.

FINGER FLATTENING

When a finger flattens out, a two-process movement results: the finger first is placed down and then flattens out. Placing the flat part of the fingertip down to cover the rings and holes causes this twofold movement, which slows the finger action and results in an uneven and laden technique instead of an even and facile technique. To correct this, place the tip of the fingers down in the natural curved position onto the rings and holes. If the placement is correct, it will be difficult to flatten the finger out.

Figure 8.6. Incorrect flattening of the finger

TOO MUCH FINGER PRESSURE

Beginning students often push too hard to close the holes on the clarinet. They do not trust that anything less than hard pressure will close the holes. This results in a laden and slow technique. Have the student work slowly from note to note, experimenting with how little finger pressure is necessary to cover the hole.

Younger students might have a problem covering a hole because their fingers are either too small or too thin. They need to be careful in the placement of their fingers or wait until they are older when their fingers have grown wide enough to close the holes comfortably.

A related problem is the tendency to push the fingers down harder when one is playing in a louder dynamic. The fingers should always work with the same pressure whether playing loudly or softly. The player must divorce the energy needed to create the air support to play loudly from the pressure of the fingers. This is a difficult concept for most students, who want to give the same energy with the entire body, fingers included. To demonstrate this concept, have the student softly play a d^2; as they are playing, have him push harder on the fingers covering the holes on the clarinet. Ask if pushing harder changed the dynamics. Of course, the dynamics will not change unless the student also increases the air flow. The finger pressure has nothing to do with the dynamics of a note.

RAISED AND BUNCHED-UP FINGERS

It is often difficult for students to keep their fingers in the proper position over the keys and holes. Tendencies to extend the fingers in the air when they aren't being used and to bunch up the fingers, moving them away from their proper position, are often the result of compensating for the weight of the clarinet. This is especially true in the right hand, where many students are inclined to bunch up their fingers, when idle, to help stabilize the clarinet. Sometimes the student will rest the lowest right-hand side key (key #8; see key numbers chart on p. 153) on the side of the first finger. Both raising and bunching up the fingers place the fingers out of position and must be avoided.

To demonstrate to students how far their fingers stray from the clarinet, hold your hands about an inch above their fingers as they play. Their fingers will be stopped from going too high by your hand, thus showing them the proper height. To help with the bunching of the fingers, have the student work note to note, attempting to maintain the proper finger position between notes.

Breathing

Proper breathing is basic to playing any wind instrument and should be taught from the very beginning. Breathing for playing a wind instrument is different from normal moment-to-moment breathing. Wind players must think about breathing deeply, filling the lungs to full capacity from the lower part of the lungs upward. Although at first it takes a conscious effort to breathe properly, it eventually becomes second nature and, in fact, becomes the way the player breathes all the time. The difference is in the amount of air taken in; much more air is needed for playing than for regular breathing.

Learning to take in the amount of air necessary for correct wind playing is difficult for many people because it involves relearning how to breathe. The teacher must help the student locate the lower part of the lungs and the abdominal muscles and diaphragm surrounding the lower lung area.

Here are some suggested exercises to help students learn this process:

1. Have the students stand, focus their air, and blow short gusts of wind at a relatively quick rate as if blowing out a candle or as if out of breath. As the students locate and feel the abdominal muscles, have them slow down their gusts of wind and begin to fill up the lower lung area with air.

2. Have the students stand and slowly draw in air through a straw, thinking of breathing deeply and filling up the lower part of the lungs from back to front. As air enters the lower lungs, the abdominal muscles and the diaphragm will expand. The teacher can tell if the air is filling up by visually checking the expansion of the lower lung area. It is important to make sure the students are filling up with air and not just pushing out their abdominal muscles.

3. Suggest to the students that they practice at home by lying on their back on the floor or a hard mattress. They should take a heavy book and rest it on the stomach. As they slowly inhale and exhale, the book will rise and fall as the area is filled and emptied. The book gives a resistance against which to breathe. It is important for the students to focus on the air coming and going to lift the book and not just push out their abdominal muscles.

After students are able to inhale the air into the lower part of their lungs, they must continue the intake of air to fill both the middle part and the upper part of the lungs to complete the process and take in the maximum amount of air.

It is critical to have students do some form of exercise involving long tones, such as the one illustrated in Figure 8.7, to increase their air intake capacity and to develop the diaphragm muscles so they can support and control the movement of air. The number of counts this long tone lasts is arbitrary, but I suggest a smaller number counted slowly rather than a higher number counted faster. Start the long tone with the tongue as softly as possible, keeping in mind that the volume at each given number during the crescendo must be the same during the diminuendo. (For example, the volume at number 3 in the crescendo must be the same as the volume at number 3 in the diminuendo.) The crescendo must be even and reach the loudest possible controlled sound at the peak of the long tone. The long tone must be symmetrical, with the length of the diminuendo matching the length of the crescendo. The student should strive to make this tone longer and louder each time, controlling both the sound and the intonation.

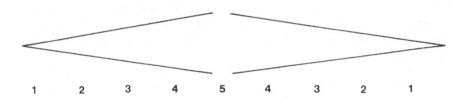

Figure 8.7. Long tone exercise

This long tone exercise develops many important facets of clarinet playing:

- Greater air intake capacity
- Embouchure stability
- Ability to start notes very softly with assurance
- Even crescendi and diminuendi
- Tone control
- Intonation control
- Greater control of the extremes of the dynamic ranges

Tonguing

The sound of the clarinet initiates with the flow of air and the movement of the tongue away from the reed. Starting the sound with only the air and without the tongue takes away control of the exact beginning of the note, the clarity of attack, and the type of attack. An advanced player develops variations on initiating a note, but it is important that the student develop the standard method of tonguing.

Four factors must be considered when tonguing:

1. The part of tongue making contact with the reed
2. The part of the reed where the tongue makes contact
3. The strength of the stroke of the tongue
4. The air support when tonguing

Although there is some difference of opinion about tongue placement, most teachers would agree that the clarinetist should use the upper tip of the tongue to touch the upper part of the flat of the reed when tonguing. Demonstrate the tongue placement by asking the student to say a syllable such as "tuh" or "tee" without the clarinet in the mouth.

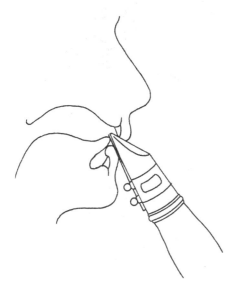

Figure 8.8. Correct tongue position

The tongue should touch the reed gently, with just enough strength to completely stop the reed from vibrating. The tongue should not be forceful except when the music calls for a harder attack such as an accent or a sforzando, markings that usually do not appear in beginning-level music. The soft tongue stroke creates flexibility, control, and speed.

It is of utmost importance to continue the airflow from note to note when tonguing. Many beginning students stop the airflow between notes.

COMMON ERRORS OF TONGUE PLACEMENT

Common errors of tongue placement include the following:

1. Tonguing into the opening at the tip of the mouthpiece and reed
2. Starting each note with new air
3. Scraping the tongue against the reed as it moves away from the reed
4. Holding the tip of the tongue against the lower teeth and touching the reed too far back on the tongue, known as "anchor tonguing"
5. Striking the reed with too hard a tongue stroke

A good staccato exercise is to have the student try the staccato with the clarinet out of the mouth. Have the student take a big breath and exhale, focusing the air as if he or she were playing the clarinet. As the air exits,

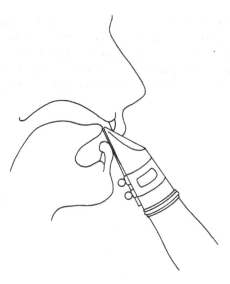

Figure 8.9. The tongue is too close to the mouthpiece tip

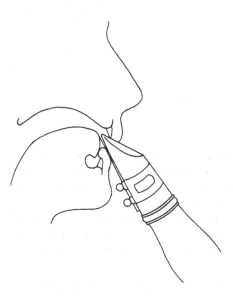

Figure 8.10. "Anchor tonguing," with the tongue against the lower teeth

have the student interrupt the airflow by touching the roof of the mouth with the tip of the tongue with the syllable "tuh." This way the teacher can tell if the air is being exhaled in a continuous flow or if the student is stopping it between the "tuhs."

Another excellent staccato exercise is to have the student play an open throat tone g¹ and interrupt the sound at odd intervals with the tongue against the reed while continuing the flow of air. Thus, when there is no sound, the tongue will be against the reed. Air will escape from the side of the mouth, since it must go somewhere. When the tongue draws back from

Figure 8.11. Staccato exercise

the reed, the sound will start. This gives the student the time to perfect tongue placement and calculate how softly he or she can touch the reed to stop the sound completely. This exercise will help the student develop clean, clear, and secure staccato.

CHAPTER 9

Technique

The Registers

The registers of the clarinet are as follows:

Chalumeau: from the lowest note e to b♭¹

Example 9.1. Chalumeau register

Throat tones: a subregister of the chalumeau register, from g¹ to b♭¹

Example 9.2. Throat tones

Clarion: from b¹ to c³

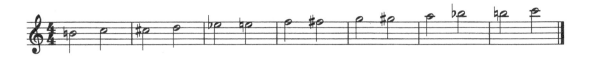

Example 9.3. Clarion register

Altissimo: from c♯³ and higher

Example 9.4. Altissimo register

110

These registers are quite different from those of the other woodwind instruments because the clarinet overblows a twelfth instead of an octave. Thus when the clarinetist plays a c¹ and then opens the register key, the resulting note is a twelfth higher, g², not an octave, c².

Learning the Chalumeau (Low) Register

The notes below b♭¹ include those notes played without use of the register key. These notes should be learned by starting on open g¹, played with no fingers depressing a key or covering a tone hole, and descending in order by adding a finger at a time until one arrives at g. Note that the right-hand fingers are not placed down in order because the b is played with the middle finger of the right hand.

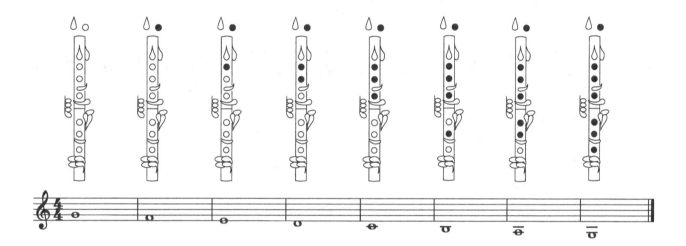

Example 9.5. The basic lower octave

Practicing this octave from the top, working downward one note at a time, gives the student the opportunity to learn the feel of each hole and ring in order and helps the fingers find their proper position. If a note does not respond or results in a squeak, go back to an easy note and try again until the notes respond properly. When the descending scale is produced comfortably, start at the bottom of the scale and work upward. This is more difficult because the student must begin with the fingers covering all the holes so the g will respond properly.

Exercise 9.1. Introducing g¹, f¹, and e¹

Exercise 9.2. Introducing d¹

Exercise 9.3. Introducing c¹

Weissenborn

Exercise 9.4. Introducing b

Weissenborn

Exercise 9.5. Introducing a

Exercise 9.6. Introducing g

THE FINGERING FOR F♯¹   The first finger of the left hand plays f♯¹. When playing this note, make certain that the left thumb stays in position to close the thumb hole when needed.

Exercise 9.7. The G major scale

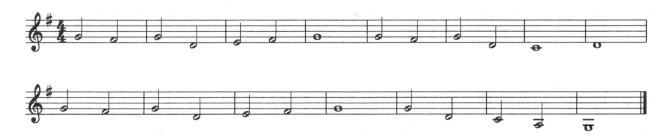

Exercise 9.8. Returning to the open g¹

THE FINGERINGS FOR F AND E   Play the f with the right-hand little finger (key #15). Then e can be played by adding the left-hand little finger (key #12) while the right-hand little finger keeps the f key depressed.

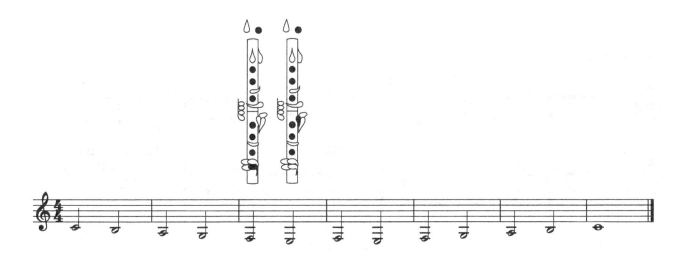

Exercise 9.9 Introducing f and e

Tunes in the Chalumeau Register

Mary Had a Little Lamb

French Tune

Twinkle, Twinkle, Little Star

Hudson River Steamboat

Joy to the World

The Remaining Notes in the Chalumeau Register

Exercise 9.10. Introducing b♭

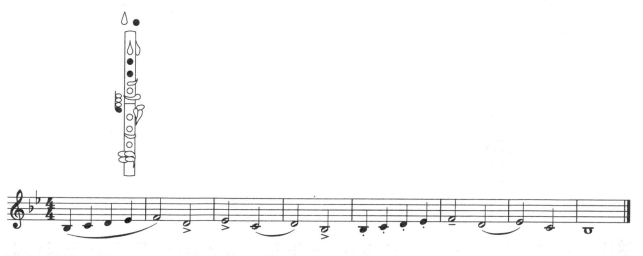

Exercise 9.11. Introducing e♭

Exercise 9.12. Introducing a♭

Exercise 9.13. Introducing f♯

Exercise 9.15. Down to e

The Chromatic Scale

The following chromatic scale from e to g¹ includes the chromatic fingerings.
These fingerings should be introduced from the outset so they become habit.

Example 9.6. Chromatic scale with chromatic fingerings

Tunes in the Chromatic Chalumeau Register

Hot Cross Buns

The Scale Song

The Bells

Mi Gallo

Deck the Halls

My Bonnie Lies Over the Ocean

O Come All Ye Faithful

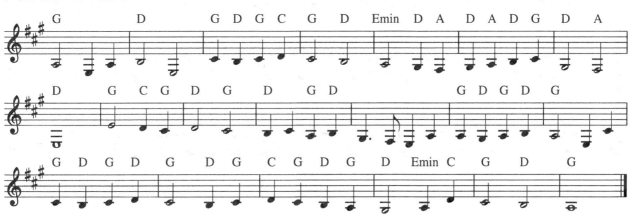

De Colores (Duo)

(*continued*)

De Colores (*continued*)

Learning the Throat Tones

When playing the throat tone a[1], roll the left first finger onto the *a* key (#2) and depress it with the side of the finger instead of lifting the finger and placing it flat on the key. This allows the finger to roll back and forth from the key in one smooth, uninterrupted motion.

To allow this first finger movement, the other fingers on the left hand rotate in concert upward from their normal position. They should stay in the same relative position so they will automatically return to their proper position when the first finger rolls back onto the first hole. Use this same motion when playing the g#[1].

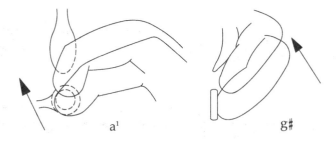

Figure 9.1. Finger movement for a[1] and g#[1]

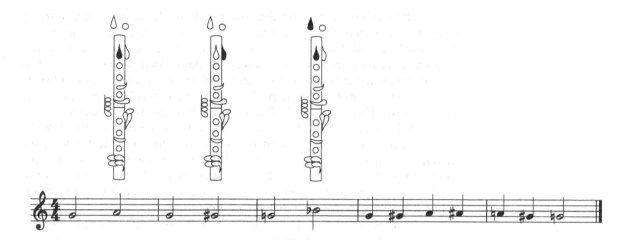

Exercise 9.16. Introducing g♯¹, a¹, and b♭¹

Learning the Clarion (Upper) Register

THE BREAKS

The two "breaks" of the clarinet occur between b♭¹ and b¹ and between c³ and c♯³. These breaks occur when the clarinetist goes from using few fingers to using many fingers. For example, b♭¹ is fingered with the thumb and first finger of the left hand and b♮¹, a half step above, is fingered with all five fingers on the left hand and three on the right hand.

Learning to get across the breaks smoothly and without a timbre change is one of the biggest challenges on the clarinet. It involves coordinated finger movement, air support, and a firm embouchure.

THE LOWER BREAK

With Example 9.7, which allows the fingerings to remain the same with only the addition of the register key on the upper notes, the student can begin playing from register to register without worrying about the break.

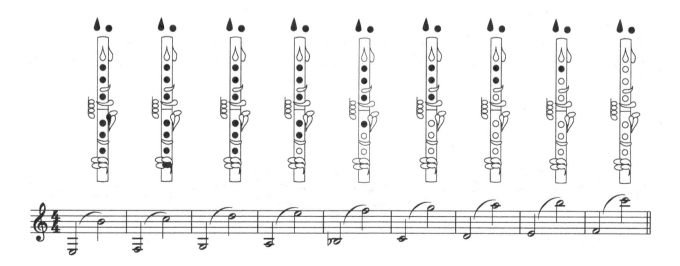

Example 9.7. Introducing the break and the clarion register notes: b¹, c², d², e², f², g², a², b², and c³

As the student slurs from the lower note to the upper note, nothing should move except the left thumb to depress the register key. The thumb hole must remain fully covered as the register key is depressed by the thumb. A continuous flow of air must be maintained between the notes, and the embouchure must remain firm, with no movement between notes. Most students will try to "help" the upper note speak by moving their embouchure. This often results in a break or hitch between the notes.

To help demonstrate this concept, have the student turn the mouthpiece around and blow into the instrument as you finger the notes. Keep an arrhythmic pace going from the lower notes to the upper notes so the student will not have time to "set" the embouchure for the upper notes. If the student is supporting the air correctly, the upper notes will respond properly and easily without embouchure movement.

In Example 9.8 the student slurs back to the lower note. This exercise is more difficult because there must be a very slight movement of the embouchure to help the lower note speak. If this minuscule movement is allowed to be exaggerated, it will not only encourage excess embouchure movement in other situations but also affect the intonation of the lower note.

Example 9.8. Slurring down from the clarion register

Lower Break Exercises

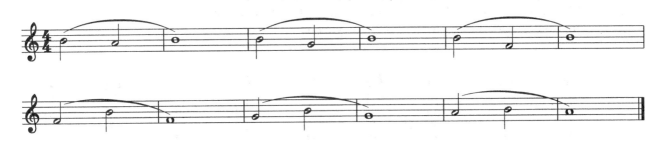

Exercise 9.17. Break exercise #1

Exercise 9.18. Break exercise #2

Exercise 9.19. Break exercise #3

It is important that these exercises be practiced slowly, making certain that all the fingers are coordinated and cover the holes and keys at the same time. As always, it is essential that the air support continue between notes. Again, to demonstrate this, have the student turn the mouthpiece around and blow into the instrument as you finger the notes in the exercises.

The Remaining Notes in the Clarion Register

Exercise 9.20. Introducing c#²

Exercise 9.21. Introducing e♭²

Exercise 9.22. Introducing f#²

Exercise 9.23. Introducing g#²

Exercise 9.24. Introducing b♭²

The Clarion Chromatic Scale

The following chromatic scale from b¹ to c³ includes the chromatic finger-ings. As with the chalumeau chromatic scale, these fingerings should be introduced from the beginning so that they become automatic.

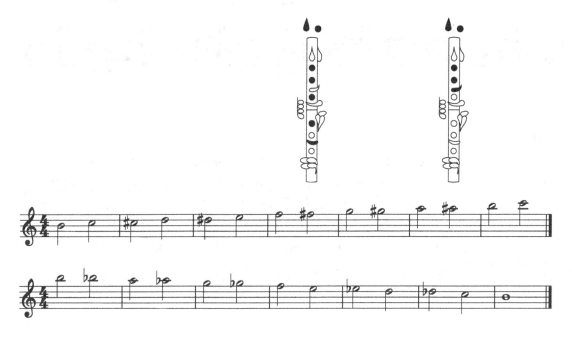

Example 9.9. Clarion chromatic scale with chromatic fingerings

Tunes in the Clarion Register

Joseph Dearest, Joseph Mild   Traditional German Carol

German Folk Song

Lightly Row

We Shall Overcome

Simple Gifts

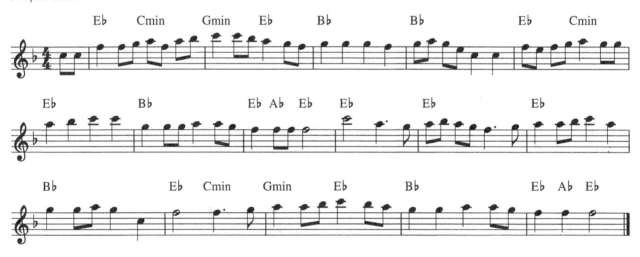

Scarborough Fair   English Folk Song

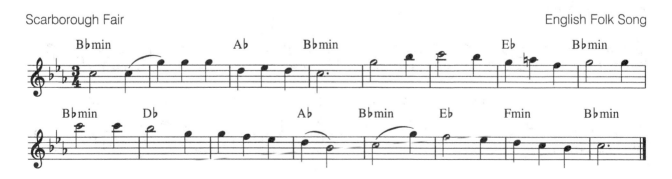

Blow, Ye Winds

Johnny Has Gone for a Soldier

Little Annie Rooney

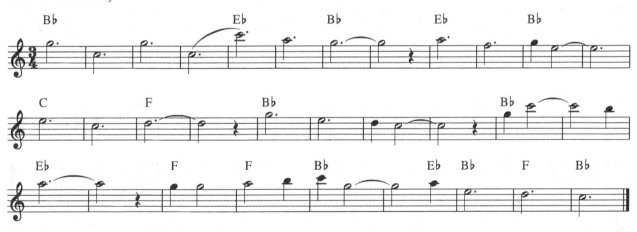

Dos y dos   Mexican Folk Song

130 Clarinet

Chester (Quartet)   William Billings

The Altissimo Register

The altissimo range is from c♯³ upward. Although fingerings for the notes up to c⁴ are included in the reference, for the purposes of this section I will limit my comments to g³. The notes in the altissimo register are considered the most difficult to produce and to play beautifully. High notes can sound as beautiful and be controlled as easily as the lower notes with the proper production and practice.

The production of high notes creates a set of problems all its own. However, many of these problems are mental. The production of high notes involves the same elements as the notes of any other register: air support, finger coordination, and embouchure. These elements must be in place for all fine playing, and this is particularly true of the higher notes. It is also necessary that the student should have progressed sufficiently to be using a reed that is hard enough to produce the upper notes. A reed that is too soft will close when the air support necessary to produce the upper notes is given.

Most students approach high notes with fear and trepidation. As with any technique on the clarinet, it is a mistake to tell the student how hard something is: "The break is the hardest thing on the clarinet. The upper notes are difficult to get and always sound bad"—familiar words, creating mental blocks that often take years to break down.

In truth, there are difficulties in producing the high notes: their response, the difficulty of attacking and playing them softly, their intonation and their sound quality.

The response of the high notes depends on the basic elements mentioned above: air support, finger coordination, and embouchure. The embouchure is often the cause for high notes not speaking, speaking late, or being out of tune. It seems to be human nature for the body to do everything possible to help with these high notes. Thus the student will try to "help" the note speak with embouchure movement. This is exactly the wrong thing to do. When the embouchure remains firm and unmoved, the air support remains steady, and the fingers are coordinated in their movement, high notes will speak and have the same basic sound quality as the lower notes.

Refinement of sound quality and volume control of the high notes comes with time and patience. If the student approaches these notes with the proper attitude, this refinement will take far less time than if mental blocks are built.

Unfortunately, the intonation of some of the high notes is a real concern, owing to the imperfections of the instrument itself. Several notes are inherently out of tune in the upper range, and the player must find a way to accommodate these notes. When learning the fingerings of the altissimo register, the clarinetist must remember to use the e♭² key (key #14) as a vent key on every note with the exception of c♯³, the first note in that range. The addition of this vent key raises the otherwise flat pitch and improves the quality of sound. If the vent key is used for c♯³, the resulting note will be very sharp.

The notes d³, e³, and f³ are not particular problems on most clarinets. However, d♯³/e♭³ using the traditional fingering—the register key and thumb and covering the second and third holes on the upper joint and the middle hole on the bottom joint, with the little finger opening the vent key—is generally flat. I recommend using the forked fingering—the first finger hole of the lower joint with the addition of the sliver key (key #13) played by the third finger and the vent key along with the normal upper-joint fingering—whenever possible. An alternative is to cover the bottom hole of the lower joint with the third finger plus the vent key of the right hand along with the normal upper-joint fingering. These two fingerings are much more in tune than the middle, and either can be approached from any other note (see the section on alternate fingering).

Another problem note is f#³. This note, using the traditional fingering of register key, thumb, and middle hole of the upper register, is very flat on most clarinets. I recommend using the full or long fingering for this note whenever possible (see the alternate fingering section).

THE UPPER BREAK

Exercise 9.25, which works on perfecting the upper break of the clarinet, should be practiced slowly. It is important that all the fingers are coordinated and cover the holes and keys at the same moment.

Exercise 9.25. Introducing d³ with upper break

When one moves upward into the altissimo range from below, the embouchure must remain firm, without movement, and the air support must be continuous. In slurring, the downward movement from the altissimo range might involve a slight downward movement with the lower lip to help the lower note speak. This exercise must be practiced slowly, experimenting with how little movement is necessary to have the lower note speak clearly without a break or hitch between notes.

Exercise 9.26. Introducing c#³, d#³, e³, f³, f#³, and g³

The Fourth-Finger Keys

The right- and left-hand fourth fingers each have four keys to play. Three of these four keys have a corresponding key on the other side that plays the same note (see Figs. 9.2, 9.3, and 9.4).

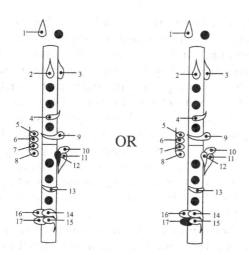

OR

Figure 9.2. Key #12 or #17 plays e/b¹

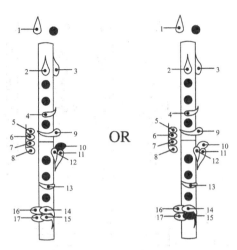

Figure 9.3. Key #10 or #15 plays f/c²

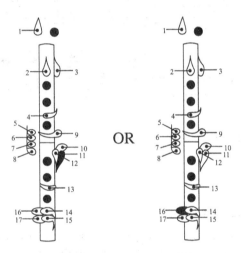

Figure 9.4. Key #11 or #16 plays f♯/c♯²

This allows the clarinetist the choice of which key to use in any given combination of notes. The student usually begins by learning to play e/b¹ with the left fourth finger and to play f/c¹ with the right fourth finger. It is also possible to play e/b¹ with key #12 and key #15 depressed, since all the holes are closed anyway and putting the right-hand fourth finger on key #15 can prepare it for the next note if it is f/c². Some methods teach that the fingering for e/b¹ is always to use both fingers. This is not correct, as the next note is often not f/c¹, in which case both fingers must be lifted or an unnecessary slide must be made to another key to play the next note. When learning these notes, the student should be aware of this possibility so he or she can take advantage of leaving the finger on key #15 if the note combination accommodates this. This, however, should not become the sole way to play e/b¹.

The remaining keys on each side are unique in the notes they produce (see Figs. 9.5 and 9.6). This sometimes creates the need to plan ahead on which side to start a group of notes. One of the first such problems a beginner will encounter when learning to play in the key of B♭ is going from c² to e♭². The clarinetist must play c² with the left hand (key #10) in order to play the e♭² with the right hand, the only option.

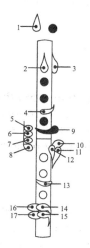

Figure 9.5. Key #9 plays c#¹/g#²

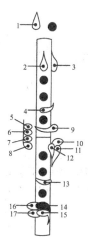

Figure 9.6. Key #14 plays a♭/e♭²

Example 9.10. Using the left-hand c² key

Another example of having to plan ahead is shown in Example 9.11.

Example 9.11. Using the right-hand b¹ key

I can't recommend enough that, from the outset, the student learn the habit of marking fingerings. If the first note of a passage is marked to indicate on which hand to start, the rest of the sequence will work itself out and the player will never be caught in a wrong combination of fingers.

SLIDING

Certain combinations of notes necessitate sliding, in which the clarinetist literally slides the same finger from one key to another key while continuing to play. This occurs in a sequence of notes where there is no alternative to sliding. The most common slides are from key #14 to key #16, back and forth between keys #14 and #15, and from key #12 to key #11.

Example 9.12. Various slides

There are certain slides that don't work. It is impossible to slide from the lower right-hand keys (#16 and #17) to the upper ones (#14 and #15) without a break. On the left hand, sliding from keys #9, #10, or #11 to key #12 creates a break.

Chromatic and Alternate Fingerings

CHROMATIC FINGERINGS

Bb/A♯ TO B♮; F¹ TO F♯¹ (FORKED FINGERING)   To play from bb/a♯ to b♮, finger the Bb/a♯ normally and then play the b♮ by adding the lower-joint sliver key (key #13). The fingering is the same in the upper register going from f¹ to f♯¹ with the addition of the register key. This avoids the flip-flop between the first and second fingers of the right hand and creates a much smoother interval.

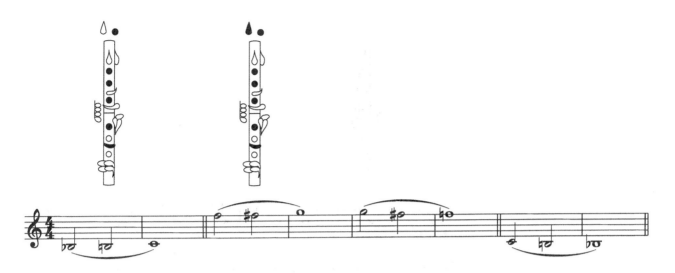

Example 9.13. Using chromatic fingering for b♭/a♯ to b♮ and f¹ to f♯¹

D♯¹/E♭¹ TO E♮¹; B♭²/A♯² TO B♮²   To play from d♯¹/e♭¹ to e♮¹, finger the d♯¹/e♭¹ by depressing the upper-joint sliver key (key #4) with the third finger of the left hand instead of using the first side key (key #8). For the e♮¹, just lift the third finger from the sliver key. This is also true in the upper register (b♭²/a♯² to b♮²) with the addition of the register key. This keeps all the movement in one hand and is thus easier to coordinate.

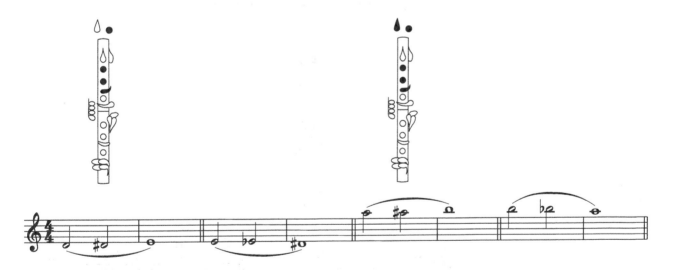

Example 9.14. Using chromatic fingering for d♯¹/e♭¹ to e♮¹ and b♭²/a♯² to b♮²

F♯¹/G♭¹ TO G♮¹   To play from f♮¹ to f♯¹/g♭¹, finger the f¹ normally with the thumb and then for the f♯¹/g♭¹ add the two lowest right-hand side keys (keys #7 and #8), played by the first finger of the right hand. This avoids the flip-flop between the thumb and first fingers of the left hand and makes a much smoother interval.

Example 9.15. Using chromatic fingering for f♯¹/g♭¹ to g♮¹

COMMONLY USED ALTERNATE FINGERINGS

B♭²: FORKED FINGERING OR 1 AND 1   This fingering is used when going between the b♭² and another note that can be reached from this fingering without sliding. The advantage of using this fingering is that it eliminates coordinating the use of the right-hand side key with the left-hand movement. To use this fingering, the clarinet must be in good adjustment, since the fork fingering depends on the proper connection between the upper and lower joint. This fingering must not be used in the lower register because the resulting e♭ is flat in pitch and fuzzy in tone.

Example 9.16. Using chromatic fingering for b♭²: forked fingering or 1 and 1

E♭³   The e♭³ is normally fingered two different ways depending on what note precedes it and what note comes after it. Fingering #1 in Figure 9.7 is the most in tune and should be used whenever possible. Fingering #2 is flat in pitch on most clarinets and should be avoided and replaced by fingering #3 whenever possible. One example of the use of fingering #3 is going from c² to e♭³. The player should use the left-hand c² and the fourth-finger e♭³.

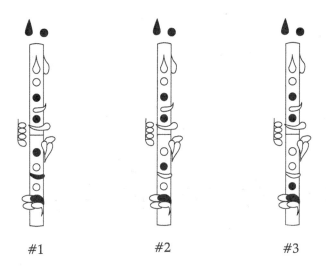

Figure 9.7. Alternate fingerings for e♭³

F#³   The full or long fingering for f#³ is used for two reasons. On most clarinets, this note is very flat when fingered with the normal fingering. Using the full fingering raises the pitch, and the note speaks easily and clearly when coming from the lower registers. This fingering should be learned in slow passages. As students gradually become more familiar with it, they will be able to determine when to use it.

Example 9.17. Alternate fingering for f#³

F³   The full or long fingering for f³ is used because it speaks easily when approached from the lower registers. The pitch usually is the same as the normal fingering, so intonation is not a factor here. Once again the student will gradually learn to decide when it is appropriate to use this fingering.

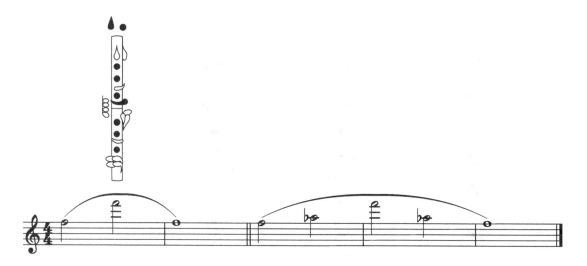

Example 9.18. Alternate fingering for f³

Tuning and Intonation of the Clarinet

General tuning of the clarinet is accomplished by adjusting the barrel in or out at the upper joint. Most clarinets are manufactured to play a little sharp when the barrel and upper joint are flush. This leaves the flexibility to pull the barrel out to lower the pitch, especially after the clarinet warms up. The barrel should be pulled out no more than one-sixteenth of an inch. If the cork of the upper joint tenon is exposed, the barrel is out too far. This will affect the intonation of individual notes in the clarinet's scale and throw off entire registers.

If the clarinet is still sharp after the adjustment at the barrel, the mouthpiece can be pulled out the slightest amount, not more than one thirty-second of an inch. Once again, if the mouthpiece is pulled out too much, the intonation of the entire clarinet is affected. If the clarinet remains sharp, the upper and lower joints can be pulled apart, but not more than one thirty-second of an inch. Make sure the connecting bridge between the two joints still functions properly. If the clarinet is consistently sharp to A = 440, the purchase of a longer barrel is necessary.

Flat intonation on the clarinet is often related to the embouchure. A loose embouchure produces a flat pitch. Firming up the embouchure will raise the pitch. If the clarinet is consistently flat to A = 440 when warmed up and played with a correct embouchure, the purchase of a shorter barrel is necessary.

Adjusting the clarinet to the tuning note is only the beginning of solving the intonation problems on the clarinet. To flatten an individual note, move the lower lip out and down in a subtle movement until the desired pitch is reached. This is an easy adjustment because the embouchure is quite flexible in this direction.

To sharpen an individual note, the embouchure must be tightened and stretched out and back. This is a more difficult adjustment because the embouchure should already be firm.

Although each clarinet has its own individual intonation problems, some problems are often common from clarinet to clarinet. The following techniques for solving these problems are for those students who have advanced enough to have a good sense of pitch and intonation and a firm but flexible embouchure. Working with a tuner is necessary to discover the pitch tendencies of any individual clarinet and the individual notes on that clarinet.

Common intonation problems include the following:

- The throat tones (g^1 to $b\flat^1$) are often sharp.
- The low notes (e to a) are often flat in a *forte* dynamic and sharp in a *pianissimo* dynamic.
- The notes b^2 and c^3 are often sharp.
- The altissimo register can be either sharp or flat, depending on the player's embouchure and the individual clarinet.
- When played with the middle finger of the right hand, $e\flat^3$ is usually flat.
- When played with the middle finger of the left hand, $f\sharp^3$ is usually flat.

Sharpness of the throat tones can be adjusted by putting a variety of fingers down on the right-hand tone holes to lower the pitch. The student whose ear is developed enough to discern the subtleties of intonation can experiment on his or her instrument with a variety of fingers down to find the tendency of the relative pitch of any given throat tone.

Possible fingerings for the throat tone a^1 are shown in Figure 9.8.

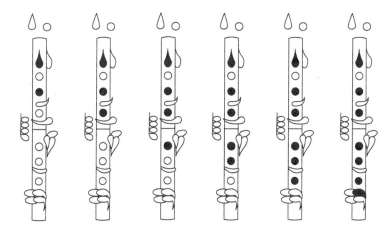

Figure 9.8. Alternate fingerings for a^1

When playing the lower notes at a loud dynamic, the student must maintain the embouchure at its firmest, not allowing the notes to become flat. In the *pianissimo* range, the embouchure must be flexible enough to make the normal adjustment for sharp notes (i.e., slightly pushing the lower lip out and down).

To correct the sharpness often heard on b^2 and c^3, the embouchure must loosen slightly and the lower lip must be pulled slightly down and out as with other sharp notes.

The altissimo register is often very flat with beginning players because their embouchures are not developed enough and they are still learning to breathe properly. As the embouchures and breathing techniques develop, the high notes will gradually be easier to produce and be more in tune. Because many of the altissimo notes tend to be sharp when produced properly, the clarinetist must be careful to control the intonation with lip adjustment and alternate fingerings. Working with a tuner is mandatory. Most clarinets have inherent intonation problems in the altissimo register; these problems and possible solutions are discussed above under "Alternate Fingerings."

CHAPTER 10

Reeds

The clarinet uses a single reed. It is made of cane, from the plant *Arundo donax*, specially grown and cured to be used for the manufacture of clarinet reeds. Clarinet reeds come in strengths from 1 to 5. The response and strength of a reed is largely determined by the thickness of the vamp and the tip of the reed: the thicker the vamp and tip, the harder the reed; the thinner the vamp and the tip, the softer the reed. The strength rating of reeds varies slightly from manufacturer to manufacturer, but in all cases, the higher the number, the harder the reed.

Choosing Reeds

The beginning student who has never played a reed instrument before should begin with a $1\frac{1}{2}$, 2, or $2\frac{1}{2}$ strength reed and gradually work up to a 3 or $3\frac{1}{2}$ as the embouchure muscles develop and the breathing technique advances. A student who has played a reed instrument before should try different clarinet reed strengths to see which one works best for him or her.

The ideal reed is one that responds well in both legato and staccato and produces a beautiful sound in all ranges and dynamics. Finding the ideal reed is a constant search. Even though it is the sound-producing mechanism of the clarinet, a reed is usually a compromise—a little too hard or a little too soft. Those reeds that produce the requisite qualities such as good staccato, dynamic range, and high note response must be sought. The ability to distinguish a good reed from a bad one grows correspondingly with the development of the embouchure and the ability to distinguish between a good and a bad clarinet sound. At first, it is difficult for students to know what qualities a reed does or does not have because they are not proficient in those techniques requiring a good reed.

The reed must be moistened before playing on it. When trying out a reed, dip it into a small glass of water so it will be supple enough to respond properly when played. It is fortunate if out of a box of ten reeds, five can be used. The mystery of reeds has yet to be solved. Two reeds from the same piece of cane made exactly the same way will respond differently. Although beginning students will not be able to discern these subtleties in reed response, they will certainly notice if the reed is too hard. As they progress, the students will become more astute in their choice of reeds to produce the sound and response they are seeking.

At all times the clarinetist should carry at least two or three functioning reeds. Because of the unpredictability of reeds, one never knows which reed will work where. Changes of weather and humidity affect the reed greatly. The acoustics of one room might accommodate one reed; another room, another reed. The more acoustically live a room, the harder the reed one can use, and vice versa. Once a player develops some discrimination in reed choice, it is a good idea to do most reed testing in the same room. This allows a consistency of acoustics.

Reed Placement

The placement of the reed on the mouthpiece is extremely important. The tip of the reed should be lined up with the tip of the mouthpiece with just a hint of the tip of mouthpiece showing above the reed. As the following list shows, a reed that is not placed on the mouthpiece correctly can cause a variety of problems.

Common Reed Problems

Many of the problems here attributed to the reed may also be caused by a bad embouchure and poor finger coordination.

No sound
1. The reed is too hard.
2. The reed is placed incorrectly on the mouthpiece.
3. The reed is broken or chipped.

A fuzzy, breathy sound
1. The reed is too hard.
2. The reed is placed incorrectly on the mouthpiece.
3. The reed is broken or chipped.

Flat pitch
1. The reed is too hard.
2. The reed is placed incorrectly on the mouthpiece.

Sharp pitch
1. The reed is too soft.
2. The reed is placed incorrectly on the mouthpiece.

Thin sound
1. The reed is too soft.
2. The reed is placed incorrectly on the mouthpiece.

Squeaks
1. The reed is either too hard or too soft.
2. The reed is chipped or broken.
3. The reed has an inherent chirp in it and should be discarded.
4. The reed is placed incorrectly on the mouthpiece.

High notes not speaking or very flat
1. The reed is too soft.
2. The reed is placed incorrectly on the mouthpiece.

Care of Reeds

The clarinet reed is fragile. It is easy to chip, crack, or break a reed because of the thinness of the tip. The reed will probably become damaged and useless if the tip bumps up against the lip, the teeth, or the end of the mouthpiece.

When the clarinet is in the case, the reed should be placed in some type of reed case or reed envelope to prevent it from being damaged while in the case.

REED LONGEVITY

It is difficult to say how long any given reed will last. One reed might last just a few days, another, several days. A reed that starts on the hard side will last longer than the softer reed because, as the reed is used, the cane gradually breaks down. It is best to pick a new reed that is just slightly harder than is comfortable, as it will last longer.

To keep the reed clean and thus increase its longevity, students should brush their teeth and remove any lip products such as lipstick or lip balm before playing the clarinet.

CHAPTER 11

Additional Information

Choosing a Clarinet

Clarinets are made of both wood and plastic. Professional instruments are made of wood, and student instruments are made of both wood and plastic. There are several excellent lines of student clarinets.

When choosing a clarinet, several factors must be considered:

* Response
* Intonation
* Mechanics
* Where it will be used
* Cost

The response is measured by the resistance of the clarinet when you blow into it. Do you have to blow very hard to get a sound? Is it too easy to play? When choosing a student clarinet, find one that plays relatively easily but has some resistance to it.

The inherent intonation of a clarinet is important. Check the intonation with a tuner to find out if the clarinet has a good scale and if any individual notes are disproportionately sharp or flat.

The key mechanism on the clarinet is also important. Be certain that it functions properly and that the keys are strong enough to take the abuse they will suffer from the beginning student without getting out of adjustment.

Generally, a plastic clarinet is a good idea for a beginner, partly because the investment is smaller. In many ways it is a better school instrument because it does not stand the risk of cracking when used outdoors as a marching band instrument.

Clarinetists are fortunate in that the clarinet remains one of the least expensive instruments. The best professional clarinet costs far less than other woodwind instruments of comparable quality. If an instrument is being purchased for a serious and talented student, a good used wooden professional clarinet might be a better buy than a new student line clarinet. If several clarinets are being purchased for a school, however, it is best to purchase good student line plastic clarinets.

Be sure to use your own mouthpiece and reed when testing new clarinets. This allows for consistency.

A teacher who is unsure about which clarinet(s) to buy should consult with a local symphony player, college professor, or private clarinet teacher.

Student Clarinets

Bundy
The Selmer Company, Inc.
P.O. Box 310
Elkhart, IN 46515-0310
(219) 522-1675

Evette
Boosey & Hawkes/Buffet Crampon Inc.
1925 Enterprise Ct.
P.O. Box 130
Libertyville, IL 60048
(708) 816-2500

Noblet and Vito
G. Leblanc Corporation
7001 Leblanc Boulevard
P.O. Box 1415
Kenosha, WI 53141-1415
(414) 658-1644

Yamaha
Yamaha Corporation of America
Band & Orchestra Division
3445 E. Paris S.E.
Grand Rapids, MI 49512-0899
(616) 940-4900

Professional Clarinets

Buffet
Boosey & Hawkes/Buffet Crampon Inc.
1925 Enterprise Ct.
P.O. Box 130
Libertyville, IL 60048
(708) 816-2500

Leblanc
G. Leblanc Corporation
7001 Leblanc Boulevard
P.O. Box 1415
Kenosaha, WI 53141-1415
(414) 658-1644

Selmer
The Selmer Company, Inc.
P.O. Box 310
Elkhart, IN 46515-0310
(219) 522-1675

Yamaha
Yamaha Corporation of America
Band & Orchestra Division
3445 E. Paris S.E.
Grand Rapids, MI 49512-0899
(616) 940-4900

Others

The Mouthpiece

It is important to realize that, with rare exceptions, the mouthpiece included in the case when a clarinet is purchased is a throwaway. Therefore it is necessary to purchase a new mouthpiece along with each clarinet.

Each mouthpiece is graded as more open or more closed depending on the opening between the reed and the mouthpiece at the tip of the mouthpiece and the length and depth of the lay or facing. For students, it is best to purchase a medium-faced mouthpiece, not too open or too closed.

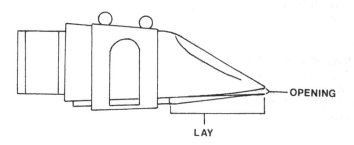

Figure 11.1. Mouthpiece dimensions

There are numerous student mouthpieces on the market. The Mitchell Lurie and Vandoren B45 mouthpieces are two of the most commonly used student mouthpieces.

Methods and Etudes

Below are three clarinet methods that can be used for beginning students depending on their general musical knowledge, previous musical study, and talent.

CARL BAERMANN. *Complete Method.* Carl Fischer. Books 1–2 combined, *Theory and Preparatory Studies;* book 3, *Technical;* book 4, *Etudes.*
This method moves along quickly and would be best for someone who shows a great deal of talent or has played another instrument. Book 1 is rudimentary, with explanations of various aspects of music and clarinet playing. Book 2 contains finger exercises and études that increase in difficulty at a rapid pace. Book 3, used by many people as the bible for building the basic technique, features scales and arpeggios up to very high notes and written in sixteenth notes. This book should be used when the student is ready for faster finger work. Book 4 has twenty études.

HYACINTHE KLOSÉ. *Celebrated Method for the Clarinet.* Carl Fischer.
Part 1 of this method works on the rudiments of playing. It includes two sets of short finger exercises, fifty duets, slow scale and arpeggio exercises in all major keys, articulation and various other exercises, and five easy solo pieces.
Part 2 includes major, minor, and chromatic scale and arpeggio work, fifteen Grand Duets, two sets of études, book 2 of Fritz Kroepsch's studies (see below), and four intermediate pieces.
This is an excellent basic method book for the serious beginner. It moves at a slower pace than the Baermann method, but quickly enough not to be boring.

NILO HOVEY. *Rubank Elementary Method for Clarinet.* Rubank.

J. E. SKORNIKS. *Intermediate Method for Clarinet.* Rubank.
The Rubank method is for the beginner who has no previous knowledge of music. It teaches the basics of music (notes, rhythm, etc.) as well as the basics of clarinet performance. It was written with class instruction in mind and is often used as the beginning book in school groups.

OTHER IMPORTANT STUDIES

CAVELLINI, ERNESTO. *Thirty Caprices.* Ricordi/Carl Fischer.

HERFURTH, C. PAUL. *A Tune a Day.* 3 books. Barton Music.

KLOSÉ, HYACINTHE. *Twenty Etudes.* International.

KROEPSCH, FRITZ. *416 Progressive Daily Studies.* 4 books. International.

LANGENUS, GUSTAVE. *Complete Method for the Boehm Clarinet.* Carl Fischer.

RODE, P. *Twenty Grand Studies,* arranged by Harry Bettony. Cundy Bettony.

ROSE, CYRILLE. *Forty Studies.* 2 books. Carl Fischer.

———. *Thirty-two Etudes.* Carl Fischer.

STARK, ROBERT. *Twenty-four Studies in All Keys.* Cundy Bettony.

———. *Twenty-four Grand Virtuoso Studies.* 2 parts. Cundy Bettony.

———. *Daily Staccato Exercises.* International.

Uhl, Alfred. *Forty-eight Etudes.* Part 1. Schott.

Voxman, Himie. *Classical Studies.* Rubank.

It is important that beginning students be exposed to solo works for clarinet as well as étude and scale books. They should begin enjoying their instrument as soon as they are technically capable of playing simple solo works.

The solo works listed below are appropriate for beginning and intermediate clarinetists.

ADLER, SAMUEL. *Harobed: Seven Studies for Clarinet Alone.* Southern.

AMANI, ARR. HITE. *Ancient Menuet.* Bourne.

BACH, J. S., ARR. VOSMAN. *Minuet and Allegro.* Rubank.

BORDNER, GERALD. *Clarinet Solos for the Young Player.* 2 books. Southern.

DeCOSTA, LEON. *Clarinette Dansant.* Belwin.

DIABELLI, ARR. HITE. *Introduction and Rondo.* Southern.

DRUCKER, STANLEY. *Easy Original Clarinet Solos.*

FAURÉ, GABRIEL, ARR. HARTMANN. *En Priere.* Edition Musicus.

GEE, HARRY. *Twelve Progressive Pieces.* Southern.

HAYDN ARR. WILLAMAN. *Serenade Op. 76 #5.* Southern.

HOVEY, N., ARR. B. LEONARD. *Progressive Solo Series.* Rubank.

LANGENUS, GUSTAVE. *Six Easy Solos Series.* Carl Fischer.

LULLY, ARR. D. KAPLAN. *Air and Courant.* Jack Spratt.

PIERNÉ, GABRIEL. *Piece in G Minor.* Southern.

ROBINSON, STANFORD. *Rondo.* Southern.

STOCKS, ARR. BONADE. *Wessex Pastorale.* Southern.

VOXMAN, H. *Concert and Contest Collection for Clarinet and Piano.* Rubank.

WALTERS, DAVID. *Episode.* Southern.

WEINBERGER, J. *Sonatine.* Carl Fischer.

Selected Repertoire for Clarinet

The clarinet has a wealth of repertoire, including solo pieces, sonatas, and concertos. There is also a vast repertoire of chamber music including the clarinet. The following is an annotated list of some of the most frequently performed pieces for clarinet. Piano reductions of the orchestra parts are available for all of the concertos.

W. A. MOZART. CONCERTO IN A, K.622, FOR CLARINET AND ORCHESTRA   Composed for the clarinet virtuoso Anton Stadler very late in Mozart's life, this was the first important clarinet concerto, establishing the clarinet as a solo instrument. Mozart's concerto, written for the A clarinet, is the most performed clarinet concerto and is difficult technically and musically. Because the original manuscript has never been found, there are numerous highly different editions. I recommend the Breitkopf edition. Mozart also wrote another very important work for Stadler, the Quintet for Clarinet and Strings, K.581.

CARL MARIA VON WEBER. CONCERTINO IN E♭ FOR CLARINET AND ORCHESTRA OP. 26; CONCERTO NO. 1 IN F MINOR FOR CLARINET AND ORCHESTRA OP. 73; CONCERTO NO. 2 IN E♭ FOR CLARINET AND ORCHESTRA OP. 74; GRAND DUO CONCERTANT FOR CLARINET AND PIANO OP. 28   Inspired by the clarinet virtuoso Heinrich Baermann, Weber wrote several important works that have become basic works in the clarinet repertoire. The Concertino is one of the first solo pieces for the young player to study. The two concertos and the Duo Concertant should follow. Again, there are many editions of these works. For the Concertino and the Duo Concertant, I recommend either the version in the G. Schirmer publication *Masterworks for Clarinet* or that published by Carl Fischer. For Concertos No. 1 and 2, I recommend the traditional Carl Fischer editions.

CARL NIELSEN. CLARINET CONCERTO, OP. 57 (1928)   Nielsen's Clarinet Concerto came as a direct result of having heard the Copenhagen Wind Quintet practicing some Mozart. Nielsen (1865–1931) was so impressed with the group's sound that he wrote a wind quintet for them shortly thereafter. He then began a project of writing concertos for each of the players, but only the concertos for flute and clarinet were completed before his death. The clarinet concerto, published by Peters, was composed as a portrait of Aage Oxenvad, the clarinetist in the Copenhagen Wind Quintet. It is a very difficult work technically and should be attempted only by the most advanced players.

AARON COPLAND. CONCERTO FOR CLARINET, STRINGS, HARP AND PIANO   The great jazz clarinetist Benny Goodman commissioned this concerto, published by Boosey & Hawkes. Copland (1900–90) uses jazz elements in it, although he once told Phillip Ramey that "the jazz elements in the Clarinet Concerto have nothing to do with the 'hot jazz' improvisation for which Benny Goodman and his sextet were noted." It is the most frequently performed contemporary clarinet concerto. Its single movement opens with a long lyrical section, leading into a lengthy cadenza, followed by a final section marked by pointed notes and jazz-type rhythms. Although this concerto is not as difficult as the Nielsen Concerto, it is for the advanced player.

PAUL HINDEMITH. SONATA FOR CLARINET AND PIANO   Paul Hindemith (1895–1963) wrote solo sonatas for many instruments. The Clarinet Sonata, published by Schott, has become one of the staples of the repertoire and serves as a good introduction to contemporary music. Although not difficult technically, this sonata's idiom will be new to the younger player.

FRANCIS POULENC. SONATA FOR CLARINET AND PIANO   One of Poulenc's (1899–1963) last works, this is a wonderful sonata and is often included in clarinet recitals because of its audience appeal. This sonata, published by Chester, serves as a good introduction to the French style. Although it has some tricky moments, it can be played by an advanced student.

JOHANNES BRAHMS. SONATA IN F MINOR OP.120, NO. 1; SONATA NO. 2 IN E♭ OP. 120, NO. 2   Inspired by the clarinetist Richard Mühlfeld, Brahms (1833–97) wrote some of the greatest works for clarinet. Besides these two sonatas, Brahms wrote the Trio Op. 114, for Clarinet, Cello, and Piano and the Quintet for Clarinet and Strings Op. 115, two of the greatest pieces in the chamber music repertoire. The sonatas are not particularly difficult technically but call for a musically mature performer.

CLAUDE DEBUSSY. PREMIERE RHAPSODIE FOR CLARINET AND ORCHESTRA   This piece was originally written for clarinet and piano as a contest piece for first prize in clarinet at the Paris Conservatory. Debussy (1862–1918) later orchestrated the piano part. This beautiful piece, published by Durand, is very difficult technically, calling for a player with excellent breath control and advanced technique.

IGOR STRAVINSKY. THREE PIECES FOR SOLO CLARINET   This is the first work written for unaccompanied clarinet. Published by Chester and International, each of the three pieces creates a mood of its own. The second and third pieces are difficult both technically and rhythmically. Stravinsky (1882–1971) asks that the first two pieces be played on the A clarinet and the last piece on the B♭ clarinet. Some students have difficulty understanding this piece musically.

Other Works for Clarinet

INTERMEDIATE

ARNOLD, MALCOLM. *Sonata in B♭.* Lengnick.

BERNSTEIN, LEONARD. *Sonata for Clarinet and Piano.* Witmark.

BOZZA, EUGENE. *Idylle.* Leduc.

DEBUSSY, CLAUDE, ARR. PIQUET. *First Arabesque, Second Arabesque.* Durand.

DELMAS, MARC. *Fantaisie italienne Op. 110.* Alfred.

DONDEYNE, DÉSIRÉ. *Concertino for Clarinet and Piano.* Leduc.

FINZI, GERALD. *Five Bagatelles for Clarinet and Piano.* Boosey & Hawkes.

GROVLEZ, GABRIEL. *Lamento and Tarantelle.* Leduc.

KALLIWODA, I. W., REV. S. BELLISON. *Morceau de salon Op. 229.* Carl Fischer.

KROEPSCH, FRITZ, REV. S. BELLISON. *Fantasie from the Opera "Der Freischutz."* Carl Fischer.

LEFÈVRE, XAVIER. *Sonata No. 7.* Galaxy.

LITAIZE, GASTON. *Récitatif et thème varié.* Leduc.

LUTOSŁAWSKI, WITOLD. *Dance Preludes.* Polskie Wydawnictwo Muzyczne.

MARTIN, PHILIP. *Six Dances* (1976). Boosey & Hawkes.

MARTY, GEORGES. *First fantaisie.* Leduc.

MENDELSSOHN, FELIX. *Sonata.* G. Schirmer.

MILHAUD, DARIUS. *Sonatine* (1927). Durand.

MOZART, W. A., ARR. S. BELLISON. *Concerto Rondo in B♭ Major.* Carl Fischer.

———, ARR. SIMON. *Duo for Clarinet and Piano.* International.

MÜLLER, IWAN. *Romance de Blangini.* Ricordi.

PENDERECKI, K. *Three Miniatures.* Belwin Mills.

RABAUD, HENRI. *Solo de concours.* Leduc.

REISIGER, C. G., REV. S. BELLISON. *Fantasie Op. 146.* Carl Fischer.

RODE, P., REV. S. BELLISON. *Air varié.* Carl Fischer.

STEVENS, HALSEY. *Suite.* Peters.

WEBER, C. M., ARR. H. KLOSÉ. *L'invitation à la valse.* Leduc.

———. *Variations Op. 33.* G. Schirmer; Peters.

ADVANCED

ARNOLD, MALCOLM. *Sonatine*. Lengnick.

BABIN, VICTOR. *Hillandale Waltzes*. Boosey & Hawkes.

BAX, ARNOLD. *Sonata for Clarinet and Piano*. Chappell.

BENNETT, RICHARD. *Duo Concertante*. Novello.

BERG, ALBAN. *Vier Stücke Op. 5*. Universal.

BUSONI, FERRUCIO. *Concertino Op. 48*. Breitkopf.

CAHUZAC, LOUIS. *Variations sur un air du Pays d'Oc*. Leduc.

CASTELNUOVO-TEDESCO, MARIO. *Sonata for Clarinet and Piano Op. 128*. Ricordi.

DEVIENNE, FRANÇOIS. *Second Sonata for Clarinet and Piano*. Editions Musicales.

DELLO-JOIO, NORMAN. *Concerto for Clarinet and Orchestra*. Carl Fischer.

FAITH, RICHARD. *Concerto for Clarinet and Orchestra*. Southern.

FRANÇAIX, JEAN. *Concerto for Clarinet and Orchestra*. Editions Musicales Transatlantiques.

————. *Tema con variazioni*. (For clarinet in A.) Editions Max Eschig.

IRELAND, JOHN. *Fantasy Sonata*. Boosey & Hawkes.

KROMMER, FRANZ. *Concerto in E♭*. Music Antiqua Bohemica.

JETTEL, RUDOLPH. *Sonata*. Hofmeister.

MARTINŮ, BOHUSLAV. *Sonatine for Clarinet and Piano*. Leduc.

MILHAUD, DARIUS. *Concerto for Clarinet and Orchestra*. Elkan-Vogel.

MUCZYNSKI, ROBERT. *Time Pieces Op. 43* (1984). Theodore Presser.

REGER, MAX, ARR. PIQUET. *Romanze*. Breitkopf.

————. *Sonatas for Clarinet and Piano Op. 49, Nos. 1 and 2*. Universal.

————. *Sonata for Clarinet and Piano Op. 107*. Bote & Bock.

RIMSKY-KORSAKOV, N. ARR. KIRKBRIDE. *Flight of the Bumble Bee*. International.

REINECKE, CARL, ARR. KIRKBRIDE. *Sonata "Undine" Op. 167bis*. International.

ROSSINI, G. *Introduction, Theme, and Variations for Clarinet and Piano*. Oxford University Press.

SAINT-SAËNS, CAMILLE. *Sonata*. Durand.

SCHUBERT, FRANZ, ARR. KIRKBRIDE. *"Arpeggione" Sonata*. International.

SCHUMANN, ROBERT. *Fantasy Pieces Op. 73*. Peters.

SPOHR, LUDWIG VAN. *Concerto No.1 in C Minor Op. 26*. Peters.

————. *Concerto No.2 in E♭ Major Op. 57*. Cundy Bettony.

————. *Concerto No. 3 in F Minor*. Breitkopf; International.

————. *Concerto No. 4 in E Minor*. Breitkopf; International.

STAMITZ, JOHANN. *Concerto for Clarinet and Strings*. Belwin.

STAMITZ, KARL. *Concerto No. 1 in E♭*. Hofmeister.

TALMA, LOUISE. *Three Duologues*. Edition Musicus.

Selected Works for Clarinet Alone

BENNETT, RICHARD RODNEY. *Sonatina* (1981). Novello.

————. *Scena III* (1977). Novello.

BERIO, LUCIANO. *Sequenza IX*. Universal.

BETTINELLI, BRUNO. *Studio da concerto* (1970). Ricordi.

BOULEZ, PIERRE. *Domaines*. Universal.

DRUCKMAN, JACOB. *Animus III*. Boosey & Hawkes.

FROHNE, VINCENT. *Study for Clarinet Alone Op. 17*. Bote & Bock.

KUPFERMAN, MEYER. *Five Singles*. General.

MARTINO, DONALD. *A Set for Clarinet* (1954). McGinnis & Marx.

MESSIAEN, OLIVIER. *"Abîme des oiseaux"* from *Quartet for the End of Time*. Durand.

OSBORN, WILLSON. *Rhapsody*. Peters.

RÓZSA, MIKLÓS. *Sonatina Op. 27*. Rongwen.

SMITH, WILLIAM O. *Five Pieces for Clarinet Alone* (1959). Universal.

————. *Variants*. Universal.

SUTERMEISTER, H. *Capriccio for Unaccompanied Clarinet in A*. Schott

TOWER, JOAN. *Wings*. Associated Music.

Key Numbers Chart

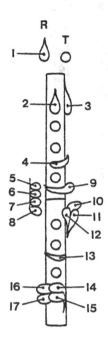

Fingering Chart

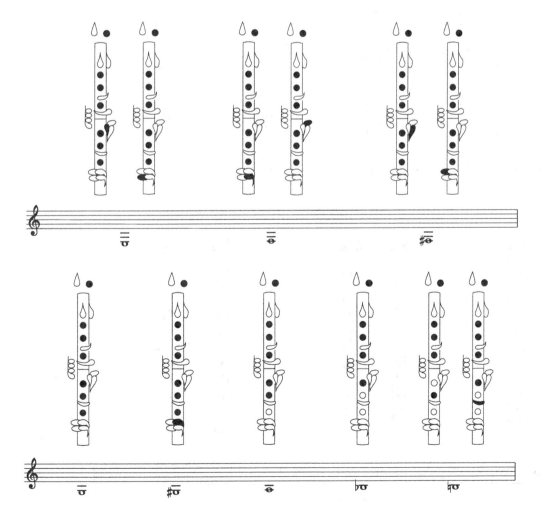

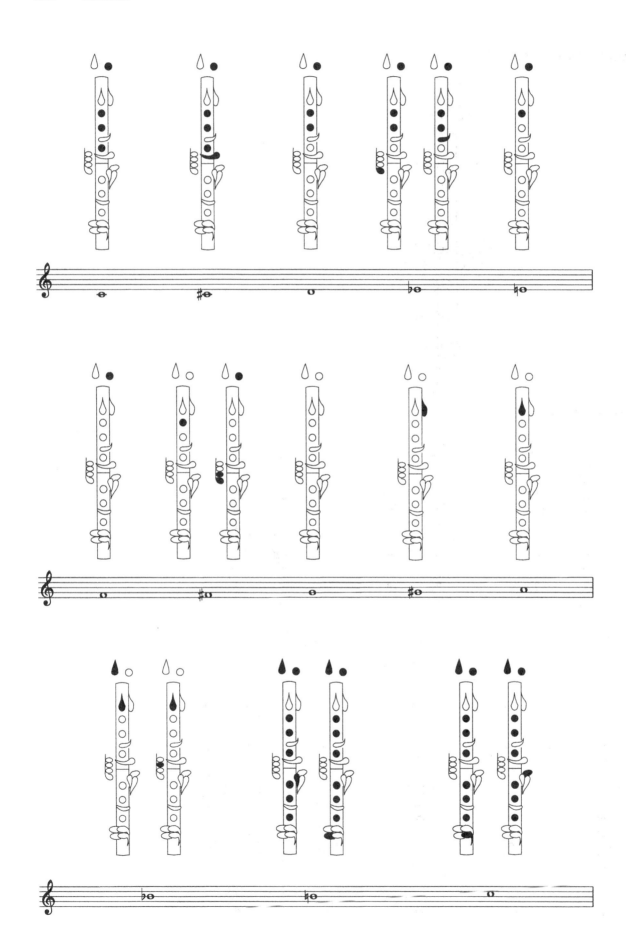

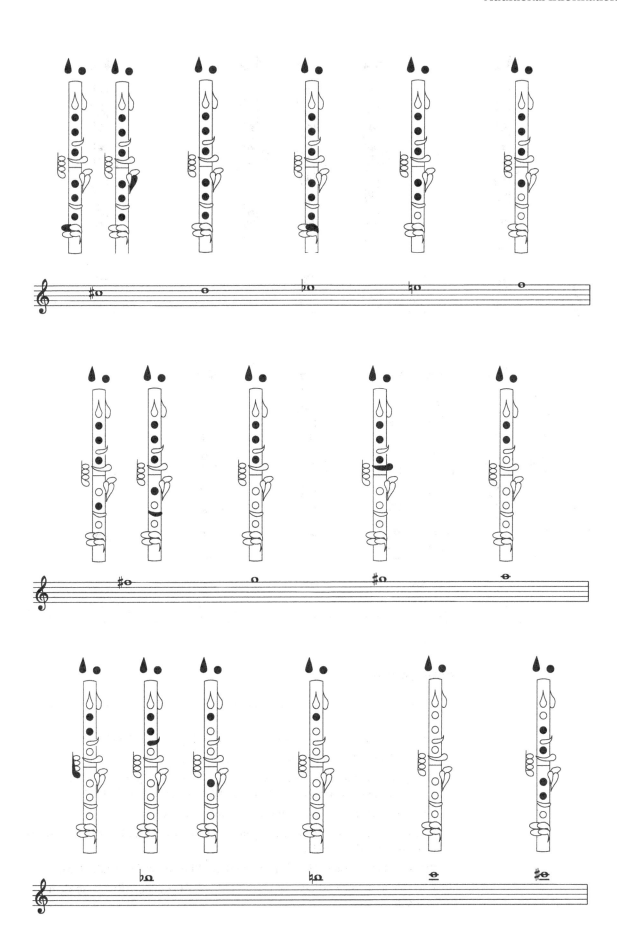

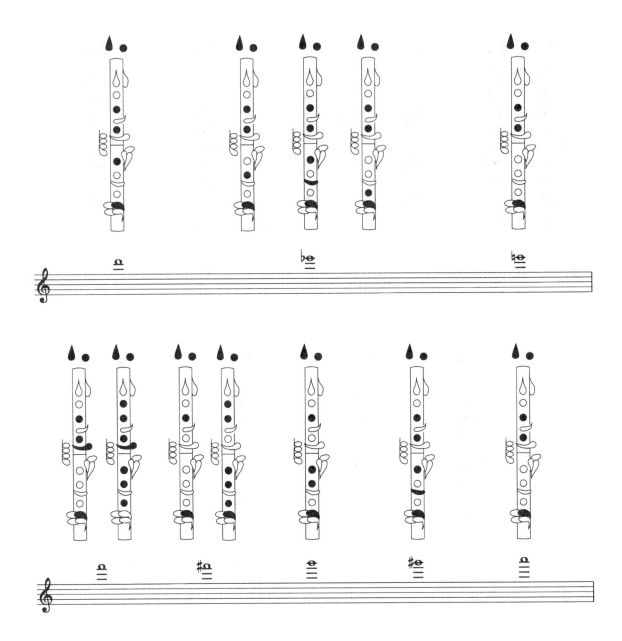

Bibliography

BAINES, ANTHONY. *Woodwind Instruments and Their History.* New York: Dover, 1967.

BONADE, DANIEL. *The Clarinetist's Compendium.* Kenosha, WI: Leblanc, 1962.

BRYMER, JACK. *Clarinet.* London: MacDonald & Jane's, 1979.

GOLD, CECIL V. *Clarinet Performance Practices and Teaching in the United States and Canada.* Greensboro, NC: Institute for Woodwind Research, 1977.

KROLL, OSKAR. *The Clarinet.* New York: Taplinger, 1968.

LAWSON, COLIN. *The Cambridge Companion to the Clarinet.* Cambridge: Cambridge University Press, 1995.

RENDALL, F. GEOFFREY. *The Clarinet,* London: Williams and Norgate, 1954.

WILKENS, WAYNE. *The Index of Clarinet Music.* Magnolia, AR: Music Register, 1975.

PART 3

Flute

<small>HAL OTT</small>

CHAPTER 12

Introduction

The present-day flute, which serves as the soprano voice in the wood-wind choir, has a cylindrical body with a parabolic head. Its overall length is approximately twenty-seven inches, and no fewer than eighteen keys are strategically placed along the body and foot joint both to fit the hands and to produce an in-tune and consistent tone in all registers. Its range extends from c^1 (b, on some instruments) to g^4. Two models are generally available, with either closed or open tone holes. The closed-hole or plateau design is most often found on less expensive student flutes, while the open-hole or French model is typically a more expensive instrument. Flutes are usually made of metal, silver being the most popular alloy employed, and they are occasionally constructed of other materials such as gold, platinum, nickel, crystal, acrylic, amber, ivory, plastics, porcelain, carbon fiber, and a seemingly endless variety of wood products. Flute prices cover the extremes: whereas student model instruments are relatively inexpensive, some professional flute models can be much more costly than any of the other wind instruments, with the exception of the best professional bassoons.

The reason for the flute's popularity is multifaceted: the flute is used in many styles of music from classical to pop and jazz; it is small and easily carried; it has a mechanical system that is the most perfected of all the woodwinds; it has an enormous repertoire; both of the sexes find it appealing; and it possesses a unique tone, one that has often been compared to that of the human voice.

History

The flute is considered to be one of the oldest instruments known. The discovery of the flute's basic principle probably dates back to a prehistoric observation of the pleasing sound of wind blowing across the open end of a reed. Evolution was slow and sporadic; it took centuries for our distant relatives to grasp the fact that different sizes of reeds produce various pitches.

Little is known about the early flute, for only a few ancient instruments have survived. Also, little existing documentation deals with flutes prior to the thirteenth century, when the flute is reported to have been widely used. The thirteenth-century instrument, or Renaissance flute, resembles a fife in that it is cylindrical and has six holes (see Fig. 12.1). Having a vocal ideal in mind, builders constructed several sizes of these flutes to correspond to the various parts of a vocal ensemble.[1]

During the last decade of the seventeenth century the transverse flute acquired a conical shape and one key; now in three sections, the flute was fully chromatic and could more easily match the expressiveness of the voice and stringed instruments. A similar instrument, divided into four sections, was the instrument for which Rameau, Bach, and Handel wrote. During the second half of the eighteenth century three additional keys were added to eliminate some of the difficult cross fingerings; more challenging tonalities were now more easily negotiated with a more consistent sound from top to bottom. Slightly later, C and C♯ keys were added to extend the range down two semitones.[2] The Industrial Revolution spawned flutes with many additional keys, but the essential design and shape of the instrument remained the same.

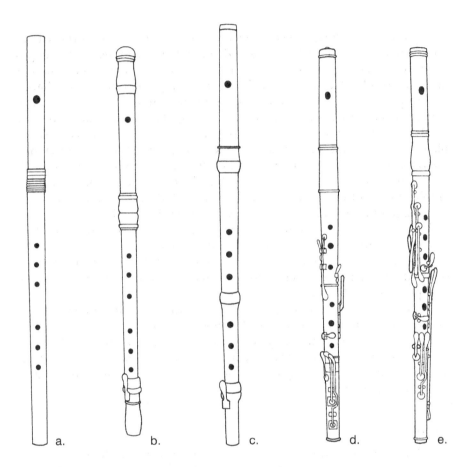

Figure 12.1. (a) Renaissance flute; (b) early Baroque flute (ca. 1690); (c) late Baroque flute (ca. 1720); (d) late Classical/early Romantic flute (ca. 1800); (e) mid-Romantic flute (ca. 1830)

The most significant development in the flute's construction since its metamorphosis during the late seventeenth century was the radical transformation initiated by Theobald Boehm (1794–1881), a builder and flute virtuoso.[3] On a trip to London in 1831 he heard the famous English flutist Charles Nicholson perform a concert on a seven-keyed flute, one with very large holes to accommodate the flutist's large hands. Boehm was so impressed with Nicholson's powerful sound that he set out immediately to remodel the flute. Had he not heard Nicholson, the Boehm flute would never have been made. In 1832 he produced his new model (see Fig. 12.2) and performed on it in a concert in Munich that same year. This wooden conical flute had large holes that were placed as closely as possible to their acoustically correct positions, and the typically closed holes were opened and regulated with rings connected to long rods. Boehm's work is

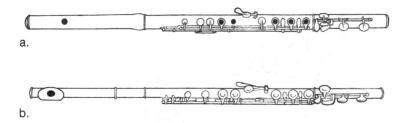

Figure 12.2. (a) Boehm's 1832 model flute; (b) Boehm's 1847 model flute

regarded as perhaps the greatest improvement in woodwind instrument history.[4]

In 1847 Boehm again went back to the drawing board. He concluded that a cylindrical bore could improve the notes at the top and the bottom of the scale. This revolutionary cylindrical instrument helped stabilize pitch and timbre throughout the various registers. Moreover, he determined that the optimum tube size is thirty times longer than its diameter; for tuning octaves, Boehm introduced the parabolic head joint, one with a slight contraction at the upper end.[5] Boehm also discovered that by making the tone holes even larger than those on his 1832 model, he could improve the scale and response while permitting a greater volume of tone.[6] Indeed, the holes were so large that the fingers could not successfully cover them. To remedy this problem, Boehm developed padded covers for the open holes to replace the rings. Boehm then devised a new mechanism that would permit each key to open independently as well as interact with others; he also concluded that silver and brass tubes produced the best tone. This more resonant sound could be created on a thin, hard, drawn tube because of the metal's increased capacity for vibration.[7] Standing the test of time, this is essentially the same flute that we have used for over one hundred years—a monument to the genius of Theobald Boehm.

Assembly and Alignment

Upon opening the case, the correct placement of the head joint, body, and foot joint should be noted prior to assembly so the parts can be replaced without forcing them into an unnatural position and thereby subjecting the flute to possible damage. When removing the flute from the case, avoid bending the keys, rods, and lip plate. Grasp the head joint on the tubing below the lip plate, the body at the barrel, and the foot joint at the bottom so as to avoid bending the keys or rods (see Figs. 12.3, 12.4). The three sections should be assembled by carefully inserting each tenon into the appropriate socket with a gentle rotating motion. The same care should be exercised when disassembling. Cork grease or other lubricants should not be used on the tenons to facilitate assembly; flutes are carefully designed to slide metal against metal, and the use of such lubricants can damage the surfaces of the metal. The tenons and sockets can be kept clean by wiping them after each use. If they persist in being overly tight, they can be altered by a competent repairman.

So often in the typical flute method the importance of proper alignment of the three sections is dealt with peripherally, and occasionally it is

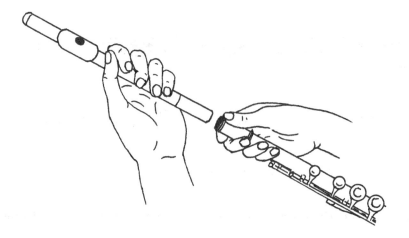

Figure 12.3. Assembly (1). Grasp the head joint on the tubing below the lip plate and the body at the barrel.

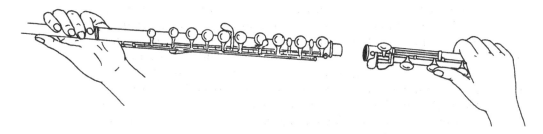

Figure 12.4. Assembly (2). Grasp the foot joint at the bottom to avoid bending the rods, tenons, and keys. The right thumb can be placed on the lowest keys for security of assembly.

ignored completely. What may seem like a minor alignment error can lead to bad habits that seriously interfere with the proper development of tone and technique. Assembled correctly, the head joint should line up with the first key on the body. Some manufacturers of student model flutes provide marks for alignment; these can be helpful but should be checked for accuracy before using them as a guide. The foot joint rod should line up with the center of the keys of the body. Considering that the little finger is significantly shorter than the other digits, this alignment allows for the best right hand position with a curved little finger (see Fig. 12.5).

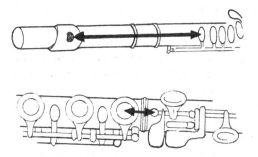

Figure 12.5 Properly aligned flute

Care and Maintenance

The flute, though relatively reliable and sturdy, requires special care to keep the instrument in good playing condition. Light finger pressure should be used in depressing the keys in performance; not only is wear and tear of the pads thus minimized, but technical efficiency is more easily attainable as well. The most critical aspect of flute care is keeping the instrument as free of moisture as possible. The interior of the flute should be swabbed with a soft, absorbent cloth threaded through the eye of the cleaning rod. The cloth should be wrapped around the rod to avoid scratching the inside of the tube (see Fig. 12.6). To avoid saturating the cloth immediately, the foot joint can be swabbed first, followed by the body and finally the head joint. Wiping off fingerprints and general grime from the exterior of the flute should follow; the sockets and tenons should be included. Circular motions used to clean the keys are to be avoided; they can loosen the delicate regulation of the mechanism. When finished, never leave the cleaning cloth or swabs inside the case; doing so defeats the purpose of keeping moisture away from the pads and mechanism.

Never attempt to clean the flute with metal polish; even the slightest contact with the pads or the inner mechanism can cause serious damage. Although the development of tarnish is inevitable, it will not damage the

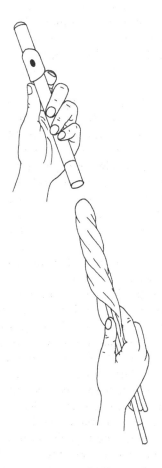

Figure 12.6. Swabbing condensation from the flute. The cloth is inserted through the eye and then wrapped around the rod to avoid scratching the inside of the flute tube.

instrument. If the flutist desires, a competent repairman can remove tarnish during routine service, but one must be aware that small amounts of silver are also taken off each time the tarnish is removed. The buildup of tarnish can be retarded by the use of a commercially available treated cloth or by the use of a small amount of denatured alcohol placed on a clean cloth; care should be taken to avoid pad edges when cleaning the instrument with these chemically treated or alcohol dampened cloths.

Occasionally the placement of the cork stopper position in the head joint should be checked by gently inserting the scored end of the cleaning rod into the head joint. This mark should line up exactly in the middle of the embouchure hole. If necessary, the cork can be adjusted by screwing and unscrewing the crown or cap at the end of the head joint. The position of the stopper, seventeen millimeters from the exact center of the embouchure hole, determines whether or not the flute will play in tune with itself. Once it is set, it should not be moved, and the stopper should never be used to make the flute generally sharper or flatter. If the cork becomes loose, it should first be removed by pushing it out toward the open end to prevent cork damage, since this end of the head joint is larger. The cork can be temporarily swelled by dipping it in boiling water, and soon thereafter it should be replaced by a competent repairman.

A variety of tools can be useful for maintenance and minor repairs. Jeweler's screwdrivers are invaluable for adjusting the screws that, on most student model instruments, fine-tune the action of keys that are coupled; it is wise to observe how these work so minor adjustments can be made. A small amount of white glue or fingernail polish can be applied to the top of pivot screws that frequently come loose. Springs can be returned to their carriages with a crochet hook. Pipe cleaners are useful for cleaning out the insides of rods.

A flame from a Bunsen burner or a lighted match can be used to reseat pads not held by a screw: heat the silver side of the pad cup and then apply gentle but steady pressure to the key until cool. Sticking pads are usually caused by moisture, and this problem can be remedied by placing an absorbent cloth or ungummed cigarette paper under the pad, applying light pressure, and gently drawing out the cloth or paper. In extreme cases, denatured alcohol applied to the cloth or paper will work; however, repeated applications will dry out the pads and cause them to tear or crack.

A small paintbrush is beneficial for removing dust and lint from inaccessible areas of the flute; dust and lint, which can work their way into the mechanism, should also be removed from the inside of the case. Additionally, it is a good idea to keep the case closed even when the flute is in use. Rubber bands and cellophane tape can come in handy in emergency situations to remedy such things as broken springs and loose tenon adjustments. Oiling the flute should be avoided. Sluggishness is often caused by dirt in the mechanism, and oil placed on the exterior pivot points attracts dirt. Springs should never be tightened to compensate for sluggish action.

Major repairs such as realigning bent posts and replacing pads should not be attempted by novices; instead, a competent repairman should routinely clean, oil, and adjust the mechanism at least once a year to keep the flute in good working order. Complete overhauls include replacing the pads, corks, and felts, as well as cleaning, oiling, and adjusting. The need for overhauling varies from person to person and is based on a variety of factors including the amount of playing, finger pressure, abuse, and neglect.

Exercising common sense can prolong the life of the flute. General suggestions for sanitation include occasionally bathing the head joint in warm soapy water followed by a thorough rinse. Brushing the teeth—or at least rinsing the mouth with water—after eating and before playing will help prevent deterioration of the pads from food acids and thereby avert costly overhauls. For the same reason, the flute should not be set down on its keys; they can become bent, and condensation can run onto and facilitate decaying of the pads. Even holding the flute vertically as opposed to horizontally when resting can channel some of the moisture out the end of the foot joint and prolong the life of pads. Another way to avoid expensive repair bills is to follow the rule that a flute never be left out of its case sitting on a chair or music stand awaiting someone to come along and accidentally kick, bump, or sit on the instrument.

The quality of the flute case and the protection it affords should also be evaluated. A case should hold its flute securely and motionlessly; a flute that rattles in its case is asking for adjustment problems. Latches should be in working order. Probably the most practical and secure way of carrying the instrument is in a commercially available case cover. Not only do such covers provide additional protection, but they also serve as excellent spaces to store saturated swabs and potentially damaging metal cleaning rods.

Notes

1. Nancy Toff, *The Development of the Modern Flute* (New York: Taplinger, 1979), 12.

2. Andrew Fairley, *Flutes, Flautists, and Makers* (London: Pan Educational Music, 1982), 13.

3. Howard Mayer Brown, "Flute," in *The New Grove Dictionary of Music and Musicians* (London: Macmillan, 1980), 6:676.

4. Sibyl Marcuse, *Survey of Musical Instruments* (New York: Harper and Row, 1975), 189.

5. Theobald Boehm, *The Flute and Flute Playing*, 1872 (Trans. and rev. Dayton C. Miller. 2d ed. 1992. Reprint. New York: Dover, 1964), 16.

6. Johann Burnau, "The Life of Theobald Boehm," *The Instrumentalist* 21 (1967): 58.

7. Boehm, *The Flute and Flute Playing*, 69.

CHAPTER 13

Fundamentals of Flute Playing

Breathing

Breathing for living is a natural, involuntary activity. Breathing for flute playing, where one has to take in a deep breath quickly and expel that amount of air over a longer period of time, is not as natural. The flute requires an enormous quantity of air to play, more than other wind instruments, because there is nothing in or on the mouth to inhibit the flow of the air. Therefore the flutist must master the process of using the air efficiently for rapid inhalation and slow, controlled exhalation. Since sufficient, well-controlled airflow is essential to the production of a beautiful tone, flutists should strive to make use of the entire lung expanse. To maximize inhalation, the flutist should try to fill up from the bottom to the top so the abdomen expands first and then is followed by the rib cage, allowing a large amount of air to enter. Expansion should be felt in the lower abdomen, sides, back, and finally the upper chest. To facilitate this expansion, imagine breathing lower than actually possible (i.e., the base of the spine or the soles of the feet).

Two sets of muscles, those including the sides of the chest cavity (intercostal) and those of the abdomen and waist (diaphragmatic), are used in controlling the airflow. A good way to become aware of these breath-supporting muscles is to pant as a dog would or by blowing as hard as possible on some object such as a thumb inserted in the mouth. When it is contracted, the diaphragm flattens and lowers the lungs, promoting the inward flow of air. When this muscle is relaxed, it pushes against the lungs and assists in expelling the air as it reverts to its natural dome shape. Since the flute lacks resistance to the airstream, except for the small amount afforded by the lips themselves, the flutist needs to learn how to control the slow, steady outflow of air as the tone is drawn from the flute, and this is where the muscles of the chest cavity, or intercostal muscles, come into play. As the diaphragm is relaxing and air is being expelled, the intercostals must resist collapsing to prevent the rapid loss of air. As the chest expansion is maintained, the air is successfully controlled and budgeted over a given space of time.

Although there are many pedagogical approaches to breathing, all professional flutists agree that in every phase of breathing and tone production it is essential to keep the throat open and relaxed. To maintain the feeling of an open throat when inhaling quickly, the mouth should form an oval shape as when pronouncing the syllable "ho." This relaxes and opens the throat and allows a large volume of air to get into the lungs. The feeling of an open throat is often compared to a slight yawning sensation. The flutist should avoid gasping when inhaling; gasping limits the quantity of air and is a sure indicator that the throat is not open. To preserve an open throat when exhaling, the air should feel warm and moist, as if one were fogging a mirror. A general rule to follow is to keep the intake passive and the output active when striving to maintain an open throat.

Good posture is important in flute playing, but exaggerated muscle tension is to be avoided; tension is a hindrance to correct breathing. Shoulders should be in a relaxed, lowered position. The chest should be held high, and the collarbone should have the feeling of actually being lifted. If one watches the performing postures of experienced opera singers, it will be seen that their shoulders are slightly down and back while their upper chests are held high so their bodies do not have to expand this area; it already is expanded. Additionally, the flutist should be careful not to pull in the abdomen while expanding the chest and rib cage. Pulling the abdomen in or raising the shoulders indicates incorrect breathing. Overinflation can also cause the shoulders to rise, and raising the shoulders can contribute to throat and vibrato tension, shallow breathing, and unwanted vocal cord noises.

Controlled breath support can be developed by sustaining long tones at one dynamic level. As a test of breath support, hold a small piece of paper against a wall by blowing on it. Slurred scales and arpeggios practiced at different speeds can also help develop excellent exhalation control. One method for improving breath capacity is to practice scales at a comfortable metronome speed where the whole scale can be performed in one breath. Gradually, with the tone remaining at the same intensity and dynamic level, the metronome should be set at slower and slower tempos. This strengthens the airflow and the resistance needed to extend the breath.

Embouchure

In ideal circumstances, the flute embouchure is best taught through actual demonstration by an accomplished flutist. In the absence of that, written directions often must suffice. Because the flute embouchure is radically different from that of any other wind instrument, the nonflutist should take great care in understanding this fundamental component of flute playing.

To produce a tone, the air is directed through a small opening in the embouchure. To form this opening, the lips need to be held together without tension, and the front upper and lower teeth should be more or less aligned. Hold the head joint alone with the open end to the right; the plate should rest gently in the cradle of the chin. The flute should be tilted slightly so the outer edge is slightly higher than the inner edge. The lower lip should be gently spread along the plate and turned out slightly in a pout formation, and some of the inner surface should be visible. Approximately one quarter of the hole should be covered with the lower lip. The lips then should be slightly parted as when forming the word "pure" or "pooh"; the feeling should be that of trying to blow across a spoonful of hot soup. In most cases, the lip aperture will naturally form near the center of the mouth, and the lip plate hole can be centered by moving the flute to the right or left as needed. To complete the process, direct a steady stream of air at the strike wall so the air is split by the sharp upper edge of the hole (see Fig. 13.1). After attempting the above steps, the student may try pretending to spit a piece of paper off the end of the tongue to produce first tones; however, it is imperative to refrain from tonguing through the lips once the ability to form an embouchure and produce a tone becomes comfortable.

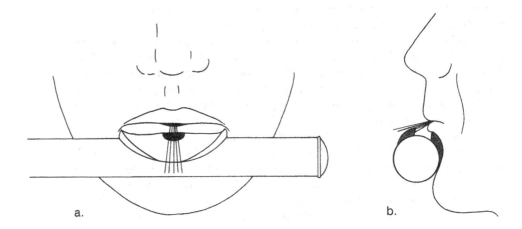

Figure 13.1 The embouchure: (a) front view; (b) side view. Note the slightly downturned corners, the lower lip in the lip plate hole, the aperture that is centered and parallel to the lip plate hole, the air blowing across the inner surface of the lips, the lower lip gently spread across the lip plate, and the air being split by the strike edge.

In general, the lips should push in an outward direction so the air stream is formed by the inner surface of the lips. These membranes are smooth and assist in producing a pure tone, while the rough texture of the outer surface is a hindrance to both purity and flexibility. Tightness, firmness, rigidity, and the use of the "smiling" muscles when playing should be avoided. The embouchure remains flexible and supple at all times, permitting each note to have a slightly different formation in order to adjust intonation, facilitate in register changes, and aid tonal color changes. Beginners should learn to exaggerate the differences, and as they advance, smaller, more economical (sometimes imperceptible) movements will suffice. Typically, the embouchure is pushed forward (the "lip tube" is extended) and the jaw is raised for softer and higher passagework, and the lips are in a more natural position with the jaw dropped for louder and lower notes (see Fig. 13.2).

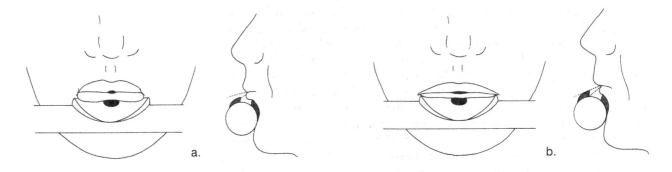

Figure 13.2. Soft and higher-register embouchure (a); loud and lower-register embouchure (b)

Although people with thinner lips are often said to be more ideally suited for flute playing, the lip structures of accomplished flutists display a variety of shapes and sizes. An even more important consideration than lip size is the shape of the airstream and how it is directed into the flute. If the student's lip is exceptionally thick, less embouchure hole should be covered; if the reverse is evident, more lip should cover the hole. These changes are minute; large adjustments often produce undesirable results.

Uncentered apertures are often caused by inappropriate holding positions. Flutists that play in cramped rehearsal conditions often push their flutes too far forward or too far backward, causing them to blow out of the side of the embouchure. A student with a natural teardrop or "Cupid's bow" formation (see Fig. 13.3) may have to learn to close one side of the embouchure, in which case an acceptable tone can be produced by making certain that the aperture remains parallel to the lip plate hole. Adaptation to this type of blowing can be expedited through frequent checks in front of a mirror. It may also be comforting for these students to know that several well-known performers have faced these challenges and with persistency have overcome them.

a.   b.

Figure 13.3. (a) "Cupid's bow" embouchure; (b) side-blown embouchure

Tone Production

To develop a basic concept of the tone that is desired, the student flutist must be given ample opportunities to listen, because tonal concepts are nearly impossible to convey through the use of written or spoken words. The modeling that the flute teacher provides is often the best and certainly the most immediate source of tone improvement. Attending live flute performances and listening to quality recordings of outstanding flutists are other excellent ways of building a mental tone picture. Additionally, solo and chamber music opportunities should be provided to insure that students have a chance to hear themselves. The typical large flute sections in most bands offer little help in this regard; in these situations individual responsibilities are nearly nonexistent and poor tonal development can easily go undetected. Another staple of good tone production is that the throat should always remain as open as possible to permit the free flow of air because the inside of the mouth, the throat, and the upper chest are resonance chambers, and they contribute greatly to the quality of the sound produced.

For many beginners, tone production is at best inconsistent. Much of the airflow is wasted because of variance in control, and these students often find themselves dizzy and discouraged. Persistence, coupled with resting periods and a mirror, breeds success. From the first notes on, the flutist will realize that refining, controlling, and enhancing the tone is a lifelong process, and as this process is pursued, the student will need less volume and velocity of air to accomplish musical goals. Suggestions to open the throat, to adjust the direction of the air column, to maintain good posture and holding positions, and to adhere to correct embouchure formation will speed the tonal refinement process.

There are four basic variables in tone control: airspeed, angle of the airstream, aperture size, and head joint placement. A different airspeed is required to produce each note on the flute. The lower registers require a slower-moving airstream than the higher ones. Moving from register to register by blowing harder or softer produces loud, sharp high notes and flat, soft lower notes. What must be learned is to control the speed of the air by altering the size of the lip aperture through forward and backward movements in relation to the strike edge of the embouchure hole.

Purity or clarity of tone is achieved, in part, by learning to deliver a "laser beam"—a constant, narrow, well-focused stream of air that splits equally on the strike edge. The air column makes contact with the strike wall at a higher point for high pitches and correspondingly lower for low tones. Air that escapes the side edges causes a hiss or airy sound, air directed too much above the edge produces a spread or unfocused tone, and air directed too far down into the flute results in a thin, nasal tone.

The aperture will change with the demands of range and dynamics. As mentioned in the section on embouchure, to ascend to a higher pitch or to play softly while still maintaining good intonation, the lips should move forward so the aperture is closer to the blowing edge. This accomplishes two things. First, the aperture becomes smaller, thus speeding up the air. Second, shortening the distance between the aperture and the strike edge increases the speed of the airflow. This phenomenon can be demonstrated by forming an embouchure and blowing across one's index finger. As the finger is moved closer to the lip opening, the airspeed will be perceived as becoming increasingly faster and more intense even though the blowing remains constant. Thus moving the lips forward provides the flutist with a faster-moving part of the airstream. The aperture will enlarge and the airstream will move more slowly as the lips are returned to a natural position for lower and louder sounds.

The head joint should be aligned on two axes: parallel to the lips and even on the chin. When this alignment occurs, the airstream has an optimum chance to make contact with the strike wall at the point where the tone can be split evenly without any excess wind noise. The flute should not be angled too far forward or backward, and if the head joint is rolled too far out, the sound will be shallow, unfocused, and out of tune with itself (generally, the octaves will be stretched). If the head joint is rolled too far in, the tone will be muffled, nasal sounding, out of tune with itself (generally, the octaves will be compressed), and apt to crack, and the dynamic range will be decreased significantly (see Fig. 13.4).

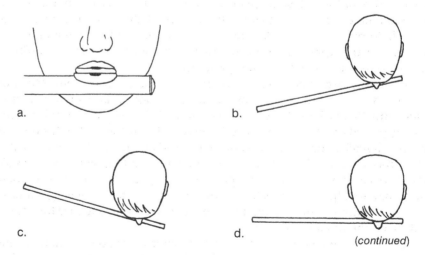

a.

b.

c.

d.

(continued)

Figure 13.4. Tone production: (a) The head joint is parallel to the opening in the lips. (b) The head joint is too far forward. (c) The head joint is too far back. (d) The head joint is aligned properly.

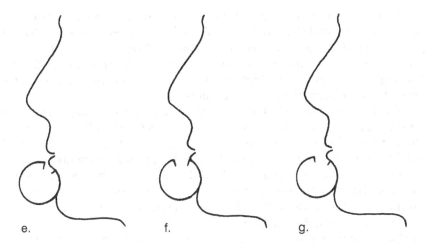

(e) The head joint is rolled in too far. (f) The head joint is rolled out too far. (g) The head joint is in the correct position.

Tonguing

The flutist uses the tongue to articulate the beginning of each note. The motion of the tongue is similar to that used when pronouncing a whispered or inaudible "du." Notice that, when pronouncing "du," the top of the tongue near the tip is striking the upper palate just behind the upper front teeth. The tongue acts as a valve releasing the air into the instrument. The student should place the tip of the tongue slightly above alveolar ridge, just behind the upper front teeth. Only the tip of the tongue should be used in this basic attack; any variation will not produce as definitive or acute an attack. Air pressure is then built behind the tongue, and when it is quickly withdrawn, the air column starts the tone (see Fig. 13.5). During this process it is important to keep the tongue as relaxed as possible and to strive for a clear beginning to each tone without creating excessive tongue noise.

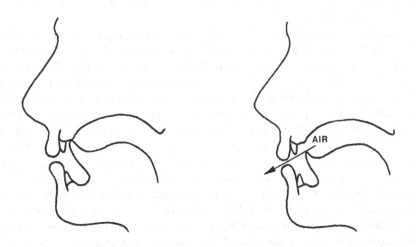

Figure 13.5. Tonguing. The tip of the tongue makes contact with the alveolar ridge. Air pressure is built, and when the tongue is withdrawn, the air column starts the tone.

As the student advances, the placement of the tongue prior to the attack will vary slightly. The tongue should strike closer to the teeth as one plays lower in range or louder in intensity, and higher up on the alveolar ridge as one plays higher in range or softer. As the student continues to gain experience, other syllables will be found to vary the sharpness of the attack to accommodate different registers.

The tongue usually should not be allowed to protrude between the lips, for the shape and size of the aperture formation may be distorted. Also, the student should not be allowed to stop the tone with the tongue, as in the syllable "tut." This release is usually too abrupt and rough and is seldom used in performance. The action of a pulsating water sprinkler can be used as a model of how the tongue interrupts the airstream without stopping it. Additionally, the student should refrain from tonguing with any portion of the tongue but the tip, anchoring the tongue to the lower teeth, tonguing by closing off the throat, moving the jaw in a chewing motion for each note, or substituting a breath attack for a tongued one. If any of these problems are left unchecked, the student may develop ingrained bad habits that are inordinately difficult and time-consuming to break.

Remind the student that the length of a note is determined by the air, not by the tongue; therefore the first type of tonguing that should be practiced is legato articulation. The syllables "du," "da," "dee," "lu," "la," and "lee" are excellent ones to use. When tonguing legato passages, the airflow is kept constant, and no breaks or stops are permitted in the sound. A very smooth connection results where the end of one note is also the beginning of the next. If legato connection is not stressed, the student will usually play each note with a separate breath attack and often will actually take a breath at every note. Learning legato articulation will not only improve tonguing techniques but also improve breath control.

Next, students should learn staccato articulation. It is important to remind the student once again that the tongue should never be used to stop a note. Rather, the tone is begun with the "tu" syllable and the air is stopped with the diaphragm for clear, even, bouncy repetitions. One way of teaching this is to have the student practice with no tongue and to articulate with short bursts of air from the diaphragm with the syllable "hah." Each note should be clearly separated. The student should avoid involving the throat in this process; it should be kept a clear, open channel for the air. Next, the syllables such as "tu," "tah," and "tee" should be added, continuing to employ the breath staccato.

Double tonguing, used for quick duple passages, is accomplished by alternating the tip of the tongue with a point further back on the tongue, resulting in pairs of syllables such as "ta-ka," "tee-kee," "du-gu," or "tu-ku." The student should use small tongue motions, keeping both of the tongue strokes close to the front of the mouth for best efficiency, and maintaining constant breath support and an open throat. Do not draw the tongue back too far, allow it to rest on the teeth, or move the lips or jaw while tonguing.

Flutists should begin learning to double tongue in their second year of playing, as soon as consistent staccato single tonguing is mastered. A slow double tongue and a fast single tongue should comfortably overlap. Many students who begin to practice double tonguing later in their development often can achieve a quick speed after considerable practice; however, their newly developed double tonguing cannot evenly negotiate passages that are slightly too fast for their single tonguing. By beginning early, double tonguing is learned slowly, and overlapping fast single tonguing with slow double tonguing occurs naturally and is unforced.

The same basic process is used to learn triple tonguing, which is intended for passages grouped in threes. A variety of syllables can be used, such as "tee-kee-tee," "ta-ka-ta," "to-ko-to," or "do-go-do." "Ta-ka-ta" followed by "ka-ta-ka" produces even articulation and is especially useful in scale passages or disjunct patterns.

As has already been mentioned, the tongue is used to start tones; it is rarely used to stop them. The overwhelming majority of releases are accomplished with the air alone; however, air-only releases tend to be flat. To combat this intonation flaw, taper releases are used. This process is accomplished by slowing down the airspeed, gradually directing the airstream upward, slightly lifting the head, and pushing the lips forward as in imitating the motion that results when uttering the syllables "ah-ooh." A variety of speeds of taper releases should be practiced to accommodate everything from slow and extended long-tone dimenuendi to staccato notes played at quick tempos.

Flutter tonguing was first notated in the early twentieth century by Richard Strauss, in his *Don Quixote*. The sound has a rapid tremolo quality because the airstream is disturbed by quick movements of the tongue. There are two generally accepted methods of flutter tonguing. The first is produced by blowing a constant airstream, relaxing the tongue, and rolling the tip of the tongue as one does when pronouncing a Spanish *r*. The second version is created in the back of the throat by the tongue. It is produced by blowing a constant airstream, relaxing the tongue, and rolling the part of the tongue that one uses in clearing the throat or gargling. Similar parts of the tongue are employed as when pronouncing a French *r*. Most students can master the former type of fluttering with little practice; others, however, find it impossible. The latter method, while more challenging to learn, can be produced with some degree of success by everyone.

Position and Balance

The prime consideration in holding the flute is to support it in the most natural and comfortable position to insure facile fingers, steady support, and freedom to breathe properly. Poor holding position can usually be traced back to inadequate supervision or student inattention during the earliest lessons. Beginners are often insecure with proper hand position, fearing that they will drop the flute. They compensate by squeezing the fingers, placing unnecessary pressure on balance points, or developing awkward holding positions that provide support but inhibit finger motion. These students must be conscientiously supervised and encouraged to practice in front of a mirror to build good habits. With so many musicians suffering from performance-related health problems, careful attention to proper position and balance can not only assist students in becoming proficient musicians but also help prevent future bouts of tendinitis, carpal tunnel syndrome, and other devastating ailments.

The flute should be held lightly with the fingers as close to the keys as possible while maintaining a sense of relaxation. Using small motions, the flutist should press only enough to overcome spring tension. Not only does this facilitate technique, but it also saves wear and tear on the pads. To teach correct position, have the student drop the hands to the sides, letting them be totally relaxed. The fingers will then curve gently while the thumbs are straight. When playing, one should try to maintain this same position (see Fig. 13.6). The left thumb should be straight and held perpendicular to the B key, and it will contact the key somewhere in the middle part of the thumb and not at the tip. The left wrist should be kept slightly bent; this will allow the left thumb to assume the correct position and will place the ring finger and pinkie of the left hand correctly on the keys. Conversely, if the left wrist is held straight, these fingers will probably be too far away from their respective keys. The right thumb should also be kept straight as it contacts the flute. If correctly positioned, it will be nearly parallel to the floor. The right wrist should be held in a natural position, which is fairly straight. Bending the right wrist causes tension and makes it difficult to position the right thumb correctly. Reaching for a pretend book that is lying flat on an elevated shelf demonstrates excellent position for the right hand and wrist.

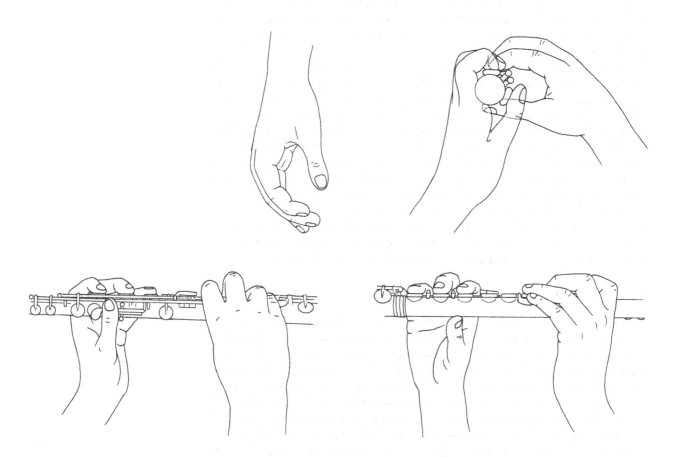

Figure 13.6. Correct hand and wrist positions. Note the natural curve of the fingers and the straight thumb.

When played, the flute is supported or balanced at four essential points: the base of the left index finger against the tube between the C lever and C hole, the right thumb against the tubing, the right pinkie on the D♯ key, and the chin (see Fig. 13.7). The position of the left index finger will be determined by size of the hand. The finger should be placed so it can operate the C key comfortably. The right thumb and pinkie apply slight pressure in a forward direction while the left index finger holds the flute gently against the chin. The left hand is placed slightly under the flute so most of the weight rests on the index finger. Excessive pressure against the chin should be avoided. When this position is achieved, one should be able to hold the flute in place without any other part of the hand touching the flute.

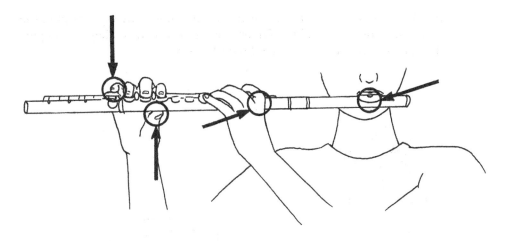

Figure 13.7. The four balance points

There are two accepted views on proper right thumb position. With the first, the right thumb is placed on the tubing under the right index finger and serves to support the flute from below. The second, often referred to as the Rockstrow position, places the right thumb on the back side of the instrument and gently pushes forward to provide secure balance between itself, the base of the left index finger, and the chin on the lip plate (see Fig. 13.8). It is considered unnecessary to employ the right pinkie as a balance point when using the Rockstrow position; the thumb-under advocates include it as a support, however, since nearly all of the notes played have the D♯ key depressed, and where it is lifted, as in d², the majority of the other fingers contribute to the balancing act.

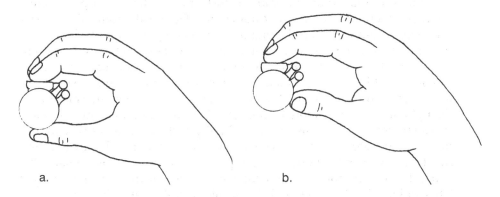

a.   b.

Figure 13.8. (a) Traditional right thumb position; (b) Rockstrow thumb position

If the right thumb protrudes beyond the tube excessively, the fingers above will be compressed and may curve in such a fashion that all the knuckles will be motion inhibited. If the thumb is placed too far to the left or the right, the fingers will lean accordingly and facility will be severely restricted. In either case, the flutist should be able to play c♯² securely without having the feeling that the flute will fall. With beginners it is also important not to allow the right index finger to touch the rods. Additionally, the keys of the flute should not be turned too far forward or backward; keys that are parallel to the floor produce the best overall balance (see Fig. 13.9).

Other hand position problems to watch for include allowing the right little finger to collapse, the left little finger to hang below the G♯ key, the fingers to be flat, and the fingers to extend over the keys.

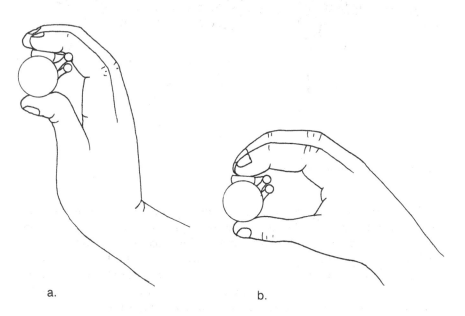

a.   b.

Figure 13.9. (a) Incorrect right hand and wrist positions; (b) correct right hand and wrist positions

As can be seen with a large number of professional performers, when the flute is positioned on the chin, the instrument is held at approximately fifteen to twenty degrees below horizontal. The head should tilt a corresponding amount to keep the embouchure plate parallel with the lips. In situations where the lips are higher at one corner or the other, the foot joint end of the flute should be raised or lowered to compensate. The head should be held up and poised as when looking forward, and it should be turned approximately thirty degrees toward the left shoulder. This affords the right and left arms more comfortable holding positions. The shoulders should be kept relaxed, lowered, and slightly back; this promotes good posture and proper breathing. The elbows should hang downward and slightly away from the body. The temptation to rest the elbows against the body, the arms on the back of a chair, or the end of the head joint on the left shoulder should be resisted. These false comforts effectively reduce air capacity and can contribute to tonal and physical problems.

Because flutists perform both in seated and standing positions, it is recommended that they practice both ways. In both cases, feet are at a forty-five-degree angle to the right. Sometimes visualizing the face of a clock can facilitate the learning of proper standing and seated positions. When standing or seated, assuming the music stand is at noon, both feet, placed comfortably apart, should point at a spot somewhere between the 1:00 and 2:00 designations (see Fig. 13.10). Additionally, flutists should make sure that any motion they make while playing doesn't affect their pitch by shifting the positions of the embouchure plate and the lips. Standing or sitting absolutely still is not recommended; being locked into place promotes tension and stiffness. Movement and musicality are inseparable, but care must be taken to move musically and subtly to the phrases, not to the individual beats or notes.

a.   b.

Figure 13.10. (a) Correct standing position; (b) correct seated position

Dynamics and Intonation

Dynamic contrasts, essential to musical expression, are relatively difficult to produce and control on the flute. Only when a flutist's embouchure, posture, and head joint placement have developed to a fairly advanced level will significant dynamic contrasts be possible. Nevertheless, tone studies should stress the use of dynamics from the earliest stages of achievement. Loud and soft sounds are created through varying the volume of air; louds use a greater volume of air than softs, and softs can be described as less air blown faster.

In practicing dynamic changes, it is beneficial to use an electronic tuning machine to insure correct intonation. The middle register is the best place to start. Notice that loud tones tend to be sharper than soft ones. Through movement of the lower jaw, the direction of the column of air and intonation can be effectively controlled. The jaw must be dropped for louder passages, with the airstream angled down. As the dynamic level diminishes, the jaw is raised and the air is angled higher. Additionally, the lips move forward as the dynamic level decreases and as the range goes up, and the lips return to a more natural position for lower and louder passages.

The head should neither raise nor lower during this process. Each note and dynamic level have a different lip formation and jaw position. Beginners should learn to exaggerate the differences, and as they advance, smaller, more economical (sometimes almost imperceptible) movements suffice. The student who can successfully control dynamics and intonation in the middle register can then apply these techniques to the more challenging lower and upper registers.

Initial tuning is accomplished by pulling out the head joint to flatten the pitch or pushing it in to sharpen it. In general, bands tune to b♭¹ while orchestras use a¹. Neither of these notes is especially stable, particularly with younger players. Often, flutists tune b♭¹ or b♭² with a full tone and are told that they are sharp; when they return to playing with the ensemble and are asked to play more quietly, however, they play flat. The notes d² or f² seem, at first, to provide the most reliable and stable guide to general intonation level.

Using the overtone series as a basis, most musicians agree that higher notes should be tuned to lower ones. Since the flute serves as the soprano voice of almost every ensemble in which it participates, it holds an unenviable responsibility of adjusting to the pitches provided by lower instruments. To be able to make satisfactory adjustments, the flutist must develop a sensitive ear as well as become intricately aware of the flute's intonation idiosyncrasies. Most flutes adhere to the intonation tendencies shown in Figure 13.11 when at a medium dynamic level without any compensation for pitch.

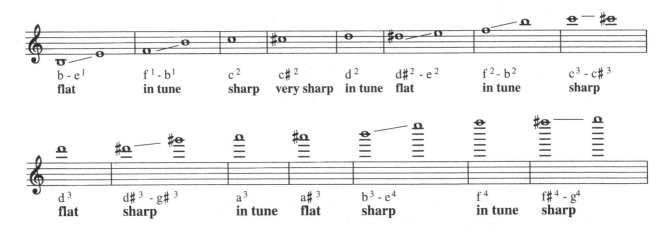

Figure 13.11. General intonation tendencies

Vibrato

Vibrato is an even fluctuation in the intensity of the air column. With proper control and good taste, it is ideally used to ornament, color, or add direction to the musical line. It should be introduced to the student when the tone in the first three registers is fairly stable. Beginning vibrato at an early stage of development also assists in further enhancing the tone. The teacher must be aware, however, that vibrato is the "icing on the cake," not the essence of the sound. It should never be allowed to compensate for or disguise faulty intonation, lack of support, or poor tone.

The first step in learning vibrato is to add pulses of intensity (usually four to six per second) to the otherwise steady airstream. Good breath support, a well-formed embouchure, and an open throat are essential. The precise muscular involvement necessary to produce vibrato has been and continues to be debated greatly. Some insist that only diaphragmatically initiated pulsations should be used, while others recommend the muscles of the throat. In truth, careful examination shows that both areas are used. The throat more easily produces narrower and faster pulses, while diaphragmatically produced vibrato is wider and slower. While the student should focus on the diaphragm area at first to avoid throat tension, the ultimate ability to control a variety of speeds and widths requires mastery of both types.

The following four-step method is one of many approaches to teaching vibrato. It is straightforward and incorporates speed and width control from the beginning. First, the student should play short, unarticulated notes on a single pitch. These should be quick and clear staccato puffs of air from the diaphragm (similar to the action of a dog panting). These should be performed at a quarter note = 60 MM in a very steady manner and with a strong tone (see Exer. 13.1). As control develops, the exercise should be repeated at faster metronome markings and eventually on several different pitches throughout the three octaves. If noises of any kind emanate from the throat, the student should stop and begin again slowly. Breaths should not be taken between puffs.

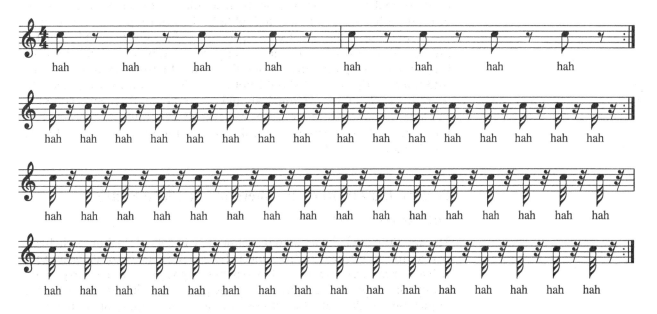

Exercise 13.1. Vibrato exercise no. 1

Second, continuing to work with a metronome, the student should begin to connect the puffs with tone in one continuous breath. The tone should now resemble a smooth wavy line. The puffs can be visualized as smooth, rounded peaks, and the connections are reminiscent of gently sloping valleys. The width of the peaks and valleys should be exaggerated, but the puffs should not become overly accented or spiky.

Third, the student should play a simple tune with a narrow range, at first applying vibrato slowly and evenly as exaggerated sixteenth-note pulsations (see Exer. 13.2). As the tempo increases, the vibrato will become smoother and somewhat narrower, but it should remain clearly audible. Although typical vibrato speeds vary from quarter note = 60 to 80 MM (sixteenth pulsations), the metronome can be set as low as 40 for the initial stages of development. Later, this exercise should be practiced both one and two octaves higher.

Exercise 13.2. Vibrato exercise no. 3, "My Country 'Tis of Thee"

Fourth, the above exercises should be applied to the student's current repertoire. At first, slow, lyrical pieces with minimal tonguing should be used. The vibrato, still clearly defined, should no longer pulsate with the beat but rather should be free to highlight the phrasing so that it complements the music, the result being purely musical, not mechanical. If the pulsations become fast and spiky, overly slow and wide, or tight-throated, fast, and narrow, the student should return to the previous exercises. Additionally, the student should not allow the vibrato to overpower the tone, especially in soft playing. It should be used with discretion and not be omnipresent; a straight tone can be remarkably beautiful and expressive. In the end, mastery of vibrato control relies on the musical sensitivity and imagination of each flutist.

Performing on Other Members of the Flute Family

THE ALTO FLUTE

The alto flute in G, the favored instrument of Theobald Boehm, is pitched a perfect fourth lower than the concert flute in C. Because of its beautifully rich lower range, composers often exploit its two lowest octaves. In general, nearly all of the same performance principles of the flute in C are applied in playing the alto flute; the alto requires a larger quantity of air, however, and it tends to respond somewhat more sluggishly, particularly in the lowest octave.

THE BASS FLUTE

The bass flute in C is pitched one octave lower than the concert flute. All of the above comments referring to the alto flute are also applicable to the bass instrument except that it requires even more air and is slower to respond than the alto flute. Some alto flutes are made with curved head joints for ease of reach; all bass flutes have this feature. Additionally, most bass flutes have embouchure holes with raised back and side walls, or wings, for ease of production.

THE PICCOLO

The piccolo sounds one octave higher than written. While some musicians specialize on the instrument, all flutists should become at least marginally comfortable playing the piccolo because it is a common double expected by many composers. Piccolo performance is essentially the same in principle as the concert flute; however, the placement of the embouchure is in proportion to the difference in the size of the hole. Because it lacks a foot joint, the piccolo's lowest note is a written d^1; this also prevents the production of notes above written c#^{4}.

Other differences from the flute include the following: most piccolos have a conical bore, and wooden piccolos have no embouchure plate. The piccolo is quicker in response, and the key action is lighter and faster. Articulation is more sensitive, as are intonation adjustments. Intonation tendencies are backward from those of the flute in that the piccolo's middle register tends to be sharp while the upper register tends to be flat. The piccolo requires a lower volume of air blown at a faster rate, greater embouchure endurance, and the use of a generally smaller aperture. It affords no place to hide because of its high tessitura; indeed, it can be heard above even the loudest of ensembles.

Piccolos are made of silver, hardened plastic, and wood. Wooden piccolos are best for concert music, while metal or plastic is better suited for marching and other outdoor performances. Cylindrical piccolos are rarer and thinner sounding but are easier to play in the upper octave. Conical piccolos produce a full sound, play better in tune, and are the preferred instrument. Professional models include those made by Haynes, Powell, Seaman, Brannen, and Burkhart; semipro models include the manufacturers Zentner and Hammig; and some student models are produced by Hardy, Yamaha, Gemeinhardt, Bundy, and Emerson.

The piccoloist follows much the same care and maintenance regimen that flutists do; however, wooden instruments require further specialized care. Wooden piccolos should be swabbed frequently, protected from drastic temperature changes, and warmed up slowly before blowing hot, moist air inside it. The inside and outside should also be oiled frequently with almond oil (especially if the piccolo is new or if the humidity level is generally dry), taking care to keep the oil from touching the pads. Care and preservation of the piccoloist's hearing often necessitates practicing with ear plugs.

CHAPTER 14

Additional Information

Selecting an Instrument

The flute has undergone relatively few changes since Theobald Boehm developed his 1847 model. Today students can confidently rely upon the product of any reputable manufacturer when selecting a student instrument. The acoustical design of the flute has been so carefully determined that basic intonation and consistency of sound are remarkably reliable.

In selecting an instrument, a trained professional flutist or flute teacher should be consulted. Several features that student model flutes should possess include a Cooper or new scale (for more accurate intonation), ease of response and tonal consistency throughout the registers and at varied dynamic levels, drawn tone holes, pads that seal well, ribbed construction (posts that are set in ribs, which are then soldered onto the tubing), light and uniform key action, and ease of assembly.

The open-hole or French model flute (five keys with open holes) is preferred by most professional flutists because of its advantages in tone production, intonation adjustment, fingering, and special effects. It also assists beginners in establishing correct hand position. Other options that can be found on many basic models include a solid silver head joint and tubing (for improved tone), a curved head joint (for small players with short arms, providing ease of production and improved access to correct hand position), gold springs (for reliability and longevity; lower-quality but still acceptable materials include phosphor, bronze, and stainless steel), an offset G key (which helps relieve strain on the left ring finger), a low-B foot extension (for better overall resonance and upper register production), and a gizmo (a small key placed on the low B to facilitate playing c^4).

Further options found on some professional flutes include soldered tone holes (for better resonance), a D♯ roller (for ease of transportation between c^1 or $c♯^1$ and $d♯^1$ and a C♯ trill key (used to facilitate certain trills and tremolos), a split E key (which helps with the production of e^3, although the tone is slightly altered), a modified embouchure hole and plate (undercutting, wing and butterfly designs, etc., for tonal color variety and to help with focus problems), a variety of tubing thicknesses (for color variety), and pointed key arms (purely decorative). Most student models are made of silver or nickel, with silver generally accepted as being superior. Most professional flutes are constructed of sterling silver, but in some cases materials such as gold, platinum, or wood are preferred.

Care must be taken when purchasing a used flute. On the negative side, some of these instruments may be in poor adjustment, and tone production can be adversely affected. Repair can be costly, and many of these instruments often have little resale value. When purchasing a used instrument, the following checklist should be helpful:

- The pads should not be torn, cracked, or grimy; they should be seated evenly with no gaps when closed.
- The springs should be strong enough to allow keys to move quickly.
- There should be no sluggish keys, no key clicks or other noises, and no side-to-side motion of keys; the key height from key to key should be even.
- The tone holes should be perfectly round, with no dents.
- The tenons and joints should be snug, neither too loose nor too tight.
- The head joint cork should not move easily (this, however, is a relatively inexpensive repair).
- The embouchure hole should have no nicks or scratches, and the embouchure plate should not be loose.
- Small dents on the body of the flute are not of consequence, although certain dents on the head joint may cause pitch and tone problems.

While most student flutes depreciate approximately 10 percent per year, many professional models appreciate in value; in fact, some instruments built in the 1950s and 1960s are now being purchased for ten times their original value. Therefore an older professional flute in need of some work is still a better value than a used student flute in good repair.

Professional makes include Haynes, Powell, Brannen, and Jack Moore. These instruments are entirely handmade and may have long waiting periods for purchase. Semiprofessional flutes include Prima Sankyo, Muramatsu, Miyazawa, Mateki, and Pearl. They can be obtained in a matter of weeks or months and are partly handmade. Dean, Emerson, Jupiter, Selmer, Yamaha, Gemeinhardt, Armstrong, Pearl, and Artley are some of the readily available student models.

Fingerings

The following chart illustrates basic fingerings for the Boehm system flute with a B foot joint and a closed G♯ key (flutes with only a C foot can negotiate almost all of them as well). In each instance, the most common fingerings are listed first; they should be learned first because they tend to produce the best tone at moderate dynamic levels. The flutist who is comfortable with these fingerings can then branch off into the seemingly endless variety of alternate fingerings used for tonal and pitch shadings as well as technical fluency. An excellent source for flute fingering possibilities is James Pellerite's *A Modern Guide to Fingerings for the Flute*. A chart for whole- and half-step trills follows the basic fingering chart.

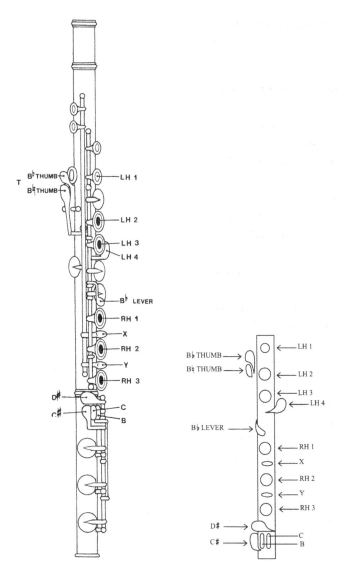

Figure 14.1. Key designations used in fingering charts.

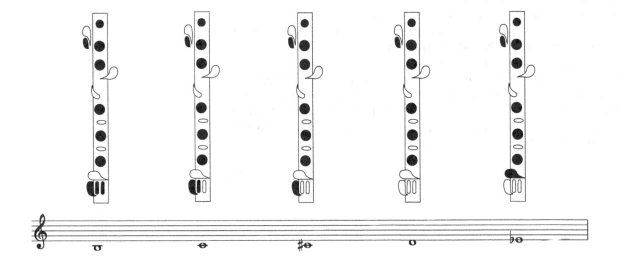

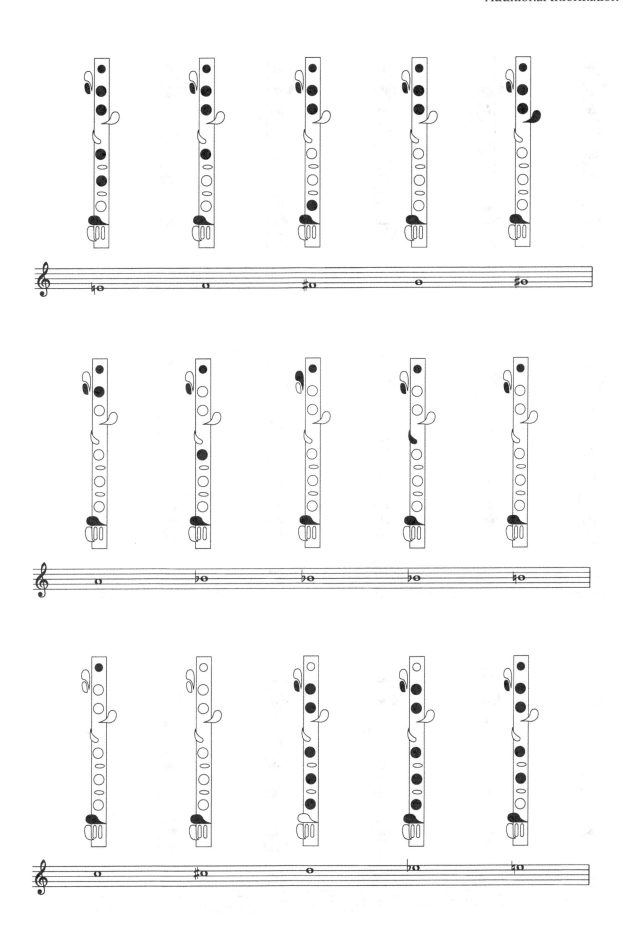

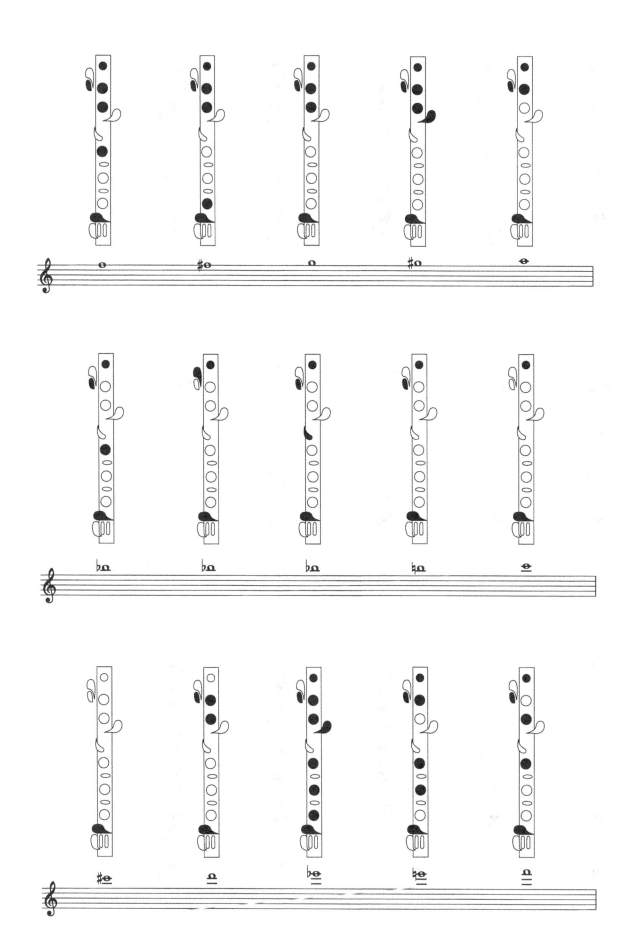

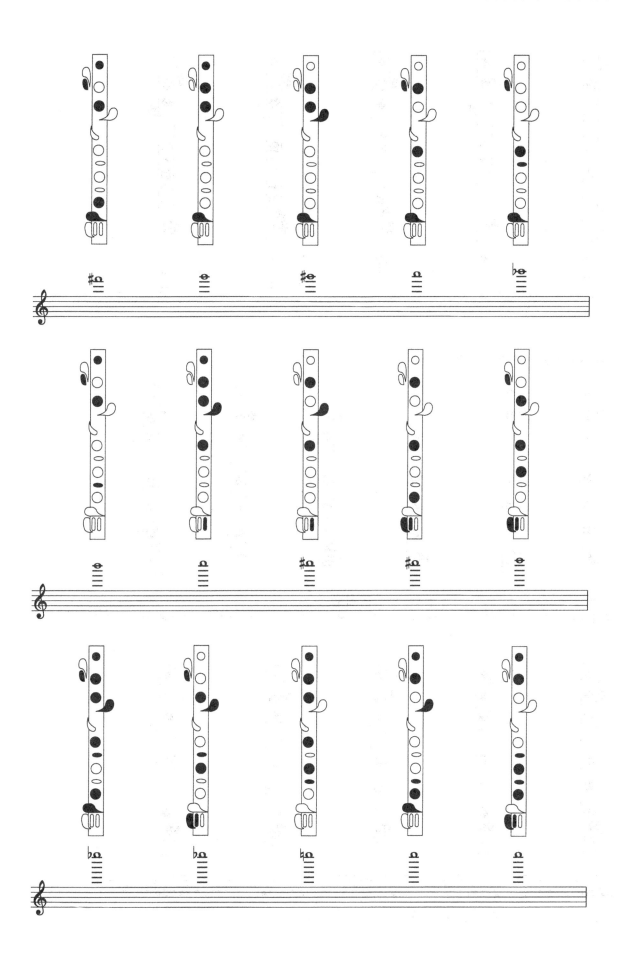

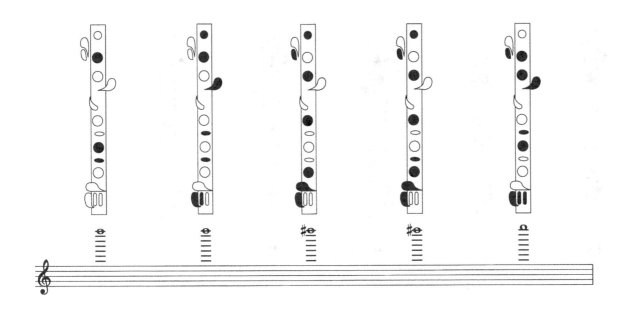

Move "arrowed" keys to execute trill

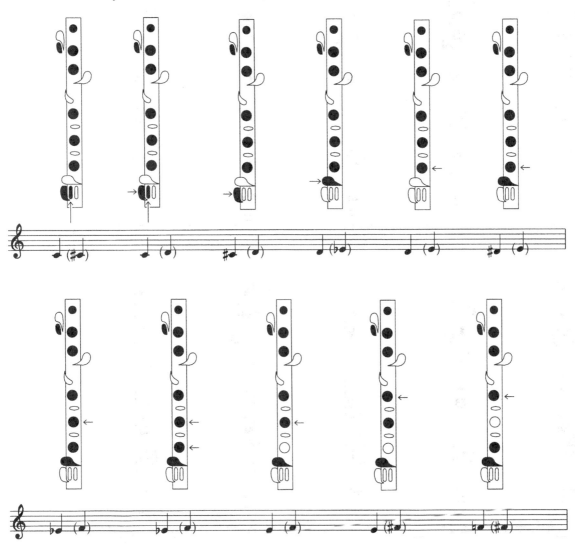

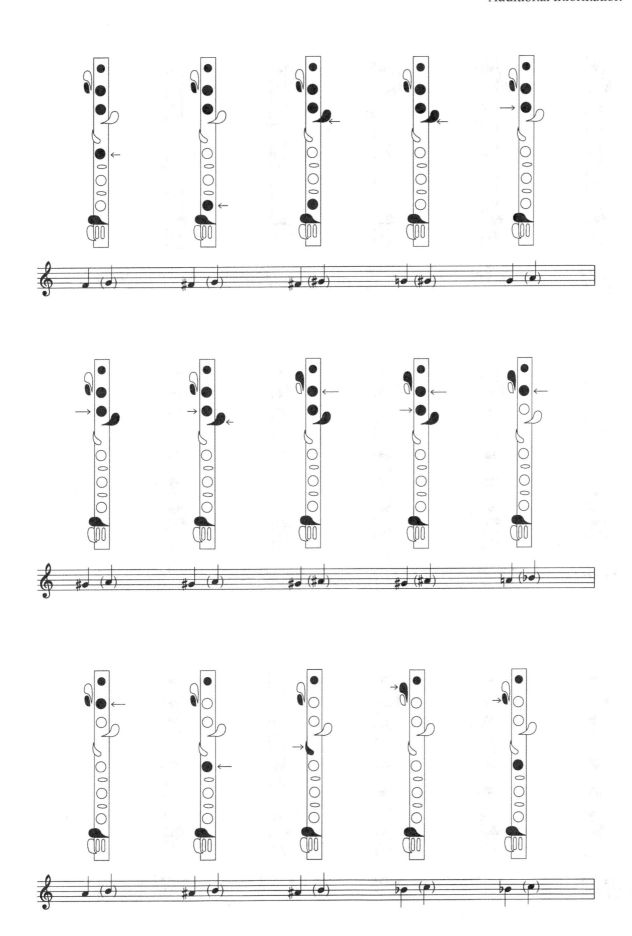

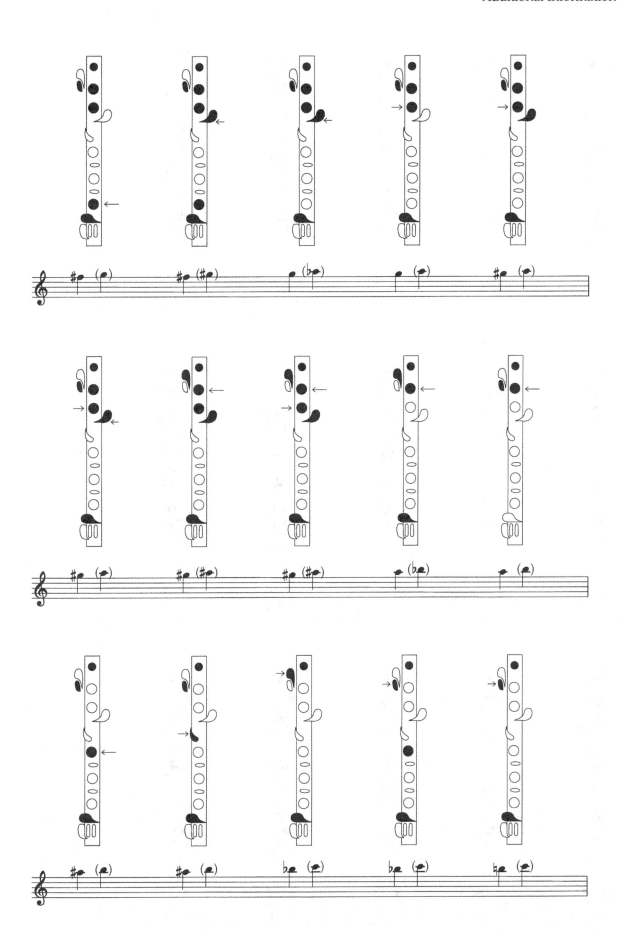

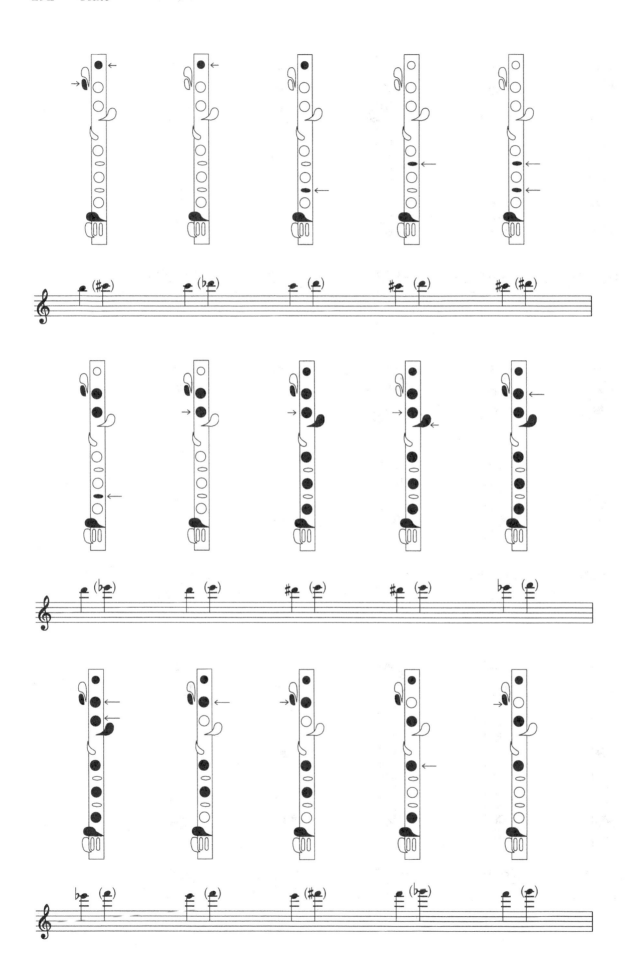

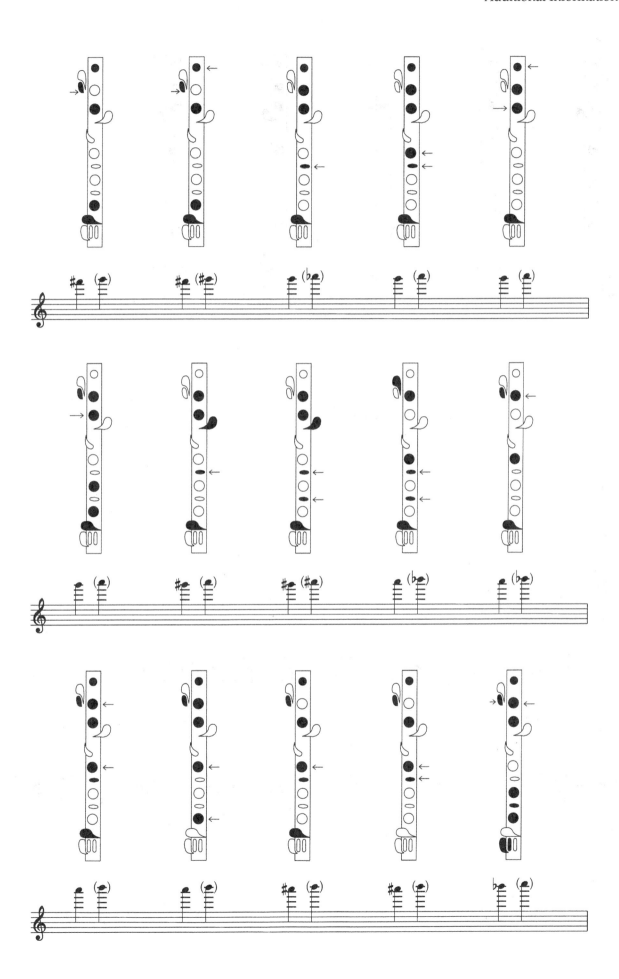

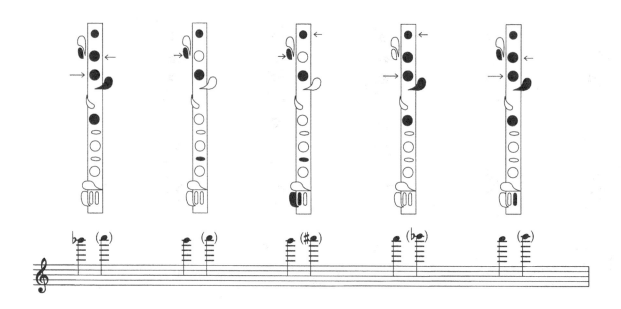

Exercises and Tunes

Exercise 14.1. Do not breathe between notes.

Exercise 14.2.

Comment: Do not tongue harder as you play faster.

Exercise 14.3.

Exercise 14.4.

Mary Had a Little Lamb

Exercise 14.5.

Exercise 14.6.

Exercise 14.7. Begin this five-note study slowly.

Duet

Exercise 14.8.

Exercise 14.9.

Exercise 14.10.

Hot Cross Buns

Exercise 14.11.

Exercise 14.12.

Lydian Waltz

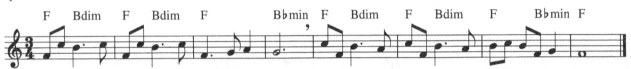

Duet

Aunt Rhodie

Comment: Tongue only the first note of each group.

Exercise 14.13.

Lightly Row

Sad Mary

Comment: Make legato connections between slurred groups.

Exercise 14.14.

Ludwig's Ninth   Beethoven

Exercise 14.15.

Exercise 14.16.

Exercise 14.17. Begin this five-note study slowly

Exercise 14.18.

Siciliano

Duet

Exercise 14.19.

Exercise 14..20.

(continued)

Exercise 14.21.

Exercise 14.21. (*continued*)

Exercise 14.22.

Siciliano (Revisited)

Exercise 14.23.

Exercise 14.24.

Exercise 14.25.

Duet

Exercise 14.26.

Exercise 14.27.

Exercise 14.28.

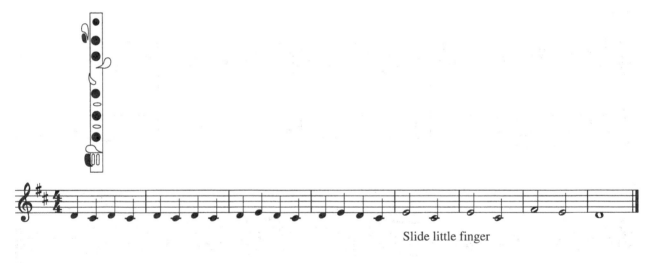

Slide little finger

Exercise 14.29.

Exercise 14.30.

Exercise 14.31.

Comment: c#^{2} is normally very sharp and unfocused.
Angle the air stream in a downward direction to compensate.

Exercise 14.32.

Exercise 14.33.

Mary (Revisited)

Comment: Maintain hand and wrist position when going over the break.

Exercise 14.34.

A-Tisket, A-Tasket

London Bridge

The Cuckoo Waltz

Exercise 14.35.

Exercise 14.36.

Simple Gifts

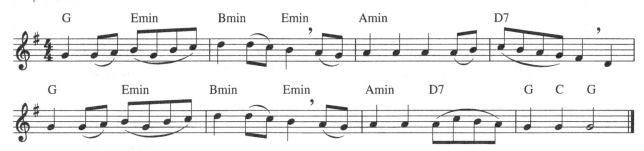

Exercise 14.37.

Exercise 14.38.

Exercise 14.39.

Exercise 14.40.

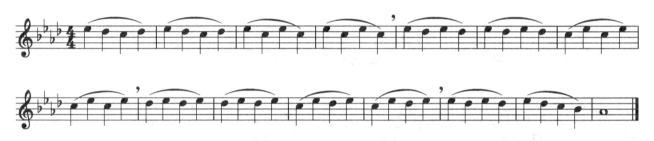

Exercise 14.41.

Twinkle Twinkle Little Star

Exercise 14.42.

Famous Melody

Duet

Jingle Bells

Exercise 14.43.

Exercise 14.44.

"Air"   Mozart

Exercise 14.45.

Exercise 14.46.

Duet

The Cuckoo Waltz (Revisited)

Exercise 14.47.

Exercise 14.48.

Duet

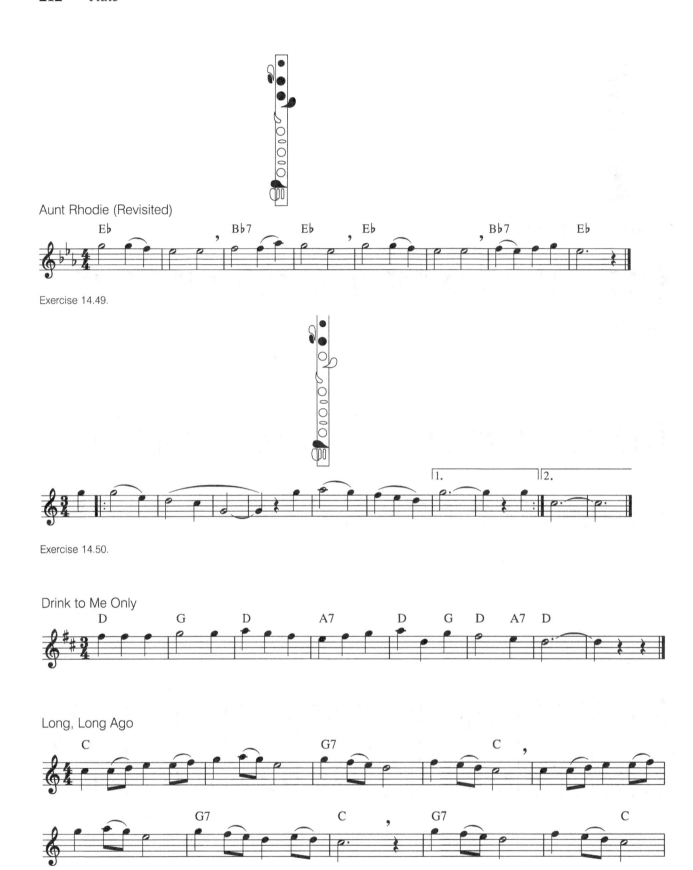

Aunt Rhodie (Revisited)

Exercise 14.49.

Exercise 14.50.

Drink to Me Only

Long, Long Ago

Duet

Exercise 14.51.

Exercise 14.52.

214   Flute

Duet

French Melody

Exercise 14.53.

Exercise 14.54.

Exercise 14.55.

Exercise 14.56.

Exercise 14.57.

Exercise 14.58.

Big Ben

Exercise 14.59.

Exercise 14.60.

Comment: To gain embouchure flexibility, play each lower-octave note
forte and each upper-octave note piano.

Exercise 14.61.

Gypsy Rondo

Exercise 14.62.

Exercise 14.63.

Andante from the "Surprise" Symphony

Exercise 14.64.

Allegretto semplice *(simply)*

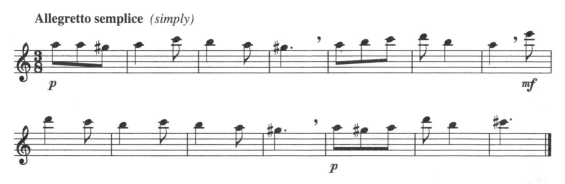

Exercise 14.65.

Exercise 14.66.

Moment Musical

Exercise 14.67.

Duet

(continued)

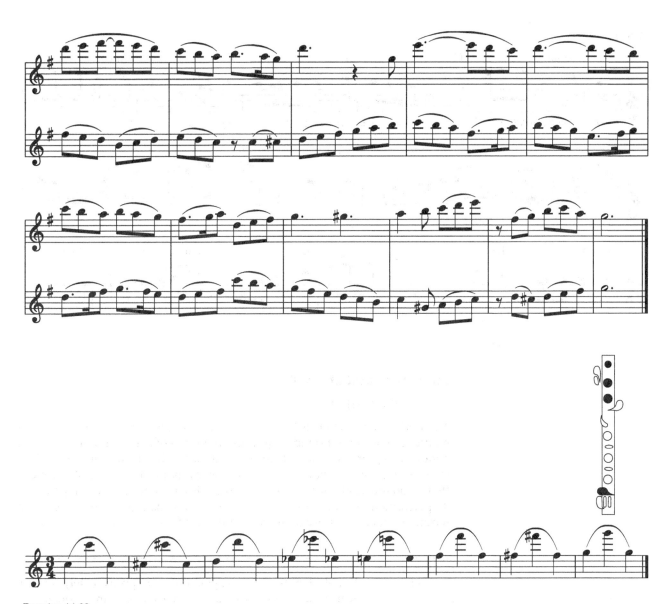

Exercise 14.68.

Minuet

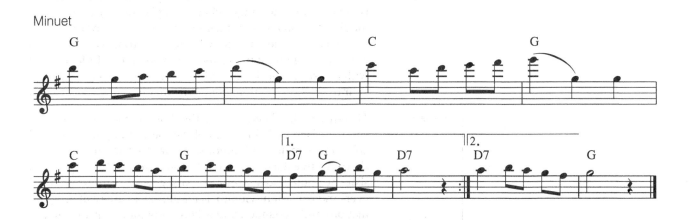

Greensleeves

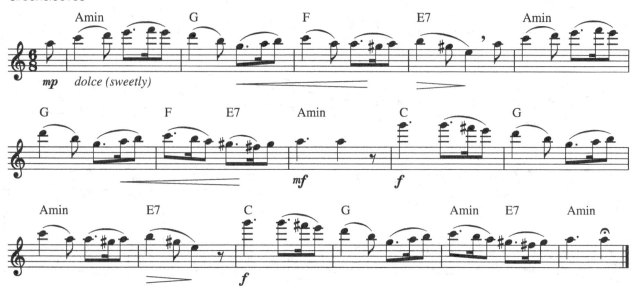

Literature and Methods

FLUTE PERFORMANCE LEVELS

The performance levels listed here are general guidelines. All level assignments are based on individual judgment. Levels of achievement vary from region to region as well as from individual teacher to teacher. Flexibility must be a prime consideration when using any graded materials. A piece that is too musically or technically challenging for one student may be easily performed by another student with the same experience, or the diverse requirements of an individual work may qualify it for a variety of levels.

Level 1	This student has been playing flute for approximately two years or less, can be classified as a beginner, can negotiate the range of b–c³ (or perhaps to e³ or f³), and can perform major scales with up to two sharps or three flats.
Level 2	This student has two to four years of playing experience, is typically in junior high school, can play up to g³, is comfortable with major scales with up to two sharps or four flats, has an elementary knowledge of rhythms and meters, is beginning to produce a vibrato, is comfortable with a variety of articulations and dynamics, and has had an introduction to intonation adjustments.
Level 3	This student has been playing the flute for about four to six years, is in early high school, can perform up to c⁴, is able to play major and minor scales with up to three sharps or five flats, is comfortable with moderate-tempo sixteenth-note and syncopated passagework, produces an even and consistent vibrato, is mastering a variety of articulations and dynamics, and is becoming more sensitive to intonation adjustments.

Level 4   This flutist has approximately six to eight years of experience, is a junior or senior in high school, can negotiate the
range to d⁴, competently performs all major and minor
scales, has an excellent grasp of advanced rhythms, possesses a basic knowledge of phrasing, is adept at changing
vibrato speed and amplitude, has a growing sensitivity to
balance requirements and varieties of attacks and releases,
and makes good attempts at intonation adjustments.

Level 5   This student has played for eight to ten years, is often in
the early years of college study, can perform the entire
range of the flute, is comfortable and familiar with technical exercises from Taffanel and Gaubert and Moyse, continues to perfect the above skills plus the self-application
of phrasing, continues to refine intonation adjustments,
and explores a variety of tone colors.

Level 6   This student has performed for ten to twelve years, is
often in the late undergraduate years, has the ability to
negotiate much of the flute repertoire, continues to refine
the above skills, possesses deeper phrasing knowledge
and sensitivity, adjusts intonation immediately and automatically, is developing further performance subtleties,
and is at ease with a variety of extended techniques.

Level 7   This student has been playing the flute for twelve or more
years, is typically in graduate school or is a professional,
performs to a high level of artistry, and is comfortable
with the gamut of the literature.

SELECTED SOLO LITERATURE
LEVEL 1

Sheet Music

Buchtel	At the Ball	Kjos
Buchtel	Celebrated Gavotte	Kjos
Buchtel	Jovial Mood	Kjos
Buchtel	Princess Helene	Kjos
Christensen	Holiday on Ice	Kendor
Guenther	Echo Song	Belwin
Guenther	La petite danse	Belwin
Guenther	March for Flutists	Belwin
Guenther	Reflections	Belwin
Guenther	Reverie	Belwin
Guenther	Spanish Folk Song	Belwin
Guenther	Yankee Dandy	Belwin
Kuhlau	Menuett	Fischer
Lancen	Ariette	Chappell
Lewallen	Notturno	Belwin

Lewallen	Poème petite	Belwin
Martini	Celebrated Gavotte	Kjos
Snell	Ballade of the Yellow Sun	Belwin
Snell	The Finial Crow	Belwin
Snell	The Peddler	Belwin
Snell	Rondo	Belwin
Snell	Three Chinese Folk Songs	Belwin

Collections

	Solo Pieces for the Beginning Flutist	Mel Bay
Moyse, L.	First Solos for the Flute Player	G. Schirmer
Moyse, L.	Forty Little Pieces in Progressive Order	G. Schirmer

LEVEL 2

Sheet Music

Bizet	Entr'acte	Editions Musicus
Bizet	Menuet	Fischer
Boisdeffre	Air de ballet	ALRY
Bournonville	Danse pour Katia	Southern
Cagnard	La flute enchantée	Lemiore
Chopin	Nocturne in E♭	Belwin
Finger	Sonata in C	Zen-On
Finger	Sonatas: d, G, and F	Boosey & Hawkes
Gluck	Minuet & Dance of the Blessed Spirits	Southern
Gossec	Gavotte	Fischer
Haydn	Serenade	Hal Leonard
Honegger	Romance	International
Laube	Alsatian Dance	Cundy-Bettoney
Lewallen	Country Dance	Belwin
Lewallen	Fantasie	Belwin
Lewallen	Romantique	Belwin
Lewallen	Valse romantique	Belwin
Pepusch	Sonata in F Major	Noetzel
Purcell	Sonata in F Major	Oxford
Rolig	A Little Shepherd Music	Concordia
Rorem	Mountain Song	Peer
Schubert	Ave Maria	Cundy-Bettoney
Tailleferre	Pastorale	Elkan-Vogel
Telemann	Sonata in F Major	Little Piper

Collections

Arnold	Easy Flute Solos No. 83	Hyperion
Cavally	Solos for the Debutant Flutist	Southern
Moyse, L.	Solos for the Flute Player	G. Schirmer
Moyse, L.	The Young Flutist's Recital Book	G. Schirmer
Vester	Fifteen Easy Baroque Pieces	Universal Editions
Wye	Flute Solos, 3 vols.	Chester Music

LEVEL 3

Sheet Music

Anderson	Scherzino	Southern
Barber	Canzone	G. Schirmer
Beethoven	Serenade Op. 41	Peters
Berkley	Sonatina	Schott
Boccherini	Concerto in D Major	International
Bozza	Aria	Leduc
Brun	Romance	Rubank
Caplet	Reverie and petite valse	Southern
Chopin	Variations on a Theme by Rossini	International
Clementi	Trois sonates	Heuwekemeijer
Cooke	Sonatina	Oxford
Debussy	Syrinx	Jobert
Diabelli	Sonatina in C Major	Schott
Donizetti	Sonata	Peters
Fauré	Morceau de concours	Bourne
Fauré	Pavane, Op. 50	Hamelle
Fauré	Sicilienne, Op. 78	Hamelle
Flotow	Martha	ALRY
Gaubert	Madrigal	Little Piper
Glass	Serenade for Flute Alone	Elkan-Vogel
Gluck	Concerto in G Major	Amadeus
Grétry	Concerto in C Major	International
Handel	Sonatas	Bärenreiter
Haydn	Adagio e Presto	Leduc
Hindemith	Echo	Schott
Marcello	Sonatas, Op. 2	Bärenreiter
Massenet	Meditiation from *Thais*	Cundy-Bettoney
Morlacchi	The Swiss Shepherd	Fischer

Mozart	Andante in C	International
Popp	La chasse	ALRY
Purcell	Sonata in G Minor	Editions Musicus
Quantz	Arioso and Presto	Southern
Ravel	Pièce en forme de habanera	Leduc
Rogers	Soliloquy	Fischer
Sammartini	Sonata in G Major	Noetzel
Telemann	Four Sonatas	Schirmer
Vanhal	Sonata	McGinnis & Marx
Vinci	Sonata in D Major	Ernst Reinhardt

Collections

Cavally	24 Short Concert Pieces	Southern
Moyse, L.	Album of Sonatinas for the Young	G. Schirmer
Moyse, L.	Flute Music of the Baroque	G. Schirmer
Peck	Solos for Flute	Fischer
Voxman	Concert and Contest Collection	Rubank

LEVEL 4

Sheet Music

Albinoni	Two Sonatas, Op. 4 & 6	Kunzelmen
Arrieu	Sonatine	Amphion
Bach, C. P. E.	Hamburger Sonate	Schirmer
Bach, C. P. E.	Six Sonatas	Zimmermann
Bach, C. P. E.	Sonata in A Minor for Flute Alone	Universal
Bach, J. S.	Sonata in A Minor for Flute Alone	Bärenreiter
Bach, J. S.	Sonata No. 2 in E♭	Bärenreiter
Bach, J. S.	Suite in B Minor	Hinrichsen
Bartók	Suite paysanne hongroise	Associated
Ben-Haim	Three Songs without Words	Leeds
Bennett	Summer Music	Novello
Bloch	Suite modale	Broude
Briccialdi	Carnival of Venice	Fischer
Dello Joio	Suite	Belwin
Doppler	Fantaisie pastorale hongroise	Fischer
Chaminade	Concertino	G. Schirmer
Enesco	Cantabile e Presto	Boosey & Hawkes
Fauré	Fantasie	International
George	Concerto	Accura
Grovlez	Romance et scherzo	Masters Music
Haydn	Concerto in D Major	International
Haydn	Sonatas	G. Schirmer

Heiden	Sonatina	Associated Music
Hindemith	Eight Pieces for Flute Alone	G. Schirmer
Hindemith	Sonata	Schott
Honegger	Danse de la chèvre	Senart
Hotteterre	Suite in D Major	Ricordi
Hotteterre	Suite in E Minor	Bärenreiter
Hue	Fantasie	Billaudot
Ibert	Pièce	Leduc
Jacob	The Pied Piper for Flute Alone	Oxford
Kennan	Night Soliloquy	Fischer
Lefèbvre	Two Pieces Op. 72	Zimmermann
Loeillet	Twelve Sonatas	Amadeus
Molique	Concerto in D Minor Op. 69	Southern
Mouquet	La flute de Pan	Southern
Mozart	Concerto in D Major	Novello
Mozart	Concerto in G Major	Novello
Perilhou	Ballade	Schirmer
Quantz	Concerto in G Major	Southern
Reinecke	Ballade	Zimmermann
Rutter	Suite Antique	Oxford
Saint-Saëns	Airs de ballet	Southern
Stamitz	Concerto in G Major	International
Telemann	12 Fantasies for Flute Alone	Bärenreiter
Varèse	Density 21.5	Ricordi

Collections

Arnold	Selected Flute Solos, Vol. 101	Hyperion
Moyse, L.	Flute Music by French Composers	G. Schirmer
Moyse, M.	The Golden Age of the Flutists, 2 vols.	Zen-On

LEVEL 5

Sheet Music

Arnold	Concerto	Paterson
Beethoven	Sonata in B♭ Major	Breitkopf & Härtel
Blavet	Concerto in A Minor	International
Boehm	Nel cor più	Edu-tainment
Bozza	Image	Leduc
Burton	Sonatina	Fischer
Busser	Prelude and Scherzo	Leduc
Dahl	Variations on a Swedish Folktune for Flute Alone	Presser

Damase	Sonata	Lemoine
Ganne	Andante and Scherzo	Fischer
Godeli	Concerto	Progress Press
Karg Elert	Sonata Appassionata for Flute Alone	Southern
La Montaine	Sonata for Flute Alone	Broude
Martinu	First Sonata	Associated
Mason	Thoughts	Warner
Mercandante	Concerto in E Minor	Zerboni
Muczynski	Three Preludes	G. Schirmer
Paganini	Caprice No. 23 in E♭ Major	Presser
Poulenc	Sonata	Chester
Reinecke	Sonata "Undine"	International
Taktakishvili	Sonata	A.M.P.
Tulou	Grand Solo No. 3	Editions Musicales
Tulou	Grand Solo No. 5	Editions Musicales
Tulou	Grand Solo No. 13	Editions Musicales
Widor	Suite Op. 34	Heugel

LEVEL 6

Sheet Music

Boehm	Grand Polonaise	International
Bozza	Agrestide	Leduc
Casella	Sicilienne et burlesque	Leduc
Copland	Duo	Boosey & Hawkes
Demersseman	Sixième solo de concert Op. 82	Leduc
Dohnanyi	Passacaglia	Broude
Dutilleux	Sonatine	Leduc
Feld	Sonata	Supraphon
Franck	Sonata	International
Griffes	Poem	Schirmer
Gryc	Five Preludes for Flute Alone	Leduc
Ibert	Concerto	Leduc
Liebermann	Sonata	Presser
Martin	Ballade	Universal
Messiaen	Le merle noir	Leduc
Muczynski	Three Preludes Op. 18	Schirmer
Piston	Sonata	Associated
Prokofiev	Sonata	International
Reinecke	Concerto	Breitkopf & Härtel
Rivier	Concerto	Billaudot
Sancan	Sonatine	Durand

| Schubert | Introduction, Theme, and Variations | International |
| Tomasi | Sonatine | Leduc |

LEVEL 7

Sheet Music

Boulez	Sonatine	Amphion
Berio	Sequenza	Universal, Zerboni
Castiglioni	Gymel	Zerboni
Corigliano	Pied Piper Fantasy	G. Schirmer
Dick	Flying Lessons	Multiple Breath
Foss	Renaissance Concerto	Pembroke
Jolivet	Chant de Linos	Leduc
Liebermann	Concerto	Presser
Nielsen	Concerto	Peters
Ran	East Wind	Presser
Reynolds	Sonata	Fischer
Rodrigo	Concierto pastoral	Schott
Sollberger	Riding the Wind	American Composers Alliance
Trombly	Kinetics III for Flute and Tape	McGinnis & Marx
Zwilich	Concerto	Merion

SELECTED DUETS

LEVELS 1 & 2

Sheet Music

Blavet	15 Duets for Two Flutes	Billaudot
Devienne	Six Duos, Op. 75, 2 books	Rubank
Gariboldi	Six Little Duets Op. 145	Leduc

Collections

Arnold	Very First Flute Duets	Hansen
Moyse, L.	40 Short Duets for Beginner Flutists	G. Schirmer
Voxman	Selected Duets, Vol. 1	Rubank

LEVEL 3

Sheet Music

| Beethoven | Allegro and Minuet | International |
| Bennett | Conversations for Two Flutes | United |

Berbiguier	Six Easy Duets, Op. 59	Editions Musicus
Blavet	Premiere recueil de pièces	Zurfluh
Boismortier	Sechs Sonaten Op. 1	Bärenreiter
Boismortier	Sechs Sonaten Op. 6	Bärenreiter
Devienne	24 Progressive Duets	Southern
Locatelli	Zwei Duette Op. 4, No. 5	Schott
Naudot	Six Sonatas for Two Flutes	Simrock
Quantz	Six Duets for Flutes Op. 5	Heinrichshofen
Soussmann	Duets Op. 53	Edu-tainment
Telemann	Six Canonic Sonatas, Op. 5	Bärenreiter
Telemann	Six Sonatas for Two Flutes, 2 vols.	Bärenreiter

Collections

Guenther	Masterworks for Two Flutes	Belwin
Moyse, L.	Album of Flute Duets	G. Schirmer
Moyse, M.	Album of 30 Classical Duets, 2 vols.	International
Voxman	Selected Duets, Vol. 2	Rubank

LEVEL 4

Sheet Music

Bach, W. F.	Sonata in D Major	Zimmermann
Berbiguier	Trois grands duos Op. 38	Heuwekemeijer
Briccialdi	Sixteen Flute Duets Op.132	International
Doppler	Andante and Rondo Op. 25	International
Drouet	Deux airs variés	Broekmans
Drouet	Six grand duos brillants et faciles Op. 74	Heuwekemeijer
Kuhlau	Duets, Opp. 10, 13, 39, 81, 87, 103, & 119	Billaudot
Kummer	Three Duets Op. 132	Belwin
Locatelli	Sonata in E Minor	Zimmermann
Muczynski	Duos for Flutes Op. 34	G. Schirmer

Collection

Moyse, L.	Album of Flute Duets	G. Schirmer

LEVEL 5

Sheet Music

Doppler	Duettino americain	Billaudot
Doppler	Hungarian Fantasy Op. 35	Musica Rara
Doppler	Rigoletto Fantasie	Billaudot
Doppler	Souvenir de Prague	Musica Rara

Doppler	Valse di bravura Op. 33	Southern
Hindemith	Canonic Sonatina Op. 31	Schott
Kuhlau	Duets Opp. 10, 13, 39, 81, 87, 103, & 119	Billaudot
Petrassi	Dialogo angelico	Zerboni
Tremblot de la Croix	Dix inventions pour deux flutes	Leduc

LEVEL 6

Sheet Music

Feld	Duo Concertante	Leduc
Migot	Six Little Preludes, Vols. 1 & 2	Leduc
Sollberger	Two Pieces for Two Flutes	McGinnis & Marx

SELECTED TRIOS
LEVELS 1 & 2

Sheet Music

Genzmer	Trio	Schott
Reinecke	At Twilight	Belwin

Collections

Voxman	Chamber Music for Three Flutes	Rubank
Voxman	First Book of Flute Trios	Southern

LEVEL 3

Sheet Music

Boismortier	Six Sonatas Op. 7, 2 vols.	Schott
Devienne	Trio in D Major	Eulenberg
Feld	Petite divertissement	Leduc
Haydn	Three Trios	International
Hook	Trios Op. 83	Rubank
Quantz	Sonata in D Major	Nagels
Zempleni	Trio for Flutes	Musica Budapest

LEVEL 4

Sheet Music

Beethoven	Grand Trio for Three Flutes	Southern
Casterede	Flutes en vacances	Leduc
Devienne	Six Trios Op. 19	Heuwekemeijer
Devienne	Trio in D Major	Eulenberg
Kuhlau	Trois grandes trios, Op. 86	Kalmus

Kummer	Trio in G Major Op. 24	Fischer
Kummer	Trio in C Major Op. 53	Fischer
Kummer	Trio in D Major Op. 58	Fischer
Kummer	Trio in A Major Op. 59	Fischer
Mercandante	Three Serenades	Belwin
Reicha	Trio Op. 26	McGinnis & Marx
Tomasi	Trois pastorales	Leduc

LEVEL 5

Sheet Music

Albisi	Miniature Suite No. 2	Fischer
Kuhlau	Grand Trio, Op. 90	Billaudot
Kuhlau	Trois trios, Op. 13	Billaudot

LEVEL 6

Sheet Music

Albisi	Miniature Suite No. 1	Fischer

SELECTED QUARTETS
LEVELS 1 & 2

Sheet Music

Corelli	Sarabande and Gavotte	Rubank

Collection

Arnold	Everybody's Favorites	Hyperion

LEVEL 3

Sheet Music

Boismortier	Sonata Op. 34, No. 3	Leduc
Dittersdorf	Notturno	Schott

Collection

Voxman	Quartet Repertoire	Rubank

LEVEL 4

Sheet Music

Bozza	Trois pièces	Leduc
Casterede	Flutes en vacances	Leduc

Dubois	Quatour	Leduc
Jongen	Flute Quartet	Southern
Kuhlau	Grand Quartet in E Minor Op. 103	Billaudot
Moyse, L.	Seven Easy and Short Trios	Presser
Wouters	Adagio and Scherzo Op. 77	Rubank

LEVEL 5

Sheet Music

Bennett	Rondo Capriccioso	Chappell
Bozza	Jour d'éte à la montagne	Leduc
Desportes	Suite italienne	Southern
Jeanjean	Ski-symphonie	Billaudot
Koehler	Grand Quartet Op. 92	Fischer
Kuhlau	Grand Quartet in E Minor Op. 103	Billaudot
Reicha	Quartet Op. 12	Fischer

LEVEL 6

Sheet Music

Dahl	Serenade	Boosey & Hawkes
Damase	Quatour de flutes	Billaudot
Schmitt	Quatour de flutes Op. 106	Durand
Sollberger	Grand Quartet	McGinnis & Marx

SELECTED WORKS FOR FIVE OR MORE FLUTES

LEVELS 1 & 2

Sheet Music

| Purcell | Chaconne | Zalo |

LEVEL 3

Sheet Music

Abt	Night	Little Piper
Boismortier	Concertos for Five Flutes	VEB Hoffmeister
Boyce	Symphony No. 1	ALRY
Fauré	Pavane	ALRY
Walters	Scenes from the West	Rubank

Sheet Music

| Boismortier | Concertos for Five Flutes | VEB Hoffmeister |
| Grimm | Five Etudes for Twelve Flutists | Southern |

Hirose	Blue Train	Ongak Tomono
Luening	Sonority Canon	Galaxy
Zaninelli	Aria	Zalo
Zaninelli	Prelude	Zalo

LEVEL 5

Sheet Music

DeLorenzo	Sinfonietta divertimento flautistico, Op. 75	Peters
Effinger	Cloud Forms	ALRY
Gates	Sails, Winds, and Echos	Southern
Missal	Rondo Caprice	Southern
Zaninelli	Three Children's Dances	Zalo

LEVEL 6

Sheet Music

Brant	Angels and Devils, Concerto for 11 Flutes	MCA
Brotons	Flute Suite Op. 41	ALRY

SELECTED TECHNICAL EXERCISES AND ETUDES

LEVEL 1

Hurfurth	A Tune a Day, 2 books	Fischer
Weber & Steensland	Flute Student, 2 books	Belwin
Weber & Steensland	Studies & Melodious Etudes, 2 books	Belwin
Weber & Steensland	Tunes for Technique, 2 books	Belwin
Gariboldi	30 Easy and Progressive Studies, Book 1	Kalmus

LEVEL 2

Cavally	Melodious & Progressive Studies, Book 1	Southern
Voxman	Advanced Method, 2 books	Rubank
Victor Salvo	243 Double and Triple Tonguing Exercises	Pro Art
Weber & Steensland	Flute Student, Book 3	Belwin
Weber & Steensland	Studies & Melodious Etudes, Book 3	Belwin
Weber & Steensland	Tunes for Technique, Book 3	Belwin

LEVEL 3

Anderson	18 Studies Op. 41	G. Schirmer
Maquarre	Daily Exercises for the Flute	G. Schirmer

| Moyse, M. | De la sonorité | Leduc |
| Taffanel & Gaubert | Complete Method | Leduc |

LEVEL 4

Anderson	24 Progressive Studies Op. 33	Southern
Boehm	24 Caprices Op. 26	International
Gates	Odd Meter Exercises	Sam Fox
Moyse, M.	Daily Exercises	Leduc
Moyse, M.	Tone Development through Interpretation	Leduc

LEVEL 5

Anderson	24 Etudes Op. 15	G. Schirmer
Casterede	Douze études	Leduc
Karg Elert	30 Caprices Op. 107	International
Falk	Quinze études atonales	Leduc
Gilbert	Technical Flexibility	Southern

LEVEL 6

| Bitsch | Douze études | Leduc |
| Jeanjean | 16 Modern Studies | Southern |

SELECTED METHODS

Altes	Celèbre methode complete, 2 vols.	Leduc
Barone	Learning the Piccolo	Edu-tainment
Brooke	Method for Flute, 2 vols.	Fischer
Eck	Method for Flute, Book 1	Belwin
Gariboldi	Complete Method Op. 128, 2 vols.	Leduc
Kincaid & Polin	The Advanced Flutist, 2 vols.	Elkan-Vogel
Kincaid & Polin	The Art and Practice of Modern Flute Technique	MCA
Kujala	The Flutist's Progress	Progress
Putnik	The Art of Flute Playing	Summy-Birchard
Soussman	Complete Method for Flute, 3 vols.	Fischer
Taffanel & Gaubert	Methode complète, 2 vols.	Leduc
Toff	The Flute Book	Scribner's

Flute Resources

HISTORY AND DEVELOPMENT

BAINES, ANTHONY. *Woodwind Instruments and Their History.* New York: Norton, 1962.

BATE, PHILIP. *The Flute.* New York: Norton, 1969.

BOEHM, THEOBALD. *An Essay on the Construction of Flutes.* Ed. W. S. Broadwood. 1882. Reprint. Saint Clair Shores, MI: Scholarly Press, 1976.

———. *The Flute and Flute-Playing* (1872). Trans. and rev. Dayton C. Miller. 2d ed. 1992. Reprint. New York: Dover, 1964.

BROWN, HOWARD MAYER. "Flute." In *The New Grove Dictionary of Music and Musicians,* ed. Stanley Sadie, 6:664–81. London: Macmillan, 1980.

BURNAU, JOHANN. "The Life of Theobald Boehm." *The Instrumentalist* 21 (May 1967): 57–58; 22 (August 1967): 52–54.

CARSE, ADAM. *The History of Orchestration.* New York: Dutton, 1925.

COOPER, ALBERT. *The Flute.* London: Albert Cooper, 1980.

DORGEUILLE, CLAUDE. *The French Flute School, 1860–1950.* Trans. Edward Blakeman. London: Bingham, 1986.

ESTEVAN, PILAR. *Talking with Flutists.* 2 vols. New York: Edu-Tainment, 1976, 1978.

FAIRLEY, ANDREW. *Flutes, Flautists, and Makers.* London: Pan Educational Music, 1982.

FITZGIBBON, H. MACAULEY. *The Story of the Flute.* 2d ed. New York: Scribner's, 1928.

GILLIAM, LAURA E., AND WILLIAM LICHTENWANGER. *The Dayton C. Miller Flute Collection: A Checklist of the Instruments.* Washington, DC: Library of Congress, 1961.

JONES, WILLIAM J. "The Alto Flute." *The Instrumentalist* 33 (December 1978): 56–58; 33 (January 1979): 38–41.

MARCUSE, SIBYL. *Survey of Musical Instruments.* New York: Harper and Row, 1975.

MERRIMAN, LYLE. *Woodwind Research Guide.* Evanston, IL: The Instrumentalist, 1978.

MEYLAN, RAYMOND. *La flute: Les grandes lignes de son developemment de la prehistoire à nos jours.* Lausanne: Payot, 1974.

ROCKSTRO, RICHARD SHEPARD. *A Treatise on the Construction, the History, and the Practice of the Flute.* 2d ed. 1928. Reprint. London: Musica Rara, 1967.

SACHS, CURT. *The History of Musical Instruments.* New York: Norton, 1940.

SCHECK, GUSTAV. *Die Flöte und ihre Musik.* Mainz: Schott, 1975.

SCHMID, MANFRED HERMANN. *Theobald Boehm, 1794–1881: Die Revolution der Flöte.* Tutzing: Schneider, 1981.

SMITH, CATHERINE P. "Changing Use of the Flute and Its Changing Construction." *The American Recorder* (May 1979): 4–8.

TOFF, NANCY. *The Development of the Modern Flute.* New York: Taplinger, 1979.

———. *The Flute Book: A Complete Guide for Students and Performers.* New York: Scribner's, 1985.

———. "Recent Developments in Flute Design." *The Instrumentalist* 33 (June 1979): 34–37.

WELCH, CHRISTOPHER. *History of the Boehm Flute.* 3d ed. 1886. Reprint. Wakefield, NH: Longwood, 1977.

ACOUSTICS, DESIGN, AND REPAIR

BENADE, ARTHUR. "Analysis of the Flute Head Joint." *Journal of the Acoustical Society of America* 37 (1965): 679–91.

———. "The Physics of Wood Winds." *Scientific American* (October 1960): 145–54.

BOEHM, THEOBALD. *An Essay on the Construction of Flutes.* Ed. W. S. Broadwood. 1882. Reprint. Saint Clair Shores, MI: Scholarly Press, 1976.

COLTMAN, JOHN. "The Acoustics of the Flute." *Physics Today* (November 1978): 25–32.

FAJARDO, RAOUL. "Flute Resonance and Projection." *The Instrumentalist* 30 (March 1976): 62.

FARRELL, SUSAN CAUST. *Directory of Contemporary American Musical Instrument Makers.* Columbia: University of Missouri Press, 1981.

FLETCHER, NEVILLE. "Acoustical Correlates of Flute Performance Technique." *Journal of the Acoustical Society of America* 57 (1975): 233–37.

———. "Some Acoustical Principles of Flute Technique." *The Instrumentalist* 28 (February 1974): 57–61.

Langwill, Lyndesay G. *An Index of Musical Wind-Instrument Makers.* 6th ed. Edinburgh: Lyndesay Langwill, 1980.

MATHER, ROGER. "Care and Repair of the Flute." *The Instrumentalist* 27 (December 1972): 40–43; 27 (January 1973): 41–45; 27 (March 1973): 66–68; 27 (April 1973): 54–57.

MEYER, R. F. *The Band Director's Guide to Instrument Repair.* Ed. Willard I. Musser. Port Washington, NY: Alfred, 1973.

PHELAN, JAMES, AND MITCHELL D. BRODY. *The Complete Guide to the Flute: From Acoustics and Construction to Repair and Maintenance.* Boston: Conservatory, 1980.

TOFF, NANCY. "Recent Developments in Flute Design." *The Instrumentalist* 33 (June 1979): 34–37.

PEDAGOGY

BROOKE, ARTHUR. *Harmonic Fingerings for the Flute.* Boston: Cundy-Bettoney, 1925.

BRUDERHANS, ZDENEK. "Circular Breathing and the Flute." *The Instrumentalist* 36 (August 1981): 34.

CHAPMAN, FREDERICK B. *Flute Technique.* 4th ed. New York: Oxford University Press, 1973.

DELANEY, CHARLES. *Teacher's Guide to the Flute.* Elkhart, IN: Selmer, 1969.

GARTNER, JOCHEN. *The Vibrato.* Trans. Einar W. Anderson. Regensburg: Bosse, 1981.

KRELL, JOHN. *Kincaidiana: A Flute Player's Notebook.* Culver City, CA: Trio, 1973.

LEROY, RENÉ. *Traité de la Flute.* Paris: Editions Musicales Transatlantiques, 1966.

MATHER, ROGER. *The Art of Playing the Flute.* 2 vols. Iowa City, IA: Romney, 1980, 1981.

MONTGOMERY, WILLIAM. "Flute Tone Production." *The Instrumentalist* 33 (September 1978): 46; 33 (October 1978): 42.

MOYSE, MARCEL. *How I Stayed in Shape.* Trans. Paul M. Douglas. West Brattleboro, VT: Marcel Moyse, 1974.

PELLERITE, JAMES J. *A Modern Guide to Fingerings for the Flute.* 2d ed. Bloomington, IN: Zalo, 1972.

RAINEY, THOMAS E. *The Flute Manual: A Comprehensive Text and Resource Book for Both the Teacher and the Student.* New York: University Press of America, 1985.

STEVENS, ROGER S. *Artistic Flute Technique and Study.* Ed. Ruth N. Zwissler. Culver City, CA: Trio, 1970.

TOFF, NANCY. *The Flute Book: A Complete Guide for Students and Performers.* New York: Scribner's, 1985.

WARNER, THOMAS. *Annotated Bibliography of Woodwind Instruction Books.* Detroit: Information Coordinators, 1975.

WEISBERG, ARTHUR. *The Art of Wind Playing.* New York: Schirmer Books, 1975.

Woodwind Anthology: A Compendium of Woodwind Articles from "The Instrumentalist." 2 vols. Evanston IL: The Instrumentalist, 1992.

REPERTOIRE CATALOGS

Flute World Catalog. 11th ed. Franklin, MI: Flute World, 1996.

GOODMAN, HAROLD A. *Instrumental Guide.* Provo, UT: Brigham Young University Press, 1977.

HELLER, GEORGE N. *Ensemble Music for Wind and Percussion Instruments: A Catalog.* Washington, DC: Music Educators National Conference, 1970.

HELM, SANFORD M. *Catalog of Chamber Music for Wind Instruments.* Rev. ed., 1952. Reprint. New York: Da Capo, 1969.

HOUSER, ROY. *Catalogue of Chamber Music for Woodwind Instruments.* New York: Da Capo, 1973.

Musik für Flöte. Hamburg: Musikbucherei, 1974.

National Flute Association Catalog. 6th ed. Tucson: University of Arizona Press, 1992.

PELLERITE, JAMES J. *A Handbook of Literature for the Flute.* 3d ed. Bloomington, IN: Zalo, 1978.

PETERS, HARRY B., comp. *The Literature of the Woodwind Quintet.* Metuchen, NJ: Scarecrow, 1971.

PIERREUSE, BERNARD. *Flute Literature.* Paris: Jobert, 1982.

RASMUSSEN, MARY, AND DONALD MATTRAN. *A Teacher's Guide to the Literature of Woodwind Instruments.* Durham, NH: Brass and Woodwind Quarterly, 1966.

Selected Music Lists: Instrumental Solos and Ensembles. Washington, DC: Music Educators National Conference, 1979.

SOLUM, JOHN. *The Early Flute.* Oxford University Press, 1992.

SWANSON, PHILIP J. "Avante-Garde Flute Music: A Partial Bibliography." *Woodwind World* (December 1972): 19; (June 1973): 6–8.

VESTER, FRANS. *Flute Repertoire Catalogue.* London: Musica Rara, 1967.

VOXMAN, HIMIE, AND LYLE MERRIMAN. *Woodwind Ensemble Music Guide.* Evanston, IL: The Instrumentalist, 1974.

———. *Woodwind Solo and Study Material Guide.* Evanston, IL: The Instrumentalist, 1975.

WILKINS, WAYNE, comp. *The Index of Flute Music: Including the Index of Baroque Trio Sonatas.* Magnolia, AR: Music Register, 1974.

WESTPHAL, FREDERICK W. *Guide to Teaching Woodwinds.* 5th ed. Dubuque, IA: Brown, 1990.

PERFORMANCE PRACTICE

AMBROSE, JANE. "Authenticity in Performance: Where Do We Stand?" *The American Recorder* (August 1980): 67–70.

———. "Baroque Flute Performance Practice Bibliography." *Woodwind World, Brass and Percussion* 14, no. 4 (1975): 23–25.

BARTOLOZZI, BRUNO. *New Sounds for Woodwind.* Trans. and ed. Reginald Smith Brindle. New York: Oxford University Press, 1967.

CASTELLANI, MARCELLO. "The Italian Sonata for Transverse Flute and Basso Continuo." *Galpin Society Journal* 19 (May 1976): 2–10.

DICK, ROBERT. *The Other Flute: A Performance Manual of Contemporary Techniques.* New York: Oxford University Press, 1975.

DONINGTON, ROBERT. *Baroque Music: Style and Performance.* New York: Norton, 1982.

———. *The Interpretation of Early Music.* New ed. New York: St. Martin's, 1974.

———. *A Performer's Guide to Baroque Music.* New York: Scribner's, 1973.

DORIAN, FREDERICK. *The History of Music in Performance.* New York: Norton, 1942.

FLEURY, LOUIS. "The Flute and Flutists in the French Art of the Seventeenth and Eighteenth Centuries." *Musical Quarterly* 9 (1923): 515.

HOTTETERRE LE ROMAIN, JACQUES. *Principles of the Flute Recorder and Oboe.* Trans. and ed. David Lasocki. New York: Praeger, 1968.

HOWELL, THOMAS. *The Avant-Garde Flute: A Handbook for Composers and Flutists.* Berkeley and Los Angeles: University of California Press, 1974.

LASOCKI, DAVID. "Baroque Flute and Its Role Today." *Recorder and Music* (February 1967): 99.

———. "New Light on Handel's Woodwind Sonatas." *The American Recorder,* (February 1981): 163–70.

———. "Vivaldi and the Recorder." *The American Recorder* (March 1969): 22–27.

LASOCKI, DAVID, AND BETTY BANG MATHER. *The Classical Woodwind Cadenza: A Workbook.* New York: McGinnis & Marx, 1978.

MATHER, BETTY BANG. *Free Ornamentation in Woodwind Music.* New York: McGinnis & Marx, 1976.

———. *Interpretation of French Music from 1675 to 1775 for Woodwind and Other Performers.* New York: McGinnis & Marx, 1973.

———. "Making Up Your Own Baroque Ornamentation." *The American Recorder* (August 1981): 55–59.

NICOLET, AURÈLE, ed. *Pro Musica Nova: Studies for Playing Avant-garde Music for Flute.* New York: MCA, 1974.

QUANTZ, JOHANN JOACHIM. *On Playing the Flute.* 1752. Trans. Edward R. Reilly. London: Faber, 1966.

RANGEL-RIBEIRO, VICTOR. *Baroque Music: A Practical Guide for the Performer.* New York: Schirmer Books, 1981.

READ, GARDNER. *Contemporary Instrumental Techniques.* New York: Schirmer Books, 1976.

REILLY, EDWARD R. "Further Musical Examples for Quantz's Versuch." *Journal of the American Musicological Society* 17 (1964): 157.

SCHMITZ, HANS-PETER. *Querflöte und Querflötenspiel in Deutschland wahrend des Barockzeitalters.* Kassel: Bärenreiter, 1952.

SEYFRIT, MICHAEL. *Musical Instruments in the Dayton C. Miller Flute Collection at the Library of Congress: A Catalog.* Vol. 1: *Recorders, Fifes, and Simple System Transverse Flutes of One Key.* Washington, DC: Library of Congress, 1982.

SMITH, CARLETON SPRAGUE. "Haydn's Chamber Music and the Flute." *Musical Quarterly* 19 (1933): 341–50, 434–55.

SOLUM, JOHN. *The Early Flute.* Oxford University Press, 1992.

STOKES, SHERIDON W., AND RICHARD CONDON. *Special Effects for Flute.* Culver City, CA: Trio, 1970.

VEILHAN, JEAN-CLAUDE. *The Rules of Musical Interpretation in the Baroque Era.* Trans. John Lambert. Paris: Leduc, 1982.

Vinquist, Mary, and Neal Zaslaw. *Performance Practice: A Bibliography*. New York: Norton, 1971.

Ward, Martha Kingdon. "Mozart and the Flute." *Music and Letters* 35, no. 4 (October 1954): 294–308.

Warner, Thomas. "Tromlitz's Flute Treatise: A Neglected Source of Eighteenth-Century Performance Practice." In *A Musical Offering: Essays in Honor of Martin Bernstein*, 261–71. New York: Pendragon, 1977.

PART 4

Oboe

MARK WEIGER

CHAPTER 15

Introduction

History

The history of the oboe dates back to antiquity. One of the earliest versions of the oboe is the Middle Eastern zurna. Still played today, the zurna is made from one piece of wood with six to seven finger holes. It has a conical bore with a flared bell and uses a double reed made from rush, corn stalk, straw, pala grass, or palm leaf. The performer's lips do not come in contact with the reed. Instead, the reed is placed in a pirouette: a metal disk with a hole in the middle against which the performer places the lips.[1] In this way, the entire reed is enclosed much like that of the modern bagpipe.

Although the shawm developed from the zurna, the use of the two instruments overlapped. The shawm, while similar in construction to the zurna, used a cane reed placed closer to the top of the pirouette. This made it possible for the performer to contact the reed with the lips. As such, the shawm proved easier to control, especially in the upper range.[2] After its heyday in the Renaissance, the shawm continued to be popular even after the development of the oboe.

The oboe, or in French, *hautbois,* was probably developed in the court of Louis XIV by Jean Hotteterre I and Michel Philidor around 1657.[3] Unlike the shawm or zurna, the oboe designed by Hotteterre and Philidor had three sections united by tenon-and-socket joints with the reed clear of the body of the instrument and without a pirouette. The conical bore was narrowed and the bell was less flared.

The oboe of the Baroque period had two to three keys and was made so that either hand could be placed on the top joint of the instrument. This contributed to its immense popularity, which, in turn, brought about the publication of numerous tutors. Eventually the placement of the left hand over the right hand became standardized (ca. 1750) and the duplicate D♯ key was removed. Around 1780 two additional keys were added: the F and B♮ keys.

The oboe underwent its greatest transformations in the early 1800s. Though still an open-holed oboe, an octave key was added to allow for easier access to the ever-expanding upper range. Keys with rod extensions were added (serving as extensions of the fingers) for the low b♭, c^1, and $c♯^1$. A closed F key was also added. Metal pillar mounts were developed for the keys as well as shallow metal cups to hold the pads. The plate, as it was called, was developed for the half hole. This made for an oboe with fifteen tone holes, of which ten were controlled by keys, an octave key, and a half-hole plate.[4] These innovations are attributed to the oboist Henri Brod (1799–1839).

In 1810 the oboist Guillaume Triébert and his two sons opened a business building oboes. It is likely that Brod worked with the Triébert family. In 1840 a second octave key was added along with a leaf-spring system, which closed the c^1 and b♭ secondary keys with the first finger on the right hand.[5] The oboe with this new type of key system was called the "Conservatoire Système Six."

François Lorée took over the Triébert family oboe business in 1881. With the help of George Gillet, the Conservatory Model oboe, the oboe that is used today, was born. In 1906 the use of finger plates instead of open rings was employed.[6] More recent developments include the addition of the left-hand F key, a forked-F resonance key, and a third octave key. Much experimentation has occurred over the years as to the type of material best suited for projection, longevity, crack prevention, and tone quality. Although today's oboes are generally made of grenadilla wood, many other woods are also in use. In addition, much progress has been made in the use of resonant plastics.

Much like the string family (violin, viola, cello, bass) and SATB (soprano, alto, tenor, bass) choir, the oboe family has four primary members: the oboe, oboe d'amore, English horn, and baritone oboe. The baritone oboe is somewhat of a rarity, as very little music has been written for it. The bassoon primarily plays the role of bass instrument for the double reed family, in great part because of its range.

The oboe d'amore serves as the alto voice of the family. It stands a little taller than the oboe and is pitched in A, a minor third lower than the oboe. Unlike the oboe, whose reed is placed into a reed well and whose bell is conical, this instrument uses a bocal onto which the reed is placed and has a bulbed bell. The oboe d'amore was a popular instrument with composers such as J. S. Bach and G. P. Telemann. It served as both a solo and obbligato instrument suitable because of its particular range, mellow tone quality, and gentle dynamics to accompany the human voice. It was often used for weddings, pastoral scenes, and cantatas. As the oboe established its place in the orchestra and as a solo instrument, the oboe d'amore lost its place in the music world. It returned to prominence in the twentieth century with the revival of the performance of Baroque music, the call for original instruments, the writings of such composers as Ravel, Strauss, and Mahler, and the rekindling of the double reed consort.

The English horn serves as the tenor voice of the family. Pitched in F, a perfect fifth below the oboe, it stands taller than the oboe d'amore and taller still to the oboe. Like the oboe d'amore, it requires a bocal onto which the reed is placed and has a bulbed bell. It is neither English nor a horn; its name may well have been derived from a confusion between the French terms *cor anglé* (angled horn) and *cor anglais* (English horn). It may also be that the modern English horn descends from the Baroque oboe da caccia, or "oboe of the chase or hunting oboe," a curved instrument that could be readily attached to a saddle. This may explain the angled element of the instrument. While there seems to be no full explanation for its name, the modern English horn, as we know it today, is recorded as receiving its debut around 1839 when Henri Brod developed a straight instrument that used a curved bocal.[7] Other sources attribute this development to Giuseppe Ferlendis (1755–1802) in the eighteenth century.

To this day, the bulbed bell, or *Liebesfuss* (love foot), of both the oboe d'amore and the English horn has remained solely owing to tradition. This manner of bell, unlike the conical bell of the oboe, serves no purpose other than as an ornament. Both the oboe d'amore and English horn use the same fingering system as the oboe and are made with a conical bore.

Assembly

The four parts of the oboe are the reed, the top joint, the middle joint, and the bell. Before taking the instrument out of the case, take note of how it fits inside.

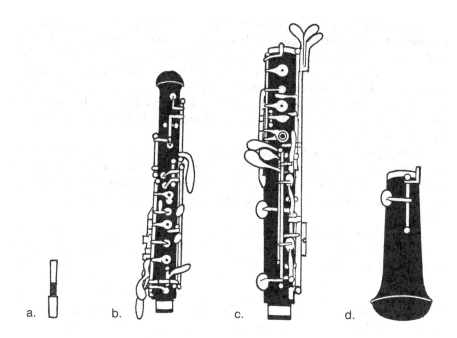

Figure 15.1. The parts of the oboe: (a) reed (b) top joint (c) middle joint (d) bell

To assemble the oboe, start by grasping the bell with one hand and the middle joint with the other hand. When holding the middle joint, your palm should be under the thumb rest so that your fingers curl over the rods and your fingertips are where the keys lie. Using a slight twisting motion, attach the bell to the middle joint so the bridge key at the top of the bell aligns with the bridge key at the bottom of the middle joint. To avoid bending this bridge connection, raise the bridge key on the bell by closing the b♭ key found on the bell with the thumb.

Next, grasp the top joint so your palm rests on the wood and your fingertips rest where the keys lie. Gently twist the top joint onto the bottom joint. The bridge keys on either side of the top joint should neatly align with the bridge keys at the top sides of the middle joint. If the oboe is assembled improperly, these bridge connections will catch and bend.

To place the reed, grasp it at the cork with the thumb and forefinger and, with a twisting motion, insert the reed into the reed well at the top of the oboe. Be sure that the reed is in as far as it will go for proper pitch. The blades of the cane should be aligned with the keywork as you look down the oboe from reed to keys. When turning the reed to establish alignment, turn from the cork and not from the cane.

Care and Maintenance

CARE OF THE REED

As reeds are somewhat delicate, it will be necessary to establish a "care and feeding" process early on. Reeds should be placed in some manner of plastic tubing or reed case to protect them from travel damage and to provide safe haven when not in use. If the plastic tube does not have an air hole of some sort, it is advisable to make one. Many oboists punch a hole in the cap. This allows the reed to dry out, prevents mold buildup, and adds to the reed's longevity.

Some reeds may come with wire or clear wrapping. These additions do not mean that the reed is good or bad. They merely serve to strengthen or seal the reed. Should the reed have a leak, however, an application of plumber's Teflon tape around the throat of the reed (just above the string) will be in order. To determine whether the reed has a leak, close the tube off with a finger and blow into the reed. A leaky reed, when dry, will produce a hiss as air escapes. When wet, it will produce bubbles or water spray from the point of exit.

Before playing, reeds should be soaked for three to five minutes in water at room temperature. The water should cover the cane portion of the reed. Soaking the reed in water rather than in the mouth is important, as saliva contains enzymes that break down the structure of the cane more rapidly.

Age and poor handling are the most common reasons for the demise of reeds. The following simple behavioral modifications will help to correct poor handling habits: brush the teeth prior to playing; avoid lipstick or lip balm, as they tend to clog the vascular bundles; and last but not least, when bringing the reed to the mouth, try to avoid making contact with the teeth. To do the latter, guide the reed to the mouth with the left hand (the right hand should be occupied holding the oboe under the thumb rest).

Often new reeds do not fit into the oboe's reed well. While some may have corks that are too narrow, most new reeds will have corks that are too thick. The narrow corks merely need to be expanded by heating them with a match. Thick corks will need to be filed or sanded down. Natural cork will last longer than compressed cork, but both will deteriorate faster with the use of cork grease. Also, as the oboe gets older, the reed well gets wider from wear.

CARE OF THE INSTRUMENT

The oboe is considered by many to be a delicate instrument, which is one reason why band directors avoid starting elementary students on it. Apart from needing periodic adjustment, however, the oboe is not the temperamental instrument that it is often accused of being.

CLEANING THE INSIDE After playing, the oboe (whether plastic or wood) will collect condensation, which can ruin pads and block vents. For this reason, the instrument should be cleaned after each use. This can be done by using a swab or feather. Although feathers do not absorb the moisture, as swabs do, they do swish it around so as not to create tracking, buildup, or deposits. Whereas a cotton swab requires the oboe to be disassembled, a pull-through silk swab can be used while the instrument is still assembled. The silk swab is useful to the conscientious player; however, if it becomes tangled or knotted, it can get stuck in the top joint of the oboe. Both swab types can be washed. Beware of bristled cleaners, "pig-stickers," and stick-swabs, as they tend to be too abrasive and often scratch both plastic and wooden bores.

Many repair technicians disagree about the usefulness of bore oil for wooden instruments. Some suggest that wooden oboes do well with regular bore oil applications as a preventive measure against cracks. Others suggest that this measure is pure bunk. And still others suggest that coating the bore with bore oil creates a coat of oils that prevents the bore from absorbing moisture.

To prevent water from gathering in vents or tracking toward tone holes, wooden instruments can be oiled or waxed. Bore oil can be a useful tool in trying to prevent tracking of condensation. If bore oil is not available, try a wax-based furniture polish. Apply the wax polish or bore oil to one side of a swab or feather and guide the treated side along the tone hole side of the bore. The wax or oil will act as a moisture repellent and should temporarily prevent the moisture from tracking into the tone holes. Another good deterrent is to position the oboe with the keys facing up, especially when setting the instrument down.

If moisture gathers in a tone hole, a gurgling effect will occur. The tone hole in question will be the first open tone hole when playing the note or notes that gurgle. For example, if gurgling occurs when c^2 is played, the tone hole with moisture will be the first open tone hole: the c^2 secondary key, which lies between the principal a^1 and b^1 keys. Or, if there is water when playing b^2, the first open tone hole will be the principal a^1 key.

CLEANING THE OUTSIDE   Many oboes have silver-plated keywork. To preserve the silver plating, the keys should be cleaned occasionally with a soft lint-free cloth. Do not use silver polish, as it will get into the key mechanism and render the instrument useless. Many repair technicians recommend against using polishing cloths, as they tend to leave lint deposits in the key mechanisms. It is, however, a good idea to brush under and around the keywork with a paintbrush. If a player's skin is particularly acidic, clear nail polish can be carefully applied to the key surfaces to protect the keys from deterioration.

The tenons and bridge key connections tend to be the most problematic areas for the novice. The bridge connections are often jammed together when the instrument is put together or taken apart. The bridges then tend to be bent or stripped of their corking, thus making adjustment, tuning, and noise control difficult. If the joints fit too tightly, students usually thickly lather the tenon corks with cork grease. Although this gesture does help for the short term, cork grease tends to cake with each new application, thus compounding the problem in the long run. Should the tenon corks be swollen, it is best to clean the corks and tenon cavities with alcohol. If this is ineffective, a non-petroleum-based lotion can be applied. (The petroleum in cork grease eats away the glue that keeps the cork on the tenon.) If the corks are too loose for the tenon cavity they can be made to swell by gently heating them with a match.

CARE OF WOODEN OBOES

Wooden instruments need to be kept in a somewhat controlled environment to avoid frequent adjustments and cracking. The oboe should not be left in a car, by a heater or air conditioner, or in any other setting that allows for drastic moisture or temperature change. If the environment is dry, the wood may crack. Using a humidifier, a Damp-it, orange peels, or some other measure to provide moisture will help to deter cracking. Applying bore oil may also help. If the weather is humid, the wood will swell and the key mechanism may rust as the wood sweats. Oiling the mechanism may be necessary.

If a wooden oboe is cold, it is important to warm it up before playing it. Do not blow warm air into the instrument. The outside of the instrument needs to be warmed before tending to the inside. Otherwise, the inside will expand before the outside expands and cracking will occur. Warming the outside of the instrument can be done by placing the joints under the arms or under a jacket. If you have a heating pad available, roll the joints in the pad and warm slowly.

Both wooden and plastic oboes respond to extreme changes in temperature and humidity. The most common reaction to these changes is the binding of keys. When the wood or plastic expands or contracts, it puts pressure on the posts. This, in turn, puts pressure on the rods. The result is limited or total loss of key movement. The only remedy is swedging—filing the rods so they fit less tightly between the posts—a process recommended for a repair technician only. It is wise to "adopt an oboist" in the community to guide you to good repair technicians.

Hand Position

In playing the oboe, the oboist's right thumb should be under the thumb rest found on the middle joint. This thumb stabilizes the oboe and bears the brunt of its weight. The fingers of the right hand should be over each of the three main keys on the bottom joint, and the right little finger should be over the three long keys: the C, D, and E♭ keys.

The left thumb should be placed beneath the octave key found on the back of the top joint. The fingers of the left hand should be over each of the three main keys on the top joint, with the pinkie over the long keys on the left side: the A♭ and E♭ keys.

COMMON HAND POSITION FAULTS AND REMEDIES

A few common faults in hand position deserve attention. Placement of the thumbs is often a point of concern. The right thumb should rest under the thumb rest so that the hand is as relaxed as possible. While some players find the placement of the right thumb to be between the nail and the knuckle, others find it more comfortable at the first knuckle, while still others prefer it by the thumbnail. The real issue is finding the position that allows for the least degree of tension and the greatest degree of facility. The natural curve of the fingers over the keys coupled with straight wrists will

Figure 15.2. Proper left hand and finger placement

Figure 15.3. Proper right hand and finger placement

help determine the correct thumb placement. Meanwhile, the left thumb should rest on the body of the instrument just below the thumb (first) octave key. Many players allow their left thumb quite a bit of traveling on and off the oboe.

The fingers should be curved and poised over the primary keys as if ready to play a low c¹. It then should be easier to travel from any note to any other note. The left ring finger and pinkie tend to be quite flat and rigid and sometimes locked at the knuckles. This will inhibit normal facility and prohibit the proper use of left E♭ and left F keys.

Figure 15.4. Proper hand and finger positions. Wrists are straight with arms at the sides. Fingers are curved and relaxed.

In an effort to relieve the right thumb of the weight of the oboe, many young players place their pinkies behind the oboe or side keys. This places their fingers so far away from the keywork that technical passages become impossible. To remedy this, try practicing in the dark. In this way, the focus becomes one of feeling the keys and springs to establish the position of each key and the distance from one to another. Students should be assigned works they can play from memory or exercises that require the use of the pinkie keys. Practice with a mirror is also useful. It may also be helpful to experiment with an adjustable thumb rest.

Figure 15.5. Proper thumb position

Posture

Whether the oboist is sitting or standing, the angle of the instrument from the body remains the same, somewhere between thirty and forty-five degrees. The wrists should be straight, allowing the upper arms to rest comfortably at the sides and establishing the distance and position the elbows will take from the body. Once the proper angle is established with the extra weight of the oboe out in front of the body, it becomes necessary to determine a new center of gravity for the body.

In the sitting position, plant the feet flat on the floor and sit squarely on the edge of the chair with the back straight. The oboe should be carried to the lips at the proper angle so the upper arms are at your sides and the head is up with the eyes forward. The bell of the instrument should be straight ahead and not resting on or toward one knee.

The standing position differs only in the distribution of body weight and point of balance. To find your point of balance experiment with the placement of the feet, the distance between them, and the direction in which each foot faces. Many students find that standing makes them dizzy. To remedy this, avoid locking the knees and pay closer attention to the breathing process.

COMMON POSTURE FAULTS AND REMEDIES

Often right-handers pull the oboe off center to the right. This puts the reed, embouchure, and direction of the air on a diagonal, which can hinder the quality of tone and pitch in the extreme ranges. To remedy this, be sure that the torso is not twisted to accommodate this posture. Turn the music stand so it is more centered or moved in the opposite direction from the player's directional tendency.

Resting the bell on one knee creates a poor body posture (slouched, head bent forward) and inhibits proper breath support. One remedy is to move the music stand higher to keep the head up. However, the usual reason the oboe ends up on the knee is to take the weight of the oboe off the right thumb. It may be necessary to try a neck strap. While the resting of the bell is not altogether common, slouching or extending the head forward is extremely common. Awareness is perhaps the best cure.

Slouching curves the spine, collapses the chest cavity, curves the shoulders, and puts the center of gravity too far forward. This, in turn, creates tension and locked muscles, which impede the breathing process and tone production. To remedy this, raise the stand, employ a neck strap, and focus on breathing exercises.

The angle at which the oboe is held can prove to be of great issue. The oboe is often held at too high or low an angle in the formative years, especially by transfers from the clarinet or flute. Too low an angle creates an exaggerated air column angle, a more closed or collapsed chest cavity, and curved back. This makes for smaller breaths and a somewhat choked playing style, with the lowest range being most affected. Too low an angle will also cause incorrect hand and wrist positions, which will impair technique. While too high a plane will create a more direct air column and a more open chest cavity, it will hinder three specific areas of play: the tone may be brash or wild, the third octave will be more difficult to manage, and large downward slurred leaps will be nearly impossible without exaggerated gestures. Many who use too high an angle place the reed against the top lip, which often allows for less tone control. Many develop a kink between the shoulder blades, tired arms, tendinitis, or carpal tunnel syndrome.

Probably the most common physical affectation adopted by wind players is the beating of time from the bell of the instrument. While freedom of movement is a healthy form of expression and release of tension, it can also be the very source of the tension. Too much movement also changes the position of the reed in the mouth and may adversely effect the sound or phrase shape. To remedy this, aim to put the focus and energies on the high points and musical shapes that exist in the music. The desire here is not to stifle the urge to emote but to harness it so it can reflect the music rather than the metronome.

RESTING POSITIONS

Poor choices for resting positions are commonplace. A good rest position protects the reed from one's neighbors and helps avoid water tracking into the usual "watering holes" such as the octave vents. A good rest position has the keys facing up and the reed removed when the oboe is resting on the lap. A preferred rest position when the reed is still in the oboe would be with the oboe standing upright on one's leg. When checking fingerings, it is important to turn the oboe away from the body so that the reed does not make contact with the body. It is always important to be aware of the reed placement when checking keys, fingerings, and so on.

Figures 15.6–17 illustrate examples of good and bad postures when standing, sitting, and resting.

Figure 15.6. A proper stance. The knees are not locked, the feet are apart, and the body is erect. The oboe is at a forty-five-degree angle from the body. The center of gravity or focus for the body is balanced. This is considered an open position.

Figure 15.7. A locked stance. The knees are locked, the feet are together, and the elbows are in against the body, locking the muscles. The position creates tension by locking the muscles. The center of gravity or focus for the body is weak and narrow. This is considered a closed position.

Remedy: Bend from the knees with the feet apart at a slight angle (not square). The arms should fall comfortably at the sides and not tucked into the body. Breathe deeply and blow fully.

Figure 15.8. A bent stance. One leg is locked; the other holds tension and needs to be relieved often. The torso is bent from the waist and the head is crooked downward.

Remedy: When bending, it is better to bend at the knees so as not to collapse or tense the breathing muscles. For the best balance, the feet should be spaced apart but not in a square.

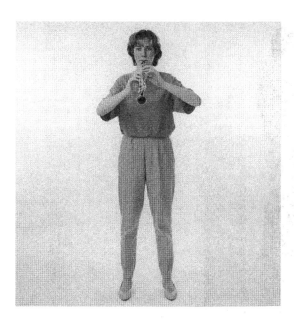

Figure 15.9. The "trumpet" stance. Arms are too high, putting the oboe at too great an angle. Legs are apart but are too square for proper balance and center of gravity. Knees are locked. All of this creates great tension, especially in the lower back and arms and between the shoulder blades.

Remedy: Use the music stand as a reference and bring the oboe bell down to create an isosceles triangle from the reed to the bell to the top of the stand.

Figure 15.10. The "stork" position. This common one-leg stance locks the lower back and the knee, creating tension and a lack of balance. Constant shifting from leg to leg will occur to relieve tension.

Remedy: Place the feet apart at a slight angle and unlock the knees.

Figure 15.11. The "leaning tower" position. This posture is deceiving because it looks comfortable and familiar. While the feet are apart and the arms are set comfortably at the sides, the locked right leg causes the body to lean and locks much of the lower back in the process.

Remedy: Place the feet another two inches apart. Feel the focus of the body on the balls of both feet and not the heels.

Figure 15.12. A poor fingering check procedure. When checking hand position or fingerings, avoid tilting the oboe so that the reed makes contact with the front of the body.

Remedy: Turn the oboe at a slight angle away from the body when checking keys, fingering, positions, or joint connections.

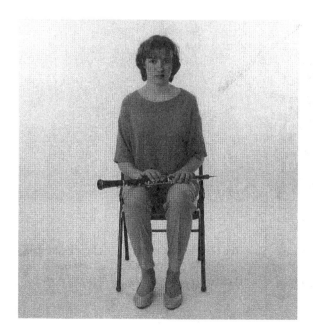

Figure 15.13. An improper position of rest. Keys are facing down so that moisture collected in the bore will track into the tone holes.

Remedy: Rest the oboe with the keys facing up or hold the oboe upright.

Figure 15.14. A proper sitting posture. The back is straight, and the arms are at the sides with the wrists straight. The feet are flat and oboe is at a forty-five-degree angle.

Figure 15.15. The elbow-on-the-knee posture. The body is bent forward with the elbow resting on the knee. This locks the abdominal breathing muscles and muscles in the lower back, twists the upper torso at an angle, and puts the oboe at too high an angle. Air support will be weak and the sound will be unsupported and blatty.

Remedy: Carry the torso up so the back is straight, with head up and eyes facing forward. Bring the arms to the sides rather than out front.

Figure 15.16. The "trumpet" posture. Although the back and head are straight and the feet are flat, the arms are too high, which puts the oboe at too high an angle.

Remedy: Bring the arms down to the sides so the oboe is somewhere between thirty and forty-five degrees.

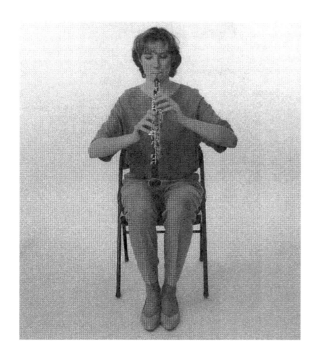

Figure 15.17. The winged posture. The arms are out from the body and too far forward. This creates tension and back strain. It also puts the little fingers too far from the body of the oboe and flattens the ring fingers.

Remedy: Bring the elbows in toward the body.

Notes

1. David Ledet, *Oboe Reed Styles* (Bloomington: Indiana University Press, 1981), 34.
2. Ibid., 35.
3. Philip Bate, *The Oboe* (London: Benn, 1956), 40.
4. Philip Bate, "Oboe," in *The New Grove Dictionary of Music and Musicians,* ed. Stanley Sadie (London: Macmillan, 1980), 13:467.
5. Ibid., 469.
6. Bate, *The Oboe,* 70.
7. Bate, "Oboe," 472.

CHAPTER 16

Fundamentals

Breathing

The art of playing the oboe involves no mystery. While oboists' techniques and approaches vary greatly and sometimes contradict one another, we do agree on one point: it is a wind instrument, not an embouchure instrument or simply a reed instrument. Tone is produced with the air, not by the mouth. The reed is made to vibrate with the air, not with the lips. Thus your method of breath control will determine what manner of oboist you are to be.

The parts of the breathing apparatus involved in playing the oboe are the lungs, rib cage, diaphragm, and abdominal wall muscles. These are the same areas involved in public speaking, singing, and playing any other wind or brass instrument. While many oboists feel "that they need breath control only to furnish breaths of suitable length, air pressure, and flow,"[1] they commonly disagree on which techniques give the best results. "This is due to differences in their training, in the conditions under which they perform, and in their ideas of how the [oboe] should sound."[2] Consequently, oboists use different breath control techniques because they have different goals.

Experiment with the process outlined below to find what works most efficiently and successfully for each individual. Practice employing all parts of your breathing apparatus in stages.

1. *Fill the lower area of your lungs.* This should push your abdominal wall outward. It should feel as though you are "filling your stomach with air." Place your hand against your stomach just above your navel. You should be able to feel and see your hand rise and fall.

2. *Fill the middle area of your lungs.* This should cause your lower ribs to expand outward. Place your hands on your sides by your ribs and then on your front and back. You should be able to see and feel your hands rise and fall.

3. *Fill the top area of your lungs.* This should cause your sternum and upper rib cage to expand outward. Place your hand on your sternum and watch your shoulders. You should be able to see and feel your hand rise and fall, but be sure not to let the shoulders rise.

In practicing this three-step approach, aim to make the inhales the same length as the exhales. Practice with a metronome exhaling for three full beats from each area and inhaling over three full beats. Next, do the same process in one gesture for an inhale and one gesture for an exhale. Experiment with inhaling and exhaling from each area separately. This experiment can then be transferred to the oboe. While these are not new ideas (see Evelyn Rothwell, *Oboe Technique*), it is a good idea to experiment to find which area (bottom, middle, or top) works best in each of the three octaves and in what contexts.

The Primary Octave

STARTING THE TONE

The tongue should not start the note. Instead, the tongue should be released from the reed tip so that the air escaping into the reed starts the tone. The tongue then serves as nothing more than a door opening to let the wind escape. When playing in the low register, the tongue should be placed so that it will rest low in the oral cavity; when playing in the upper register the tongue will rest high and to the back of the oral cavity.

Dr. Andrea Gullickson of the University of Wisconsin suggests practicing tonguing using the reed alone.[3] This is supported by many oboists, including Ray Still, former principal oboe with the Chicago Symphony Orchestra, and John Mack, principal oboe with the Cleveland Orchestra. Gullickson states that just as the brass player practices on the mouthpiece, the double reed player needs to develop an awareness of the sound and pitch produced on the reed without assistance from the instrument. Aspects of embouchure formation, breathing, blowing, and tonguing can be addressed with exercises performed with the reed alone. Begin by holding a steady pitch on the reed alone. In the beginning, ten to fifteen seconds may be a challenge, but with persistence, the amount of time the student is able to hold a steady pitch should increase. Next, play the first few notes of an ascending and descending scale. Try it by manipulating the position of the reed with the hand and then without. If this is successful, try the same with a melody. Producing a scale or melody on the reed alone will require steady air support and a flexible embouchure.

THE FIRST NOTES

The fingerings for the first and second octaves on the oboe are nearly identical, with the exception of the octave functions. For the most immediate results it is advisable to start with the notes in the staff, from d^1 to c^2.

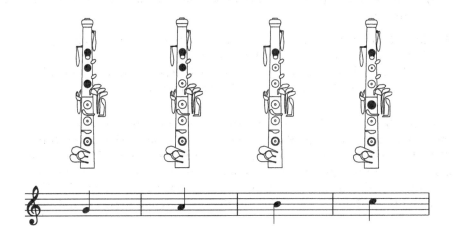

Example 16.1. The first notes for the left hand

INTRODUCTORY MELODIES FOR THE LEFT HAND

Exercise 16.1.

Exercise 16.2.

Exercise 16.3.

Exercise 16.4.

Exercise 16.5.

Exercise 16.6.

BREATH CONTROL

Oboists are the only wind players that experience being out of breath when the lungs are actually quite full. This is because the oboe, unlike the flute, works on air pressure rather than volume of air. Consequently, the act of breathing for the oboist becomes a "double action" breath: releasing the old air before taking in new air. Expelling the deoxygenated air is a most important gesture for endurance and comfort. Exercise 16.7 demonstrates a healthy approach.

Experiment with this exercise while using only step one of the three-stage breathing process. Then try it while using only step two, then step

The ↑ indicates an exhale whereas the ↓ indicates an inhale.

Exercise 16.7.

three. Do you notice any changes? Were there notes that spoke or sounded different? Better or worse? Were there notes that responded easier or harder? What were these notes?

It may be that certain notes respond better, sound better, and are better in tune when you use specific areas of breath focus. For example, the notes of the lower range may speak easier and sound richer when you use only the first step in the breathing process. Compare this with playing notes in the low register using only step three. Chances are quite good that the low notes will "chip," go up the octave, come out late, come out with a poor sound, or not come out at all.

Once the range starts growing, use the same experiment playing up the octave. Then try it on d^1 and d^3. Chances are good that d^3 will speak more easily and be at pitch when you use only step three and will respond poorly when you use only step one. The opposite may prove true with d^1. This is an important point when dealing with control. Knowing which area of the body is used to breathe and blow will assist in tone and sound production, range control, and finesse.

This approach describes how to inhale and exhale, but not where to do so in the music. While the above exercise offers plenty of opportunities, little music will be so generous or apparent. Nonetheless, music does need to breathe. The best advice is to let the music be a guide and follow the harmonic structures of the phrases. This will prove a better method than breathing in a random fashion or simply as needed.

INTRODUCTORY MELODIES FOR THE RIGHT HAND

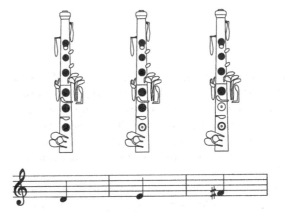

Example 16.2. The first notes for the right hand

Exercise 16.8.

Exercise 16.9.

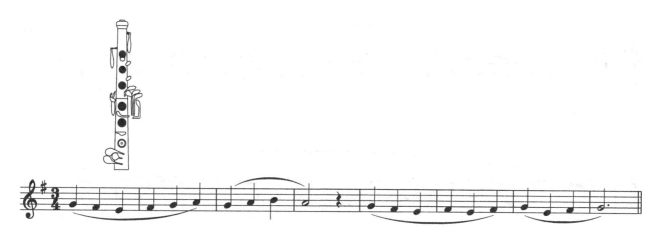

Exercise 16.10.

Exercise 16.11.

Exercise 16.12.

Exercise 16.13.

In practicing Exercises 16.14–18, exhale after each pattern and inhale before each new pattern. This will build endurance and reinforce an often over-looked and underappreciated technique: exhaling. Aim to use all of your air through the four-bar passages rather than sneaking in breaths throughout. In this way you can exhale what little remains in the lungs and take in a full comfortable breath to start the next line. Endurance will grow with every passing line if this approach is maintained.

Exercise 16.14. The ↑ indicates an exhale, the ↓ an inhale

Exercise 16.15.

Exercise 16.16.

Exercise 16.17.

Exercise 16.18.

Be sure to exhale before inhaling. It is extremely important to empty your lungs of used air each time so you can truly replenish. It is also important to practice balancing the exhales with the intakes. Accordingly, after each exercise breathe out for one beat and in for one beat.

While building the practice of "outs and ins," pay close attention to how you use your air. Are you inhaling and feeling as though you are holding your breath while you play the exercises? Are you using your throat as a valve to ration out little bits of air throughout the exercises? Do you maintain a pocket of air in your oral cavity or do you try to push it all through the reed? The best approach is to aim to maintain an even stream of air to the reed and oboe and not to try to withhold or pace it. Empty the air through the oboe, keeping it as forward in the mouth as possible.

Example 16.3. Two new notes

Exercise 16.19.

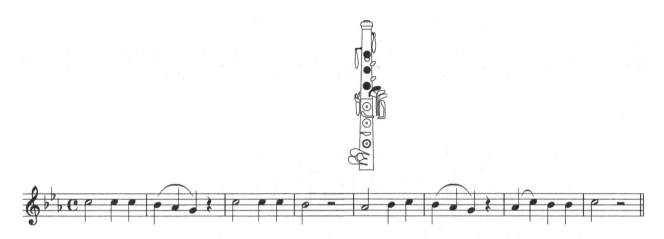

Exercise 16.20.

Exercise 16.21.

Exercise 16.22.

Embouchure

As stated earlier, the oboe is a wind instrument and not an embouchure instrument. It is the air that generates the sound, the air that starts the notes, the air that shapes the nuances, the air that shapes the phrases, the air that determines the dynamics, the air that connects the notes (whether tongued or slurred), and the air that projects the notes. Theoretically, then, it should be possible to play the oboe with any embouchure as long as the air is used well. However, a good embouchure will help to make all of the above easier and more beautiful. It is important to understand that a good embouchure is dependent upon a good and responsive reed.

In building your embouchure strength and formation, it will be necessary to check all aspects of it throughout each practice using a mirror or video camera. Because each element varies from one individual to another, and because many of the elements involved in forming an embouchure are hidden within the oral cavity, it is quite likely that embouchures will not look exactly alike. Even the most specific embouchure descriptions can only serve as a guide. Fortunately, there are commonalities in most good embouchures.

The embouchure involves the formation of the lips, the placement of the tongue, the muscles of the throat, and placement of the jaw. The muscles of the throat should be relaxed and open as if in a state of yawning. The jaw and tongue placement will depend on the notes being played. In general, however, placement of the jaw should be dropped low so the chin is flat and firm, with the tongue low in the mouth. The lips should be relaxed, not taut, to form a cushion between which the blades of the reed can vibrate.

To confirm that the throat muscles are indeed relaxed, practice producing a tone while singing into the oboe. Start by singing in your most comfortable range so that you can hear air racing through the body of the oboe. Draw a G from the oboe into play. Next, try playing a scale down from g' while singing a pitch in your most comfortable range. Ultimately, it should be possible to play entire passages while singing a pitch. If the throat muscles are not relaxed, this will be a difficult task. Further, the unrelaxed throat will, in the end, serve as a valve to control the air. Such a valve will only be intrusive and destructive to good tone, projection, vibrato, and intonation.

If the jaw is not dropped enough, the lips will flatten and spread into a smile. This will bring the teeth closer to the reed and create a hard platform rather than a cushion. The sound quality may be pinched and sharp. If the back of the tongue is too high in the oral cavity (as though saying "eek") the sound will be further pinched and sharp. The low-register notes will be more difficult to articulate if the jaw is too high, if the lips are flattened, or if the tongue is placed too high, making the back of the oral cavity too small.

Of the numerous embouchure styles, the following is a common approach in forming the lips. Form an O with the lips so the teeth are far from contact with the reed. Curl the lips in and make a cushion or pillow with the lower lip. Place the reed so the tip rests on the middle of the lower lip.

Figure 16.2. Good embouchure in normal playing position (front view)

Close the lips around the reed. The lips should be relaxed, but the muscles around the lips should be taut. The lower jaw should be dropped so the reed is resting on the lips and supported by the teeth. This drawstring style of lip formation should produce a rich quality of sound. A flatter lip surface and greater support of the teeth results in a thinner quality of sound. To get a warmer and fuller tone quality, the corners of the mouth should be drawn in and not drawn back as in a smile. Jay Light, oboe professor at Drake University in Des Moines, Iowa, suggests an "anteater embouchure."[4] Aiming

Figure 16.3. Good embouchure in normal playing position (side view)

Figure 16.4. Good embouchure for high-range playing (d³ to g³; front view)

Figure 16.5. Good embouchure for high-range playing (d³ to g³; side view)

for this image will keep the lips from rolling in too far and from spreading or flattening. If the reed seems too difficult to control with this embouchure, it is probably too hard or placed improperly in the mouth. The amount of reed placed onto the lower lip varies with the octave being played. The lower octave requires the least amount of reed to protrude beyond the lip (about one-eighth of an inch), whereas the third octave requires a good deal more reed in the mouth.

While most young players could start on the oboe, many young oboists are started on clarinet or flute. Consequently, a transfer embouchure is adopted. Although an acceptable transfer embouchure can be drawn from the clarinet or flute embouchures, the differences can also create some unacceptable sounds. Students should be encouraged to develop a true oboe embouchure. A transfer embouchure is only a vehicle of conveyance to the final formation.

Articulation

STARTING THE NOTE

While the tongue should be placed at the tip of the reed, it should not be what starts the tone. Instead, the tone should be started by the release of air as the tongue is released from the reed tip. The top of the tongue at the tip should make contact with the bottom blade of the reed tip.

It is easy enough to determine where the tongue makes contact on the reed. After a fair number of tries, check the reed for a frayed corner. This will be the point of contact. While we might aim to tongue the center of the reed, most end up tonguing a corner of the reed. Once this is established, try to feel where on the tongue contact occurs. Avoid tonguing from the underside of the tongue, as this will generate a sluggish articulation style, often with a bellied sound. Avoid tonguing from the midsection of the tongue; this will often create a locked tongue, which will be inflexible and sluggish.

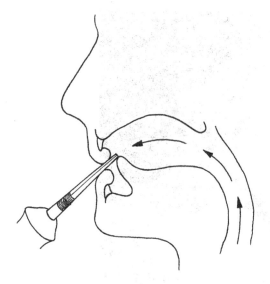

Figure 16.6. Tongue placement and the oral cavity

There are many styles of articulation that require different strokes on the reed from different points on the tongue. Experiment with producing different styles while playing a scale. Make a list of the audible differences. Using different styles can make for far more interesting performances.

Notes

1. Roger Mather, *The Art of Flute Playing*. Vol.1 (Iowa City, IA: Romney, 1989), 7.
2. Andrea Gillickson, "Playing and Teaching: Help From the Specialists." *Band Directors Guide* (Spring 1994): 32–34.
3. Jay Light, *Essays For the Oboist* (Des Moines, IA: Alborado, 1994), 5.

CHAPTER 17

Techniques

The Half Hole

The half hole is the first technical difficulty that young oboists encounter and, unfortunately, usually the last thing they learn to do well. The half hole is a function of the first plate key. Within the first two octaves the half hole addresses only three notes: $c\sharp^2$, d^2, and $e\flat^2$ (the third octave will also require the half hole). When one of these three notes is encountered, the left forefinger must pivot or roll on the pad of the fingertip to allow air to escape through the half-hole vent. If the vent is not open, the notes will remain in the lower octave. Allowing the vent to open cuts the airstream in half, causing the notes to sound an octave higher. The pivot gesture required of this finger is in great contrast to the movement of the other fingers. It is important to adopt the pivot and not to lift and then replace the finger. The pivot will generate a smoother transition from non-half-hole notes to half-hole notes and will build a technique necessary for the next octave.

In making the gesture as economical as possible, the placement of the forefinger on the plate key is an important issue. If the finger is placed too high up on the plate key, the gesture will indeed need to be a big one. If the finger is placed too low on the plate key the half hole may leak air on non-half-hole notes and the return gesture may need to be too big. The idea is to place the fatty pad of the forefinger more central to the primary plate key and the extension. In this way the pivot can be a small and simple action.

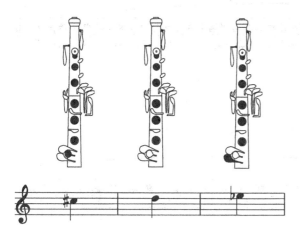

Example 17.1. Half-hole notes

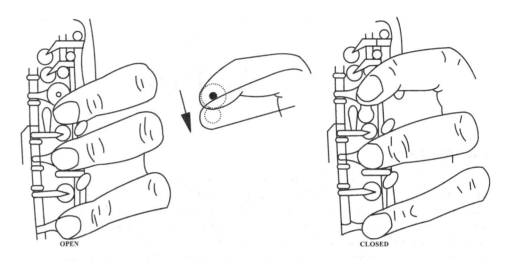

Figure 17.1. Position of the left forefinger when operating the half hole

Try using the half hole in Exercises 17.1–3.

Exercise 17.1.

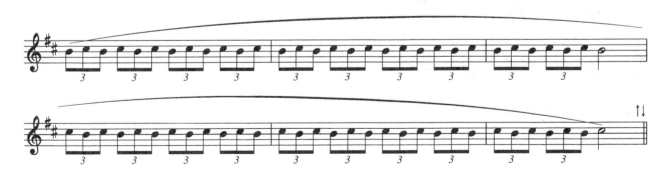

Exercise 17.2.

Exercise 17.3.

The half-hole gesture of pivoting from the pad of the fingertip does not need to be grandiose. While the plate key has an extension, the idea is simply to open and close the hole. The dilemma, however, is to open and close it in a timely manner. Most often, the half-hole action is late or too small. Either of these will cause a malfunction. Try the above exercises again. This time, focus on coordinating the pivoting action with the change of the note.

If the coordination is practiced and learned well, crossing this break will be easier when passages get more advanced and when extending the range. To establish a good half hole, try the approach outlined below.

Start by setting the metronome at a slow enough tempo to allow you to do everything well. Once you have settled on a suitable tempo, play b^1 for two counts, rolling the half hole open on the second count; then move to $c\#^2$ for two counts, closing the half hole on the second count to return to b^1. Repeat this pattern until it becomes solid. Try the same pattern starting on b^1 and moving to and from d^2. Try it again moving to and from $d\#^2$ while maintaining the same slow metronome setting.

Exercise 17.4. ◇ = opened half hole, ◆ = closed half hole

Exercise 17.5.

Exercise 17.6.

Next, play the same passage but pivot on the half hole on the and of two.

Exercise 17.7.

Next, play the same passage but pivot on the last sixteenth note of two. In each of these exercises, note that the half-hole pivot gesture is getting closer to the changing note. Eventually, the change will occur on the second beat. This anticipation of the half hole will build a better and cleaner half-hole practice.

Exercise 17.8.

TUNES FOR HALF-HOLE DEVELOPMENT

Lightly Row

My Country, 'Tis of Thee

Mary Had a Little Lamb

Balletto

Loehlein

The Dancing Master   Türk

The Octave Keys

Most student model oboes have two octave keys. Professional models often have a third octave key, for use in the altissimo range, which serves to make the altissimo range more accessible.

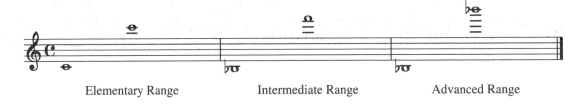

Elementary Range   Intermediate Range   Advanced Range

Example 17.2. Elementary range, intermediate range, and advanced range

These octave keys are often labeled differently in fingering charts and method books. The octave key that affects e^2–$g\#^2$ may be identified as the first octave key, octave key A, or thumb octave key. This key is, in fact, activated by the left thumb. The remaining octave key affects a^2–c^3 and is sometimes identified as the second octave key, octave key B, or side octave. This key is activated using the side of the left forefinger. For clarity, they will heretofore be referred to as thumb octave and side octave keys.

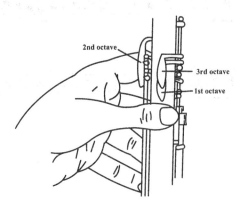

Figure 17.2. Side and thumb octave keys

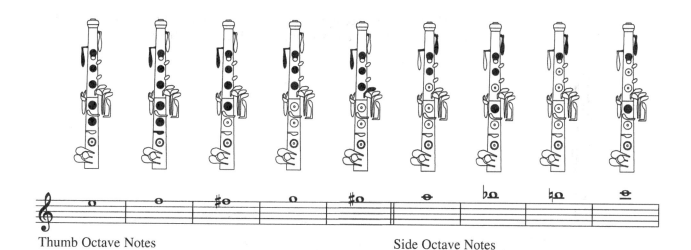

Thumb Octave Notes   Side Octave Notes

Example 17.3.

Once the half-hole pivot gesture is solid, the next technical issue to conquer will be moving from a half-hole note to a thumb octave note. The practice approach used to build the half-hole pivot gesture will be useful in
building this connection.

Half-hole to thumb octave note practice.   ◊ = half-hole open,   ♦ = half-hole closed,   T = thumb octave key.

Exercise 17.9.

The same practice approach will again be useful in strengthening the connection between the half-hole and side octave notes.

Half-hole practice to side octave notes   ◇ = half-hole open,   ♦ = half-hole closed,   S = side octave key.

Exercise 17.10.

For the oboe's octave functions, the only important numbers to remember are 3, 5, and 4: three half-hole notes, five thumb octave notes, and four side octave notes. This is also the case as you travel into the next octave. The next three notes require half hole; the next five notes will require the thumb octave and the half hole.

Example 17.4. Half-hole (H), thumb octave (T) and side octave (S) notes.

TUNES FOR OCTAVE KEY DEVELOPMENT

Hudson River Steamboat

Joy to the World

French Tune

Twinkle, Twinkle, Little Star

The Streets of Laredo

Song of the Lost Lamb

O Come, All Ye Faithful

Pivoting

Apart from the half-hole pivot, there exist only two other pivot or rolling actions on the oboe. These are chromatic movements from the low b♭ to b♮ and low c¹ to c♯¹. Pivoting is dictated by the placement of the finger on the key and the distance it needs to travel to get to the next key. When you move from b♭ to b♮, the left pinkie should be placed on both keys and rolled off the b♭.

Exercise 17.11. Pivoting from b♭ to b♮

When you pivot from c¹ to c♯¹, the right pinkie should be placed on both keys. For this pivot some advocate pivoting on the first knuckle. Not every person can manage this gesture. An alternate approach would be to roll or even slide the pinkie off the C♯ key. To do the latter, it is a good idea to "slick" the pinkie down by first rubbing it along your nose or forehead. The oils will allow for an easier slide.

Exercise 17.12. Pivoting from c¹ to c♯¹

Alternate Fingerings

Only three alternate fingerings within the first two octaves need be considered here: F, E♭, and A♭.

ALTERNATE F

On many student model oboes there are only two fingerings available for f¹ and f². Professional model oboes provide an additional key for a third fingering. The primary fingering is often identified as regular F or short F. The second fingering is usually identified as forked F, as the finger placement on the right hand, the forefinger and ring finger only, forms a two-pronged fork. The third fingering is identified as left F because the key is on the left side of the oboe and requires the left pinkie. The regular F is not normally identified, whereas the left F is often marked in elementary method and étude books with an *L* or *S* and the forked F with an *F*, ×, Ψ, or other symbol. In this text, regular F will be notated with an *R*, left F with an *L*, and forked F with an *F*.

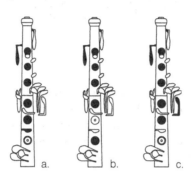

Figure 17.3. fingerings for (a) regular F; (b) forked F; and (c) left F

The passages in Example 17.4 require specific uses of the alternate Fs. Look through your own music and see if you now can better identify which F fingerings should be used when.

Example 17.5. The use and notation of the alternate Fs: forked F (F), regular F (R), and left F (L)

Though it may seem arbitrary to the beginner, there are rules for the use of these fingerings. Regular F is used most often, while forked F is used only when preceded or followed by low b♮, b♭, c¹, c♯¹, d¹, or e♭¹ and c♯², d², or e♭². This is because in each of these notes the right ring finger is employed as in the forked F fingering. It is unacceptable to slide from the regular F to these notes. However, the left F, if the oboe has one, is always to be preferred over the forked F because the natural tone quality of the forked F is stuffy, foggy, less focused, and often not as stable in pitch. Many oboists suggest adding the E♭ key when playing forked F. While this may lend better focus to the note, it often makes the forked F bright in quality and sharp in pitch.

Even if your oboe has a left F, it cannot and should not always be employed whenever preceded or followed by one of the six example notes. Moving from f¹ to low b♭, for example, will prove quite impossible. Consequently, we can only move from the forked F. Also, in very active technical passages it is best to choose forked F when needed. Thus it behooves us to learn to match the Fs so the listener cannot discern which fingering we have chosen.

Example 17.6. Six examples of when to employ forked F

Determine and mark the correct F fingerings in Exercises 17.13–14 and in "Simple Gifts."

Exercise 17.13.

Exercise 17.14.

Simple Gifts

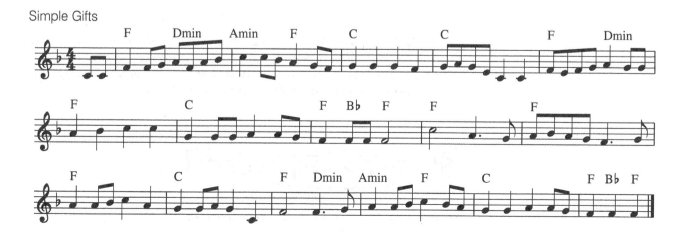

LEFT E FLAT

All oboes are equipped with both the right and left E♭ keys. The right E♭ is often identified as the regular fingering, as it is most often employed. Left E♭ is used when preceded or followed by D♭ and C, as the right pinkie is then occupied. It is unacceptable to slide from either of those notes to an E♭ or vice versa. The general rule is that if the key signature has four or more sharps or flats, left E♭ will be employed. In an article for *The Instrumentalist*, Professor Howard Niblock of the Lawrence Conservatory recommends starting students with left E♭ as soon as possible.[1] In this way it can become a regular part of their playing early on rather than something to reckon with for the rest of their playing lives. For some, this will be a physical impossibility. Nevertheless, the idea is a good one and deserves trial.

Example 17.7. When to employ the left E♭ key

Example 17.7a. Employing the left E♭ key

RIGHT A FLAT

All oboes are equipped with both the right and left A♭ keys. The left A♭ key is considered the regular fingering, as it is most often employed. The alternate right A♭ is used only when traveling to or from a left E♭.

Example 17.8. Double E♭/A♭

While Example 17.8 shows an acceptable use of the right A♭ key, some students might find a different approach easier. When playing this same exercise, employ both the left A♭ and the left E♭ keys simultaneously. This eliminates excess finger movement and hand crossovers.

Example 17.8a. When to employ the left A♭ and E♭ keys simultaneously

TUNES FOR ALTERNATE FINGERING DEVELOPMENT

Three Waltzes   Schubert

Tuning

Historically, the oboe was the first woodwind instrument introduced to the
string orchestra. Through tradition, consequently, the strings and other
winds have tuned to the oboe for centuries. Because of this responsibility,
the oboist must maintain reeds that are consistent in their quality and build,
train the ears and mind to anticipate the pitch tendencies within the instrument, and practice using a tuning fork and tuner.

REEDS

Because the following chapter treats reed making in some detail, the comments here focus on the specific question of pitch characteristics.

It is widely accepted that oboe reeds should crow a B to a C for the best possible pitch center. If the reed crows below this, the pitch center will tend to be flat and unstable. If it crows above this, the pitch center will tend to be sharp. And if the crow is late or not happening freely, the pitch center will be sharp.

If the crow is centered to a B or C but the oboe's pitch is not matching comfortably with the tuner or tuning fork, check the length of the reed (the tube should be 47mm and the total reed ca. 70mm) and the width of the shape (it should be ca. 7mm at the tip; a wide shape will be flat), and check the oboe for leaks or cracks. If these appear normal, your embouchure or breath control may be interfering with the oboe's natural pitch center.

THE OBOE

While it is true that the instruments are "tuned at the factory," they will still have notes or ranges with inherent tuning problems. Most oboes are flat in the low range ($b\flat$–d^1), sharp on e^2, $f\sharp^2$, and g^2, and flat on $b\flat^2$–c^3. To learn the extent of these tendencies, practice scales and arpeggios with a Strobo-Conn. In this way you will see the distance you need to adjust. Practice to convince your ears. Once you can see and believe the pitch discrepancies, practice with a tuner that gives off a pitch. For example, place the tuner on D and play the opening of the Marcello Concerto in D Minor. Or place it on a C and play the Cimarosa Concerto in C Minor. Train your ear to hear the pitch tendencies and build the muscle memory necessary to make the adjustments naturally and, ultimately, without much effort and thought.

PRACTICING WITH TUNERS

Many oboists argue over the use of tuning forks versus tuners. Although tuning forks are an excellent reference tool when tuning an orchestra, they also invite question, whereas a tuner is less questionable. Yet the tuning fork trains the ear while the tuner, if not used to its fullest ability, merely trains the eye. When you are tuning an orchestra or ensemble, my recommendation is to get to the rehearsal hall early enough that you have time to find your reed and your pitch center before everybody else gets there to clutter your mind and ears. Once you have done this, check your sense of where the A is. Check to see if you can hear the A every time. Can you hold a conversation and play a passage in another key and come back to the A each time? If so, then you should work toward holding that A in your mind and ear so you are able to tune the ensemble with or without the tuner. In this way, the tuner becomes only a reference tool and not the orchestra tuner.

When practicing scales and arpeggios, it is easy to become lost in boredom. Use the scale to check and build your ear. In building your scale, aim to make each succeeding note sound like the preceding note. For example, in D major the E should sound as if it came from the D in its quality, texture, timbre, and volume.

If, in your scale practice, notes sound different and "stick out," aim to find their right position with the best use of your air and embouchure. If these are working properly, it will be necessary to determine whether the problem is one of approach. If the notes work well going up but sound poor coming down, the problem may only be in your approach to the notes when descending. Try approaching each poor note from a different note above to learn the tendency and proper placement of each note in question. The goal here is to build a scale that sounds as smooth and solid as the foundation of your home. If there are uncertain notes in the scale, your foundation will surely fail you when the scales get more involved, the arpeggios start to travel farther, and intervals become bigger. Build your scale one step at a time. Use your ears, your eyes, a tuner, and a tape recorder.

Fingering Charts

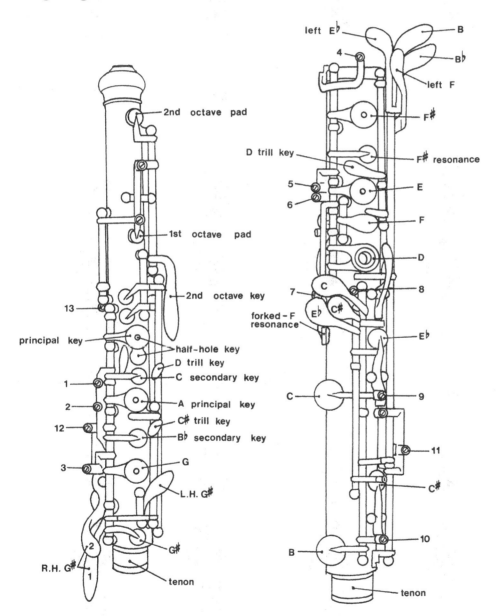

Figure 17.4. Keys and adjustment screws on the oboe

THE FIRST AND SECOND OCTAVE

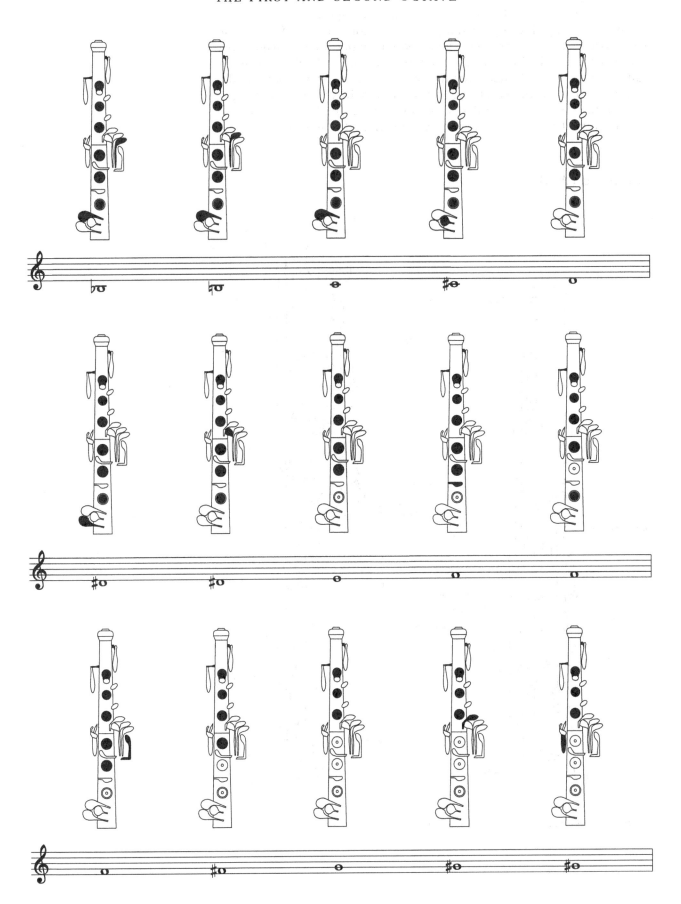

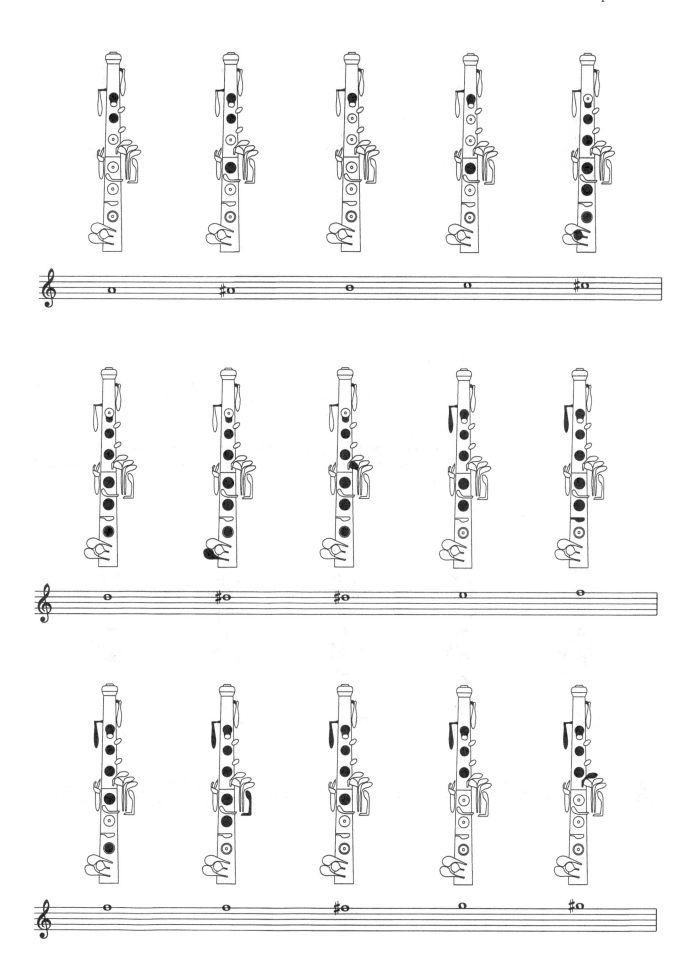

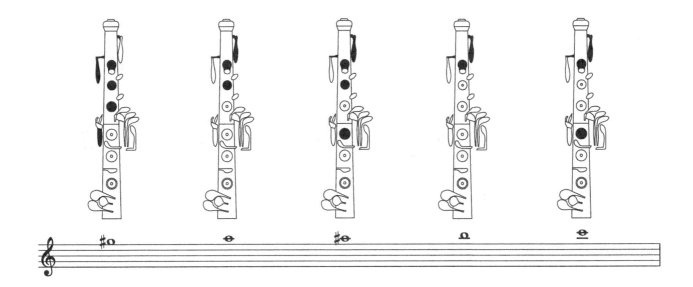

THE THIRD OCTAVE

This chart provides alternate fingerings for the third octave only. Some oboes have a third octave key, which facilitates playing in the altissimo range (e^3 and up). When using the third octave key it is not necessary to open the half hole.

Not every fingering presented here will work on all oboes. Experiment to find those that work best for your setup of oboe, reed, embouchure, and use of air.

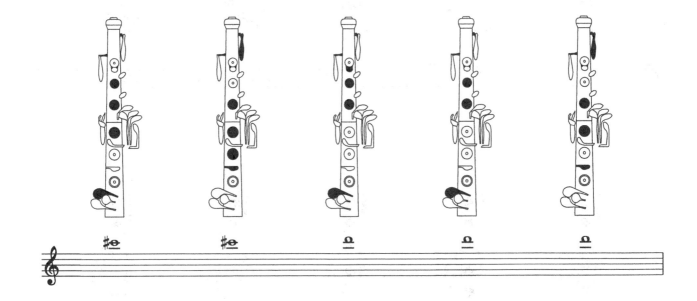

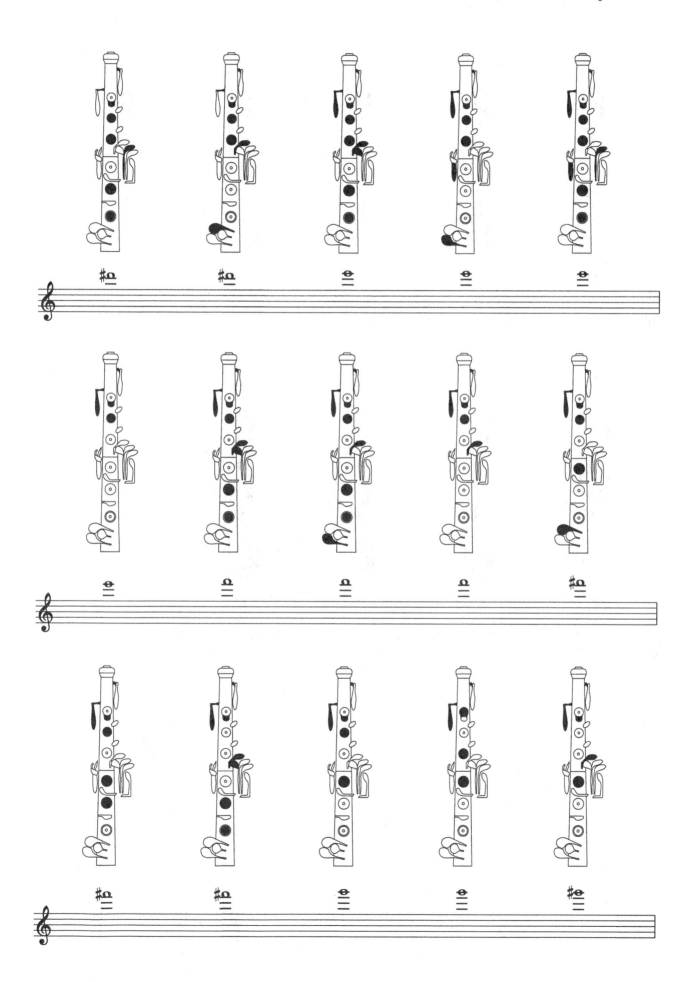

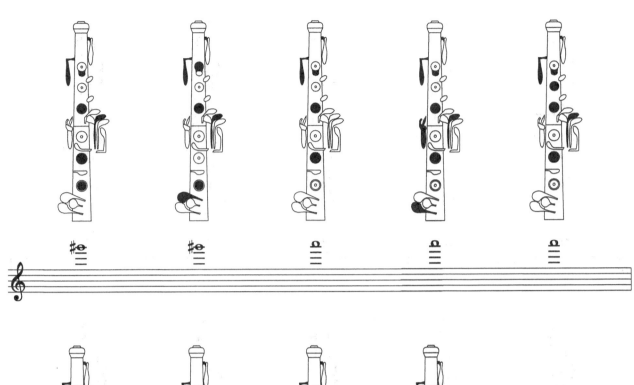

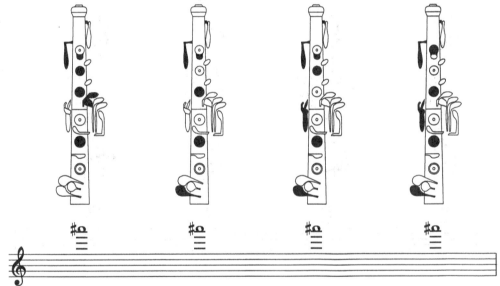

TRILLS

The arrow (←) identifies which key(s) move to create the trill.

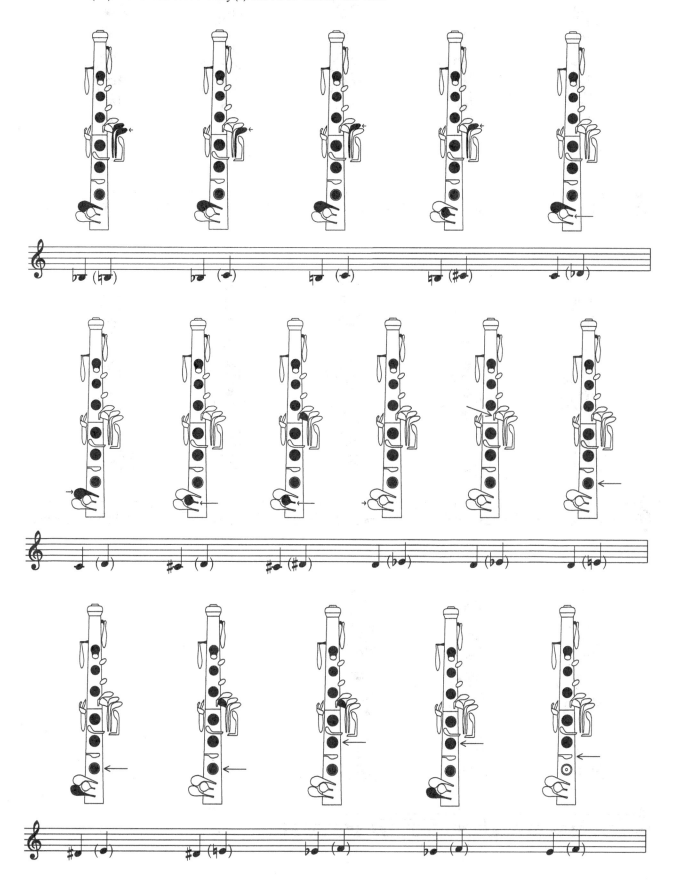

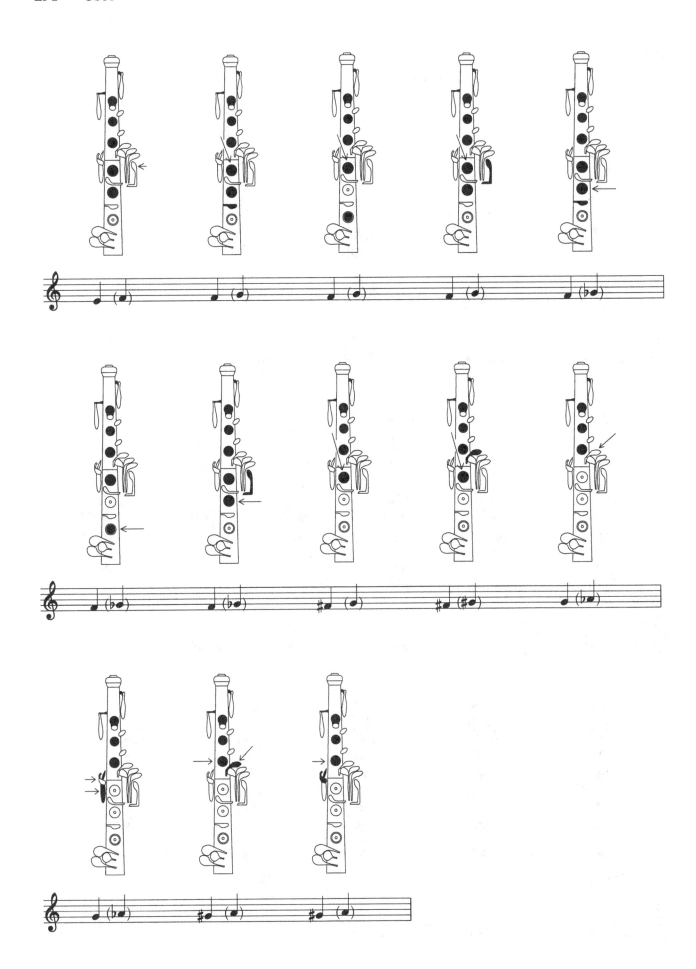

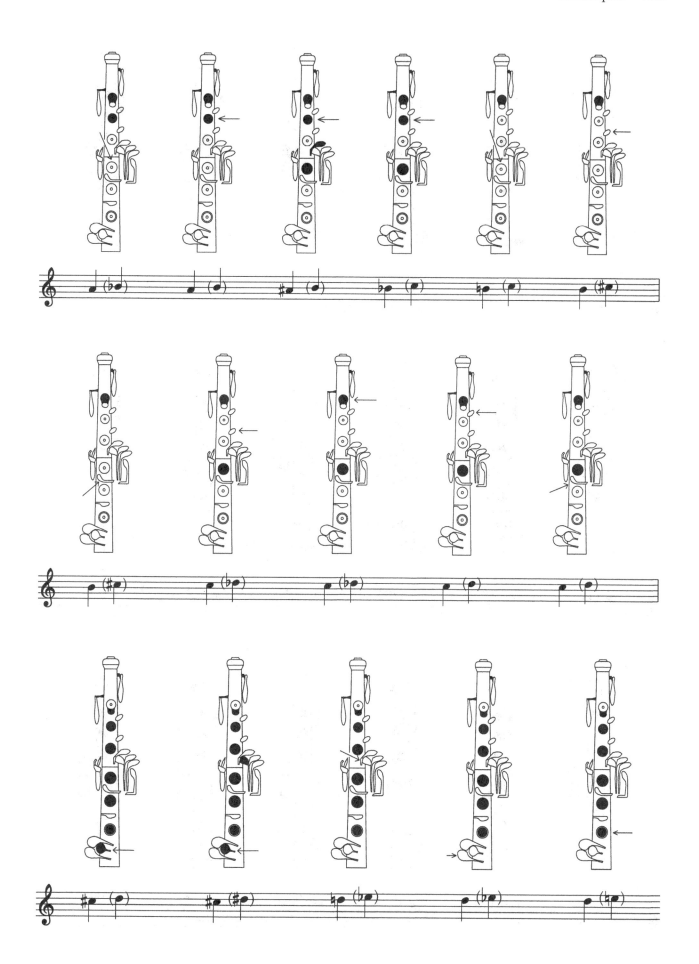

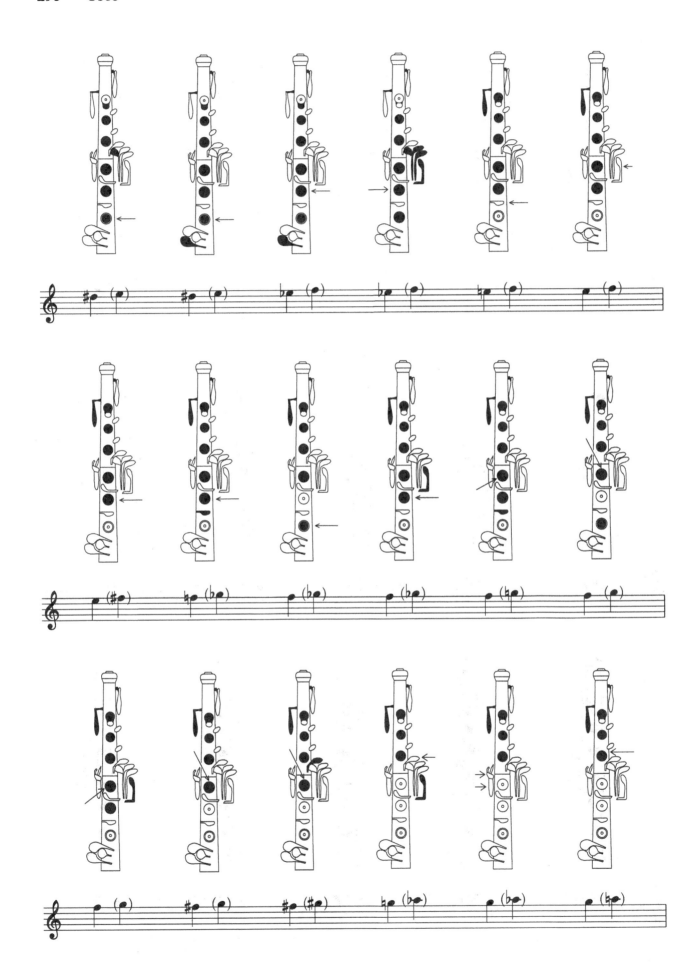

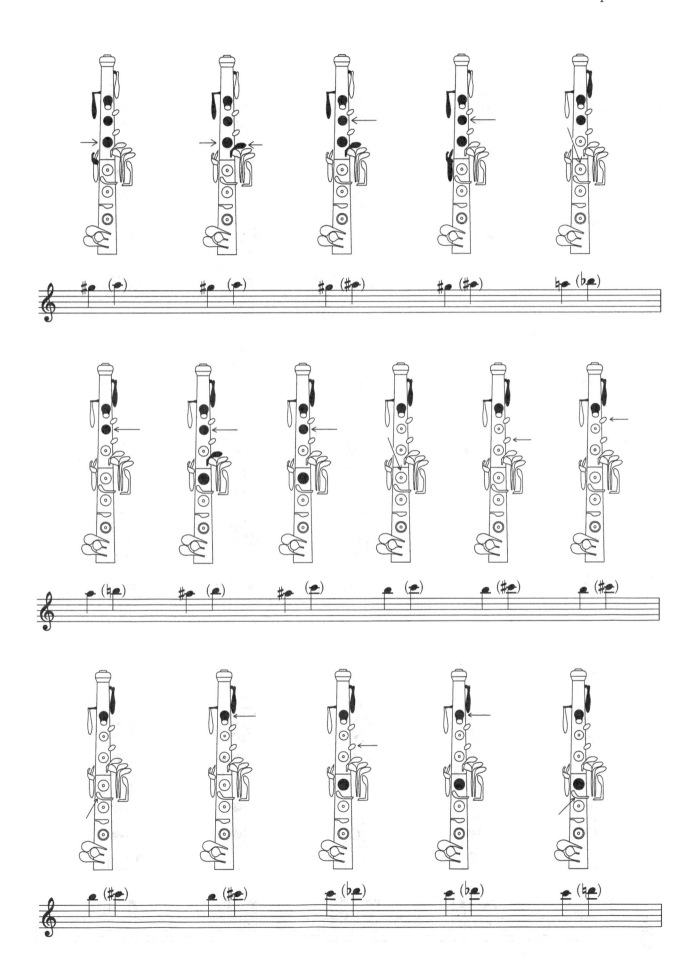

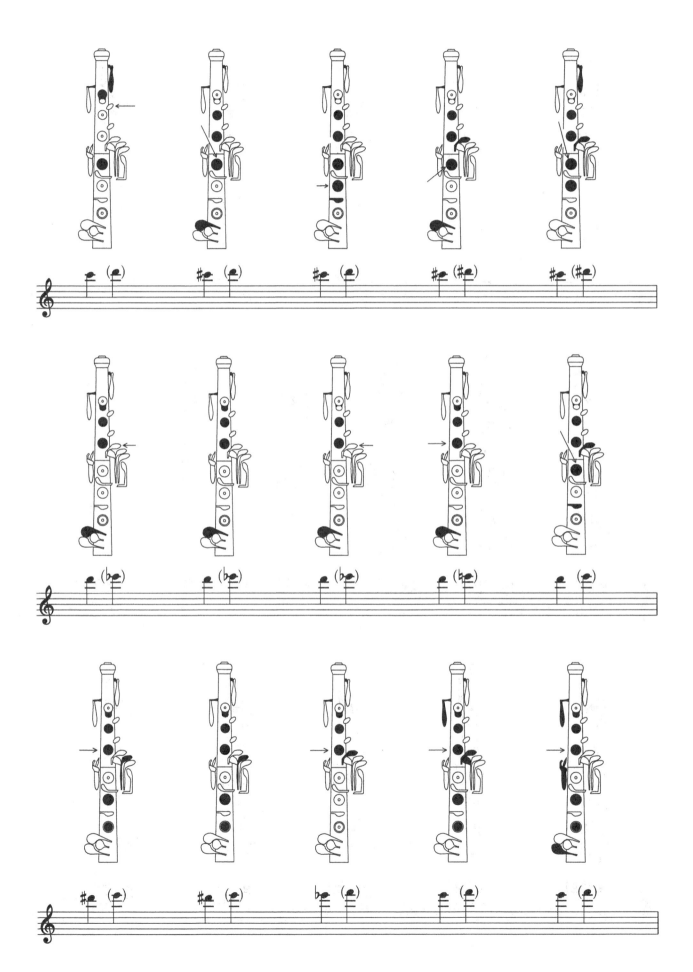

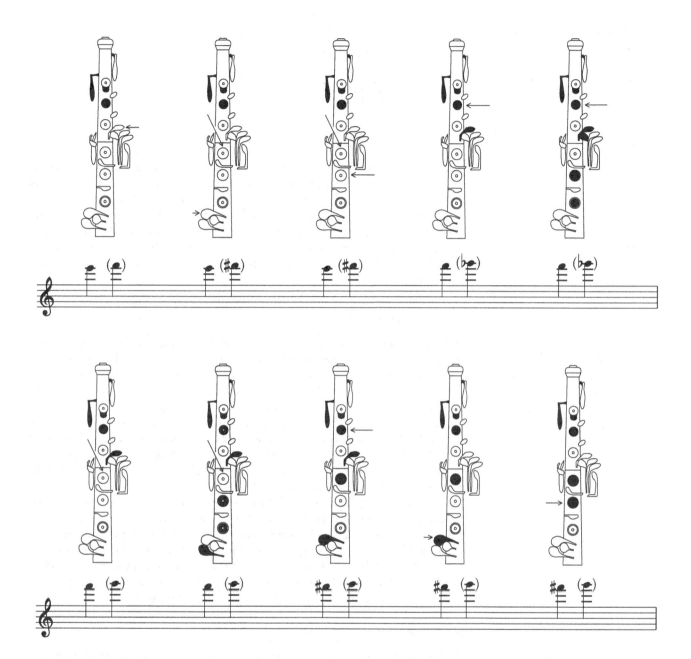

Notes

1. Howard Niblock, "Troublesome Oboe Fingerings." *The Instrumentalist*, 50, no. 4 (November 1994): 53.

CHAPTER 18

Reeds

Reeds quickly become the bane of every oboist, and adjusting reeds may at first seem an insurmountable task. When you find that you or your students are dividing their reeds into piles of "Goddess Reeds" and "Heinous Reeds," the need for guidelines will become apparent. Knowing how to identify the problems among the "Heinous Reeds" is the result of learning what a reed is supposed to do. It is important to identify the problems according to a specific order. Many of the problems are easily discernible and, in most cases, reparable.

Evaluating Reeds

Balance in the scrape, shape, and gouge of the cane is vital to building a good reed. Symmetry within each of these elements will add smoothness to the sound and scale of any reed. To a degree, some of the flaws created by a lack of symmetry can be compensated for. To do this, it is necessary to identify which is flawed: the scrape, shape, or gouge.

Through evaluating the crow you can determine what scrapes or adjustments will be necessary. Some reeds will need more of a chiropractic adjustment while others will need major surgery. Still others will need only cosmetic attention. And, of course, there will always be those reeds that do not respond despite heroic efforts.

"Deciphering the sound [of the crow] is all that is needed to determine where and how to scrape the reed. Once this is fully understood, a functional reed could be made from beginning to end without ever actually playing it."[1] The most telling sign for adjusting the reed is the crow. It is also the most misunderstood criterion and therefore the most overlooked. Most student reed makers do their reed work by eye. Sadly, the ear, and thereby the crow, is the last to be invited into the evaluation process.

THE CROW

To "crow" the reed, place the wetted reed in the mouth with the lips closed around the string and blow a stream of air through the reed. As this does not require any specialized embouchure formation, a non-oboist should have no trouble generating a true crow. However, it is important not to put pressure on the cane portion, as this will falsify the crow.

A good healthy crow consists of (a) an immediate crow response, (b) both a soft and loud dynamic level, and (c) Cs in two to three octaves. If these elements are not true, it will be necessary to determine the condition of the crow before making any adjustments. The condition of the crow is based on (1) the scrape of the reed, (2) the dimensions of the shape, (3) the gouge and diameter of the cane, (4) the opening of the reed, and (5) the wrap of the reed (length and overlap).

THE SCRAPE   While it is true that "there is no one correct way to scrape a reed"[2]—each piece of cane, reed maker, and player is perhaps too unique—

300

the fundamental principles of reed making remain the same and can be learned systematically. "For many generations reeds have had a mysterious, almost mystical aura placed about them . . . this is baloney."[3]

There exist many styles of reed scrapes and, with them, varying needs and preferences (sound quality, response, dynamics, musical demands, intonation, etc.). The more variables, the greater the variety of problems to consider with each reed; try using cane from the same crop with the same diameter, gouge, shape, staples, and measurements for the tie and scrape.

The scraping of the reed is done in three sections: the tip, the heart, and the channels. These correspond directly to the shape dimensions: tip, middle, and back. As there are only three sections that require focus, the process will be one of elimination through evaluation of the crow. If scraping is necessary, it will be important to have some proper tools (as discussed below).

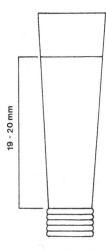

Figure 18.1. Make a straight score with the knife at 19–20mm from the string. Scrape off the bark and yellow underlay using a "straight scrape" from the score to the edge of the reed.

Figure 18.2. With a pencil, locate and draw in the spine and rails from ca. 3mm to 19–20mm above the string. These will serve as guides within which to scrape the channels. Scrape off the bark and yellow underlay between the rails and the spine. Be sure to leave bark in the rails and a narrow peak of yellow underlay for the spine.

Figure 18.3. To avoid getting nicks in the scrape, keep the knife perpendicular to the reed. If the knife is too angled, digging rather than scraping will occur. Use an X crisscross scrape to sand down the resulting nicks. Remember that nicks add resistance. At this point in the scrape the issue is to remove resistance and generate free vibration in the reed.

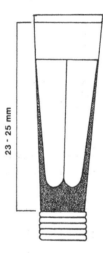

Figure 18.4. Clip the tip. While the final finished product will be ca. 70mm long, allow a margin of error and clip at 71–72mm. I use scissors, but many use a knife and cutting block. Remember that the length of the tube is 47mm and, once clipped, the cane portion should be ca. 23–25mm.

THE SHAPE   "Many results are achieved by varying the shape. A wider shape causes a lower pitch and a larger opening; a narrower shape causes a higher pitch and a smaller opening."[4] In general terms, there are three parts to the shape of a reed: tip, middle, and back (throat). The dimensions of the tip will determine the pitch and response of the low register, the middle will determine that of the middle register, and the throat will determine that of the high register.

Producing a sound is easier with a wide shape. Although this approach tends to be encouraging to the young student, it also tends to generate a lower crow, which places the pitch on the low side, with the upper register suffering the most. In the long run, the player may learn the bad habit of "biting" the pitch up. Although a narrow shape may place the pitch higher and make the upper register more attainable, it may also make playing in the low register no easy task.

REED OPENING   The reed opening is determined by the diameter of the cane, the gouge of the cane, the shape chosen, the quality of the staples used, and the wrap of the reed. The opening of the reed will determine ease of play in the lowest and highest ranges as well as the response. With a reed that has too small of an opening the crow may be high to tight with a limited rattle of one note. This will in turn imply that the general pitch may be high and the response in the low register may be minimized. A reed with too large an opening may have a fuller and possibly flatter pitched rattle in the crow, which will afford an easier low register but with a difficult high range.

In general terms, a middle-of-the-road approach to choice of cane diameter (10–10.5mm) with a moderate shape (7mm across the top) will generate a modest reed opening.

THE GOUGE   With a good gouge and diameter of cane comes a more comfortable reed opening. As a result, pitch, response, and dynamics will be more easily realized and controlled. Equalizing the contour of the cane on both sides of its center (so that the cane is balanced and consequently vibrates evenly) is the desired goal. If symmetry is not attained, the opening of the reed will be off center; one blade will be weaker and have less arc than the other. This lack of balance will affect the stability, register, and tone control. The closure of the reed also will not be as it should: it will not close from the sides to the center but rather will close flat from top to bottom.

The diameter of the tube from which the piece of cane was cut is also an important factor. A large diameter creates a small reed opening. A small reed opening will generate a small dynamic range, a tight and difficult low register (but a comfortable high range), and a sharper pitch level. A small diameter will create a large reed opening. A large opening will generate a greater dynamic range (but with difficulty playing softly), a responsive low range (but a difficult high range), and a flatter pitch level.

THE WRAP   Possibly the most common flaw in commercial reeds is the wrap. A miswrapped reed can completely misdirect your understanding of the crow. A correct wrap has the overlap of the blades in opposition to the direction of the tie. This creates a tension between the direction of the cane's displacement and the pull of the string, which helps to maintain the opening of the reed for a truer crow. To determine whether your reed is wrapped correctly, look at the sides of the reed blades. The top blade should predominate. Were the wrap displaced so that the bottom blade was the more prevalent, the reed would constantly collapse and the crow would constantly shift. Sometimes there is nothing to be done about this. Although the reed may seem good in all other respects, such a reed tends to be deceptive in its tuning: it may start out comfortably, but the pitch soon travels upward. It is sometimes possible to "slip" the reed so the top blade predominates. This can be accomplished by placing the plaque all the way down between the blades and shifting the blades across the plaque with the fingers. Be aware, however, that this venture is not often successful. Some wraps create a reed opening that is too large. This can sometimes be offset by gently massaging the back of the reed or by exaggerating the displacement of the blades.

TOOLS

The most important tool you will use will prove to be your knife. Since there are many kinds of knives with varying weight, balance, and blade styles, it will be left to the reed worker to determine which works best. It is recommended to have at least two knives: one for scraping the hard bark and clipping the tip, another for the refined, detailed work needed for finishing. Your knife sharpener will be your next most valued tool. Maintaining a sharp knife is the first reed-making lesson learned and the last remembered. Many a reed has been mutilated by those wielding a deft hand but a dull knife. Several of the items listed here are less specialized and can be found at hardware stores, whereas others will need to be obtained from a dealer. The reed worker interested only in adjusting premade reeds will need only the items listed.

Knife (2)

Mandrel

Cutting block

Razor blades

Pliers

Sharpening stone

Plaque

Scissors

File

Plumber's tape

Millimeter ruler

If the reeds you or your students are using do not seem to be of the "Goddess" variety, it would be advisable to get acquainted with the reed manuals that are available. While it has been written that "no book is ever a good substitute for a good teacher,"[5] much information can be gleaned from books (see the section "Reference Books" in chapter 19).

Troubleshooting Chart

If the Reed Crows above C:

1. There may be too much wood in the tip.	With a knife and plaque, take cane from the tip but maintain a contoured scrape in the tip.
2. The heart may be too heavy.	With a knife and plaque, dust the heart area. Taper the heart into the tip.
3. There are too many ridges or nicks, creating walls of resistance.	With a knife and plaque, scrape lightly, making Xs in a crisscross manner over the ridges.
4. The back channels may be too heavy.	Scrape cane and bark (if any) out behind the heart but be sure to leave ribs with bark.
5. The scrape style used may have too straight a heart, with too much delineation between heart and tip.	With a knife and plaque, add a V scrape and taper the heart into the tip.
6. The opening of the reed may be too closed.	Using a mandrel and pliers, squeeze the tube open near the top of the wrap. An opening that is too closed looks much like an eye that is closed at the corners.

If the Reed Crows below C:

1. The reed may be too long.

   With a razor blade or knife and a cutting block, try clipping the tip (to 69.5–70mm) at an angle, making one blade slightly longer than the other. To do this, hold the reed at a forty-five-degree angle to the cutting block and clip.

2. The opening of the reed may be too big.

   Using a mandrel and pliers, squeeze the tube closed near the top of the wrap. The opening should look like an eye, with the flatter reed blade serving as the bottom and the more arced reed blade as the top of the reed. The sides of the tip opening should meet.

3. The cane may be too broad.

   File or trim the sides of the reed with a razor so the top measures no more than 7mm across. It is helpful to clip the corners of the tip at a slight angle. This will raise the pitch of notes that commonly sag.

4. The scrape of the reed tip may be unbalanced.

   With a knife and plaque, thin the sides of the tip so that center of the tip is fuller than the sides. Clip the tip a hairbreadth.

5. The scrape of the reed may be unbalanced.

   With a knife and plaque, taper the rails and ribs and build a heart. This will help close the opening and provide more stability if the reed is wild.

6. There may be too much wood already removed.

   Clip the tip at an angle or nick a small V in the center of the tip of the bottom blade.

The size of the V is dictated by the size of the opening and the hardness of the cane. If the opening is moderate to small or the cane is soft and grainy, the size of the V will be moderate to small (less than 2mm), whereas if the opening of the reed is large and the cane is hard, the size of the V will need to be greater. The size of the V then will assist in closing the opening of the reed so it is more manageable for play. If a large V is made on a small opening, it should assist in making the opening smaller.

The plaque should be between the reed blades to support the reed while scraping. The plaque need go in only far enough that the reed blades grip it. If the V needs to be adjusted, draw a line from that center point to the sides of the reed to build an upside-down V. The scrape motion with the knife will begin from that line at that angle. Scrape up to the edge of the reed, making the sides and very edge of the reed the thinnest parts of the reed tip. Try to avoid scraping the center of the top in equal proportions. As the knife scrapes closer to the tip, straighten the angle of the scrape so the knife is scraping with the grain. Scraping with the grain will help to avoid losing the corners of the reed tip.

At this point the next question to address is how far to scrape. The answer will be based on the appearance of the reed tip as seen through the plaque and on the condition of the crow. With the plaque placed between the blades of the reed, the color of the plaque should be evident along the sides and edge of the reed tip if the reed is nearly finished. If the color of the plaque is not readily visible, more scraping in the tip will be needed. To confirm this, crow the reed. An unfinished reed tip will not crow on time or may not crow at all. When the reed is closer to being finished, the crow will occur more easily and at or close to a C. In addition, the color of the plaque should be visible along the sides of the tip and the very edge of the tip.

Use Figure 18.5 and the troubleshooting chart (on pp. 304–5) to determine what the reed should look like. Use the crow as a guide to point to what areas need to be scraped and how much scraping needs to take place. Should there be further questions, it is always a good idea to read other references and to seek out independent guidance.

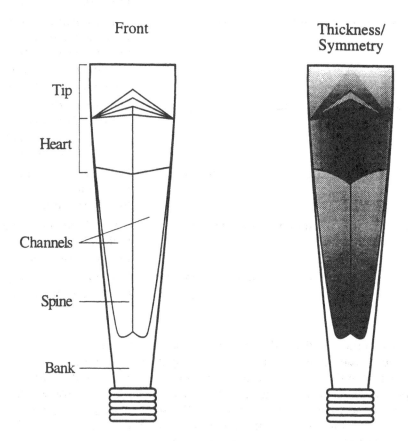

Figure 18.5. Areas of the Reed

Oboe Reed, Cane, and Tool Suppliers

Allan Double Reeds
P.O. Box 933
Hadlock, WA 98339

Allegro Woodwind Supplies
1954 Devil's Backbone Rd.
Cincinnati, OH 45238

Andre Andraud
313 Cochlin St.
Traverse City, MI 49684

Peter Angelo
P.O. Box 11476
Bradenton, FL 34282

Arundo Research Company
18082 N.W. Dixie Mountain Road
Hillsboro, OR 97124

Berdon
P.O. Box 483-D
Hobart, WA 98205

Bhosys, Inc.
123-09 109th Avenue
South Ozone Park, NY 11420

Bloom Reeds
4220 Highland Road
Minnetonka, MN 55345

John Caputo
1522-24 1st Avenue
New York, NY 10021

Charles Double Reed Supply Co.
30 Pleasant St, P.O. Box 2610
Conway, NH 03818

Cheville Double Reed Products
P.O. Box 210413
Bedford, TX 76095

Christlieb Products
3311 Scadlock Lane
Sherman Oaks, CA 91403

Mark Chudnow
P.O. Box 3886
Napa, CA 94558

Paul Covey
424 East 30th St.
Baltimore, MD 21218

Stuart Dunkel
51 Stuart Street
Watertown, MA 02172

Emerald Reeds
P.O. Box 1422
Port Townsend, WA 98368

English Horn Products
2832 Lawtherwood Place
Dallas, TX 75214

European Woodwind Instruments, Inc.
240 W. 98th St., 4G
New York, NY 10025

Forrest's
1849 University Avenue
Berkeley, CA 94703

Fox Products Corporation
P.O. Box 347
South Whitley, IN 46787

Ivan Gates/Harmony Oboe Supplies
1137 Ibex Square
Ventura, CA 93003

R.D. Gilbert
N. La Cienega Blvd.
P.O. Box 691278
Los Angeles, CA 90069

Graham Oboe Reeds
P.O. Box 6
Plymouth, NH 06354

John Hayden
P.O. Box 8126
New London, CT 06320

Hoboken Oboe Shop
Box 720034
Atlanta, GA 30324

Jeanné Double Reed Products
P.O. Box 32758
Minneapolis, MN 55432

Jones Double Reed Products
Box 3888
Spokane, WA 99220

Paul Laubin
3655 Crompound Rd.
Peekskill, NY 10566

Lesher Reed Company
P. O. Box 163
Randolph, NY 14772

Patricia Marsh
3950 Springlake Court
Clemmons, NC 27012

Master Oboe Reed
W. 615 Cotta
Spokane, WA 99204

Bruce McCall
Mundy Woodwinds
305 Riverside Drive
New York, NY 10025

McFarland Reed Shop
P.O. Box 13505
Atlanta, GA 30324

Midwest Musical Imports
2021 E. Hennepin Ave., Suite 374
Minneapolis, MN 55413

Roger Miller
P.O. Box 20054
Cincinnati, OH 45220

Edmund Nielsen
63 Park Bldg.
Villa Park, IL 60181

Don Plesnicar
P.O. Box 4880
Albuquerque, NM 87196

Fox Products Corporation
P.O. Box 347
South Whitley, IN 46787

Prestini Double Reeds
P.O.Box 2296
2301 Patagonia Highway
Nogales, AR 85621

Claude Reynolds Oboe Shoppe
P.O. Box 180005
Dallas, TX 75218

Bill Roscoe Double Reeds
P.O. Box 500
Erwin, TN 37650

Linda Roush
423 Windsor Terrace
Libertyville, IL 60048

SATCO
1670 Old Country Road, Suite 108
Plainview, NY 11803

Sorton Reeds & Supplies
5849 Lafayette Road
Granville, OH 43023

Jack Spratt Woodwind Shop
11 Park Avenue
P.O. Box 277
Old Greenwich, CT 06870

Taylor & Associates
111 W. 35th Avenue
Eugene, OR 97405

Temple Oboe Reeds
3526 Washburn Avenue North
Minneapolis, MN 55412

The Proboe Shop
1384 Filbert Avenue
Chico, CA 95926

The Reed Shop
596 Colfax
Elmhurst, IL 60126

The Oboe Shop
2405 Ardee Lane
So. San Fransisco, CA 94080

The Woodwind & Brasswind
19880 State Line Road
South Bend, IN 46637

The Woodwind Clinic
P.O. Box 1527
Memphis, TN 38101

Gail Warnaar Double Reed Shop
P.O. Box 150
Barnet, VT 05821

Frederic Weiner
92-16 37th Avenue
Jackson Heights, NY 11372

WDM Reed Supplies
P.O. Box 1648
Westford, MA 01886

Notes

1. David Weber and Ferald Capps, *The Reed Maker's Manual*, Phoenix, AZ, 1989, 70.
2. Robert Sprenkle and David Ledet, *The Art of Oboe Playing* (Evanston, IL: Summy-Birchard, 1961), 41.
3. Jay Light, *The Oboe Reed Book: A Straight-Talking Guide to Making and Understanding Oboe Reeds* (Des Moines, IA: Drake University Press, 1983), 65.
4. Sprenkle and Ledet, *The Art of Oboe Playing*, 63.
5. Peter Hedrick and Elizabeth Hedrick, *Oboe Reed Making: A Modern Method* (Oneonta, NY: Swift-Dorr, 1972), 5.

CHAPTER 19

Selected Repertoire
and Materials

The following are representative works for the intermediate oboist. For band programs, it may be more appropriate to purchase collections, since they are most cost efficient and offer a broad variety of works at varying levels. A list of collections as well as a broader listing of repertoire is provided in section "Selected Oboe Repertoire" in chapter 21.

Solo Repertoire

T. ALBINONI. *Concerti* Op. 7, Nos. 3, 6, 9, 12, and Op. 9, Nos. 2, 5, 8, 11. Musica Rara.
These works are suitable for the intermediate player. The ranges are safely limited within two octaves, and the technical and rhythmical demands are accessible. Dynamics, articulations, and ornamentation may need to be added to suit the development of the individual. Although the rhythms are basic, they are often fairly extended through melodic sequences. Phrases are often long and may need breaths. The piano reductions are generally quite manageable.

W. BARLOW. *The Winter's Passed.* Eastman Press.
This work, also available for oboe and strings, is a sweet piece that can be used to focus on dynamics and phrasing. Rhythm and range are quite manageable except for the use of hemiola suspensions over the barline at the $\frac{3}{4}$ section

D. CIMAROSA, ARR. BENJAMIN. *Concerto in C.* Boosey & Hawkes
This freely arranged four-movement (slow, fast, slow, fast) Classical work is marked by Baroque dance movements, character, and form. The opening movement has two short cadenzas. Range travels from c¹ to e♭³. The second movement, in binary form, is in the parallel major key and is reminiscent of the *opera buffa* style. This movement offers some technical and rhythmic concerns. The third movement, in the relative minor key, is in the vocal aria style. The fourth movement, in ternary form, is again in the parallel major key. Articulation may determine the speed of this dance movement. The piano reduction is very manageable.

G. DONIZETTI. *Sonata.* Peters.
The consolidated range and manageable phrase lengths make this two-movement work in operatic style most accessible. Articulations and dynamics are not marked and will need to be added. Also, mordents, trills, and appoggiaturas will need to be carefully planned for proper execution. The Allegro movement is in a light-hearted $\frac{6}{8}$ with suspensions and ties that may create rhythmic challenges.

R. FAITH. *Seven Miniatures.* Belwin.
These little pieces are delightful in every respect. Each movement is a jewel. The range is contained within two octaves with ample breathing opportunities. It is a good work to build the concepts of the "double breath" while maintaining the integrity of the phrase. Some compound meters are used, but the rhythms are quite unadorned.

G. Grovlez. *Sarabande and Allegro*. Leduc.
Subdivision will be a necessity in this charming work. The interchanges of duple and triple rhythms and the expansive range (b♭ to f³) make this a challenging work. The fast articulated passages, syncopation, and ties are plentiful but are within the means of the intermediate player.

G. F. Handel. *Concerto No. 1 in B-flat*. Boosey & Hawkes.
This is a good solid work to introduce the form of the concerto. Although some of the phrases are extended, the range is comfortable and the rhythms are straightforward. Breathing plans may need to be mapped out carefully using the double breath. This is an excellent piece for introducing the concepts of ornamentation, subdivision, and melodic sequences. Since not many articulations and dynamics are provided by the composer or editor, it may be advisable to add them. The addition of ornaments may well push these Baroque works to a higher level of difficulty. Any added ornaments should suit the level of the player.

G. Jacobs. *Ten Little Pieces*. Oxford University Press.
This set of ten pieces focuses on many aspects of playing that the intermediate player might find challenging: triplet rhythms in a duple meter, extended patterns of eighth-and-two-sixteenths, varying articulation styles, shadings of dynamics, half-hole and alternate F fingerings and use of the left E♭ key, duple and triple combinations, and so on. These pieces may prove to be very successful teaching tools.

A. Klughardt. *Concertino*. Universal.
A concertino in the German Romantic tradition. The long sustained lines will require good breathing techniques. The two-octave range and limited technical demands make this a good piece for focusing on air control and dynamics. The two quasi-recitative sections and the cadenza will prove useful for introducing a freedom of play as well as personal expression. The written preface explains the markings indicating left E♭ and forked-F fingerings.

J. Loeillet. *Sonata in C*. Chester.
While the heavy editing by E. Rothwell is not clearly marked, it is generally acceptable for performance. Breathing opportunities, range, and the moderate variety of articulation and ornamentation make this a suitable work for the intermediate player. All four movements of this standard work are beautiful and offer a great deal for the study of the French Baroque style.

A. Marcello. *Concerto in D Minor*. Musica Rara.
Of the many editions of this work, this is perhaps the most informative and accurate. Correctly, Alessandro rather than Benedetto Marcello is given credit for this work, which J. S. Bach admired. Bach's ornaments are provided as well as Marcello's original. While Bach's ornaments are perhaps more appropriate for the keyboard than the oboe, the ideas offered can be useful. This frequently recorded concerto deserves the attention afforded it.

C. Nielsen. *Two Fantasy Pieces Op. 2*. Kalmus.
The Romanza is a lovely programmatic work rich in melody and long line, whereas the Humoresque is a fast paced jaunt. The Romanza, marked con duolo (with sadness), often crosses over the half-hole break and explores a full range of dynamics. The Humoresque makes use of greater technical and rhythmic concerns. Graces and double-dotted rhythms are the most challenging elements of this portrayal of a drunken romp.

L. OSTRANSKY. *Aria and Dance.* Rubank.
While breathing, range, articulation, and tempo are certainly manageable, the compound rhythms are most challenging. Ostransky employs what is perhaps the most difficult rhythm to conquer: extended quarter-note triplets. While the changing meters in the Dance may be of moderate concern, they do create an interesting and enjoyable effect.

J. C. PEPUSCH. *Sonata in E-flat.* Nova Music.
The editorial markings of H. Voxman are clearly identified, and the preface is informative. This is a four-movement Baroque formula work. The title key of E-flat may surprise some, as the key signature only includes two flats, as was the Baroque custom. The third movement, in ¾, is in the parallel minor key, with five flats as well as the accidentals C♭ and F♭. The second and possibly the fourth movement will need articulations added, while the third will require some moderate degree of ornamentation.

A. REICHA. *Air.* McGinnis & Marx.
While this is a lovely work, some may find this edition difficult to read. The execution of graces, turns, and ornaments are not explained or clearly notated to guide the performer. Range, breathing, rhythm, and tempo are all quite manageable. Although the oboe part is not altogether difficult, the piano part will require some attention.

G. SAMMARTINI. *Sonata in G.* Oxford University Press.
While the heavy editing by E. Rothwell is not clearly marked, the general ideas are good. All four movements of this standard work are beautiful and offer a great deal for the study of the Italian Baroque style. While it may be necessary to adjust the editor's use of dynamics and ornaments, the breathing opportunities, range, and the moderate variety of articulation make this a suitable work for the intermediate player. Owing to the extended articulated passages and somewhat large leaps, the second and fourth movements are perhaps the most difficult.

C. TESSARINI. *Three Sonatas.* Harmonia.
Tessarini was both an oboist and a flutist, and these exceptionally beautiful works are functional for both instruments. Clearly of the early Baroque style, all movements are based on the same theme but are presented in different meters and tempos with moderate ornamentation. In each sonata the first movement is a slow prelude, the second is a fast dance, the slow third movement is in the relative key, and the final fourth movement is a quick duple dance. The range, breathing, tempo, rhythm, keys, and ornamentation are all well within the capacity of the intermediate player. This "urtext" edition may require the addition of articulations and ornamentation.

S. VERROUST. *Fourth Solo de Concert.* Southern.
As an oboist, Verroust was one of the finest of his day. His Solos de concert surely demonstrate his ability for fanciful contest-style writing. Nevertheless, this piece is certainly within reach of most high school players. The three movements all connect, and the work is not very long. Breathing, subdivision, rhythm, and some technical issues will be difficult but are certainly approachable for the advanced intermediate.

J. C. M. WIDERKEHR. *Duo Concertante.* Musica Rara.
Although this four-movement Classical work is of great length, the breathing, range, key, and technical issues are quite manageable for the intermediate. The greatest concern may well be endurance. Some articulations and dynamics may be needed for general interest, and repeats may need to be pared down.

Chamber Music

The basis for grading the following ensemble works is: elementary = I, II; intermediate = III, IV; advanced = V, VI.

DUETS

J. Brown, ed. *Oboe Duets.* Chester. III–IV
> The two progressive volumes contain twenty-two duets that progress rapidly in length, range, rhythm, meter, and technical issues. Volume 2 is quite a bit more difficult than the first. The prefaces offer biographical information about the various composers.

C. Gordon, and E. London. *Twelve Oboe Duets.* Janus Music. II–IV
> These duets appear easy at first glance because they are short and lie within a narrow range in the limited keys of C and G. However, the range is often too low and the dynamic too soft for all the needed articulation. Perhaps if slurs were added the pieces would be more comfortable for the novice, for whom they are clearly intended. At the elementary level, the dynamics will prove to be a challenge, since not too many can make or understand the difference between mf, mp, and p.

E. McCarty, arr. *Oboe Duets and Trios.* Southern. III–IV
> While the range, length, and dynamics are quite contained, the articulations, meters, and suggested stylistic changes provide a different sort of challenge in duet writing and reading. The preface is wordy but informative regarding the origin of these Baroque English country dances. The seven trios interspersed throughout the book are easier than the duets.

D. Owens, arr. *Twenty-one Duets for Oboes.* Kendor Music. III–IV
> This collection contains mostly arrangements of Baroque works. Consequently the range is rather contained, and rhythms and meters are standard. Some ornaments and trills may need to be worked out. The parts are equally balanced and work well for oboe. Although there are some poor page turns, some lovely music is offered.

A. Stoutamire, and K. Henderson. *Duets for All.* Pro Art. II–IV
> These eighteen duets maintain equal parts within three flats and standard meters. The range is quite contained, as are the rhythms and technical demands. This collection offers a variety of musical styles, articulations, and dynamics. The preface explains how best to use the book.

TRIOS FOR THREE OBOES

J. Brown, ed. *Oboe Trios.* Chester. III–IV
> These seven trios are by such eighteenth-century composer/wind players as Sellner, Vogt, and Aber. They are rich in melody and are equal in all aspects other than range. The oboe I travels from c^1 to e^3. Perhaps the greatest difficulty is endurance, as all parties play with little opportunity for rest throughout these works.

P. M. Dubois. *Lou Cascarelet: Danses provençales.* Leduc. IV
> This set of six dances for three oboes (optional English horn) includes a tambourin ad libitum, which adds color and interest to the work. The parts are quite equal, although the first voice generally carries the primary melody. With the exception of the fourth and fifth movements,

whose range opens up to g#^{3}, the ranges are contained, with the third voice playing the lowest. An ossia part for that upper range is much more manageable, keeping the level of difficulty at IV.

J. J. QUANTZ, ED. D. Lasocki. *Sonata in D* and *Sonatina in D.* Nova. III–IV
Each of these works contains five Baroque dances. While they are equal in all voices, the first voice hangs a bit higher than the other two (to d^3 and e^3). Though ripe for ornamentation and articulation, none have been provided. The editor states in the preface that performance "should obviously be based on Quantz's own principles of articulation and ornamentation," which have been clearly documented by Quantz. In this way the work's level of difficulty will surely rise. They are well worth the effort.

J. SELLNER. *Six Easy Trios for Three Oboes.* McGinnis and Marx. III–IV
While several of these can be found in the Oboe Trios edited by Brown, it is nice to have the complete set from which to draw. These are three-voice fugues that always start in the third voice. Rhythm, meter, and the general range are all quite manageable. The persistent low c^{1}s, c#^{1}s, and b^{1}s in the third part are all piano and offer a true challenge. Number 6 is by far the most difficult, owing to the key (E major), double sharps, extended phrases, endurance, tuning, and constant low range at piano.

QUARTETS FOR FOUR OBOES

G. POWNING. *Quartet for Four English Horns.* III–IV
Although for four English horns, this quartet works well for four oboes. Range is quite comfortable in this fun, jazzy work. Written by an oboist, the quartet is quite suitable in terms of breathing, technical issues, and style.

A. VIVALDI, TRANS. Q. Maganini. *Giga.* Edition Musicus. III
Available only in score form, this short work is easy and fun to put together. The $\frac{12}{8}$ meter may at times prove unwieldy for the novice. The first part reaches to e^3 at one instance but otherwise functions well for a young ensemble.

Standard Methods for Oboe

In choosing a method it is important to find one that is not simply a collection of excerpts and études. A method should be a clear, progressive, and organized approach to instruction. It should provide resources and materials to guide the learner beyond the pages and the practice room. An introduction explaining how to use the method is often useful, because the notes on the page do not necessarily tell the whole story or offer an approach or means to an end. While there is no such thing as a complete method, there are some strong materials out there. How you choose to use them will prove to be the key.

ANDRAUD. *Practical and Progressive Oboe Method.* Southern.
This method is best suited for an advanced beginner to intermediate. It is essentially a compilation of materials from other sources, much of which was borrowed from still other sources that were previously borrowed, and not always accurately. Although there is nothing new in this book, the material is tried and true.

ANDRAUD. *Vade-Mecum of the Oboist.* Southern.

This method book comprises two parts. The first is essentially scales and arpeggios intended primarily as velocity exercises with a number of études. The second part is all orchestral excerpts. These excerpts are overwhelmed with errors and misquotes. Although it is fairly limited as a method, it has nevertheless found its way into the library of nearly every oboist.

BARRET. *Method for Oboe.* Boosey & Hawkes.

This is an excellent book written with a philosophy espousing that if you can play in a musical context you can play in any and all contexts. The book is smartly divided into three segments preceded by a lengthy and poorly translated introduction. The technical and articulation exercises in the opening segment, while not overly interesting or new, are basic to development. The middle segment is rich with melodic exercises that involve all of the previous studies and are complete with a bass line for further musical instruction. The final segment is for the advanced player. Here the forms are expanded, as are the technical demands, harmonic implications, phrase shapings, articulations, and breathing and endurance demands.

EDLEFSEN-WEBER. *Elementary (Intermediate, Advanced) Oboe Student.* Belwin.

Each of these three methods has up to four developmental divisions that can be used for class or individual instruction. They contain much material for teaching rhythm and notes values, a variety of articulation, tempi, and dynamic contrasts. This, in turn, provides ample material for the development of embouchure and breath control and serves well as supplementary material for any specific issues of concern. The books are well organized, progressive, and thorough. The one-page fingering chart is easy to read and is attached to the book. In the elementary book, new fingerings are introduced and notated on each page for easy access and application.

KENNETH GEKELER. *Books I and II.* Belwin.

These include melodic étudelike studies built around specific issues such as articulation. There is less focus on scale development but more on intervals and melodic shape. Although this is a nice change, the melodies not borrowed from Barret are generally ugly, awkward, and uninspired. Much of what is useful can be found with better presentation in other methods. The student is left to look elsewhere for fingering charts and general information of any sort. Book 2 is stated as being the "logical next step to follow any elementary method"—a difficult claim for any intermediate book.

LANGEY-FISCHER. *Tutor for Oboe.* Carl Fischer.

This is considered to be a "complete" method, which is to say that it offers material for the elementary to the advanced student. A fairly brief foreword addresses rhythm, notation, and an introduction to the oboe. It is organized by key difficulty and rhythmic levels. The exercises in each key are structured to cover the easy to the difficult intelligently. These include scale, interval, and technical patterns. While there are some wonderful duets, melodic études, and even orchestral excerpts, supplemental materials for reinforcing concepts are extremely limited. Ornaments, trills, and alternate fingerings are explained, illustrated, and applied throughout the book.

CARL NIEMANN. *Practical Method.* Carl Fischer.

This method is much like the Fischer-Langey Tutor in its concept and structure. Although considered a complete method, it offers a limited base from which to develop. The introduction is fine and informative. Although the melodic études are drawn from a great many standard oboe étude books, they make for good studies. The fingering chart and technical studies are well organized and will prove useful.

WILLIAM HOVEY. *Elementary Book.* Rubank.

SKORNICKA AND KOEHNER. *Intermediate.* Rubank.

GOWER AND VOXMAN. *Advanced Book.* Rubank.

These three methods can serve as individual or class guides. However, they are not well organized to suit embouchure development or to overcome technical difficulties in a progressive manner. While no definable format or structure exists within the methods, with some careful planning, they can be useful and effective tools. The fingering charts are not entirely accurate and are usually lost early because they are not attached to the book. The intermediate and advanced books are far more complete and structured than the elementary book.

Reference Books

BAINES, ANTHONY. *Woodwind Instruments and Their History.* New York: Norton, 1957.

BATE, PHILIP. *The Oboe.* London: Benn, 1956.

GOOSSENS, LEON, AND EDWIN ROXBURGH. *The Art of Oboe Playing.* Menuhin Series. New York: Schirmer Books, 1977.

HAYNES, BRUCE. *Music for Oboe, 1650 to 1800.* Berkeley, CA: Fallen Leaf Press, 1994.

HEDRICK, PETER, AND ELIZABETH HEDRICK. *Oboe Reed Making: A Modern Method.* Oneonta, NY: Swift-Dorr, 1972.

HOSEK, MIROSLAV. *Oboen Bibiographie I.* Amsterdam: Heinricksofen, 1975.

JOPPIG, GUNTHER. *The Oboe and the Bassoon.* London: Batsford, 1988.

LARSON, GLEN, AND HARRY BAXTER. *Oboe Reed Techniques.* Los Angeles: Baxter-Northup, 1933.

LEDET, DAVID. *Oboe Reed Styles.* Bloomington: Indiana University Press, 1981.

LIGHT, JAY. *Essays for Oboists.* Des Moines, IA: Alborada, 1994.

———. *The Oboe Reed Book: A Straight-Talking Guide to Making and Understanding Oboe Reeds.* Des Moines, IA: Drake University Press, 1983.

MATHER, BETTY BANG, AND DAVID LASOCKI. *Free Ornamentation in Woodwind Music.* New York: McGinnis & Marx, 1976.

MCFARLAND, PATRICK. *The Oboist's Adjustment Guide* Atlanta: McFarland Double Reed Shop, 1981.

PRODAN, JAMES. *The Third Octave.* Greensboro, NC: Spectrum, 1989.

ROTHWELL, EVELYN. *Oboe Technique.* London: Oxford University Press, 1985.

———. *The Oboist's Companion.* London: Oxford University Press, 1977.

SAWICKI, CARL. *The Oboe Revealed.* Delhi, NY: Sawiki, 1988.

SNODGRASS, VIRGINIA GIFFORD. *Complete Bibliography for the Double Reed Player.* Westport, CT: Greenwood, 1983.

SPRENKLE, ROBERT, AND DAVID LEDET. *The Art of Oboe Playing.* Evanston, IL: Summy-Birchard, 1961.

TIEDE, CLAYTON. *Practical Band Instrument Repair Manual.* Dubuque, IA: Brown, 1962.

University of Iowa. *Music Source Book: Wind and Percussion Materials.* Iowa City, IA: University of Iowa Press, 1994.

VOXMAN, HIMIE, AND LYLE MERRIMAN. *Woodwind Music Guide.* 2 vols. Chicago: The Instrumentalist, 1984.

WEBER, DAVID AND FERALD CAPPS. *The Reed Maker's Manual,* 70.

WESTPHAL, FREDERICK. *Guide to Teaching Woodwinds.* Dubuque, IA: Brown, 1985.

CHAPTER 20

Guidelines

Guidelines for Choosing an Instrument and a Player

Today there are quite a number of brands of oboes suitable for all levels of players. Consequently, choosing an instrument is often confusing. Whether you are a high school band director or a parent, having guidelines to follow should help. First, it will be important to determine whether the child has what it takes to be an oboist.

CHOOSING TO START AN OBOIST

When thinking about starting a child on the oboe, it is important to recognize the child's demeanor, persistence, and physical stature. The young oboist's demeanor must be that of a patient problem solver. This is because the oboist, unlike the flutist or trumpeter, encounters daily changes in sound quality and production due to the reeds' reactions to changes in weather, the way they are soaked and cared for, and the often poor quality of student instruments. Although band directors are usually good about sending oboes out to repair shops regularly, the shop technicians do not necessarily know enough about maintaining oboes. Wooden oboes tend to be the instruments that suffer the most because of cracking, constriction and contraction, and age.

Because of the inherent problems of band program oboes and available reeds, the young oboist must show a level of persistence. In the beginning, unlike the flute or trumpet, perseverance and persistence will make getting a sound—let alone getting a beautiful sound—a challenge.

Physical stature is an issue because playing the oboe is a physical activity. Hand size is the first outward point of concern. Although the hands do not need to be large, the pinkies need to be able to reach the lowest keys. Lip formation is also an issue. If the top lip is not able to roll over the top teeth at first, it may happen with time as the lip stretches. A cleft palate, however, is sure to make correct embouchure formation difficult if not impossible. Many parents become concerned when braces are introduced. This is not an issue. In fact, once the braces are removed the embouchure should be vastly improved. The final issue is lung capacity. Again, unlike the trumpet or flute, the oboe functions on air pressure, not volume of air. If the breathing muscles are not developed enough to support a sufficient speed of air, playing the oboe should be postponed.

Many band directors discourage students from starting on the oboe, recommending instead that the student begin on the flute, clarinet, or saxophone. Perhaps this is because of the difficulties mentioned above; students may be more likely to continue in instrumental music when their first experiences are with the more easily managed flute, sax, or clarinet. Or it may be the band directors who are discouraged by the oboe. With a good instrument and some acceptable choices in reeds, however, the oboe

319

can be a great joy with which to make music. If the child has the right demeanor, persistence, and physical stature, starting on the oboe should not be a problem.

CHOOSING AN OBOE

Choosing an instrument should be a joint effort between the parents, the band director, the student, and a local oboist or private oboe teacher. Some band programs have oboes available; others have rental programs through a local music store. Clearly both of these are inexpensive methods of obtaining an oboe. Band and rental program instruments tend to be rather poor, however, even though they may come with a repair contract.

As most band programs function on a bidding system, it is important to have some information to support your choices. While it is a good idea to call the local music store for guidance and advice, it is just as important to speak with a local oboist. Generally, an oboist teaching within the community will have a sense of the level of players and instruments within your schools as well as the current prices and repair records through dealers as well as the local music store.

It is important that the band director have the current stock of oboes evaluated. This will help to determine whether any instruments should be removed or involved in a trade. This will also provide a status report for future needs and identify any problems that may have come about with the past purchases. From this juncture, it is necessary to determine how many oboes to buy, what level of oboe to buy (beginner model, intermediate, or full conservatory system), quality of oboe (warranty, crack potential, tuning, longevity/history), and whether it should be wood or plastic.

Wood oboes, while often waving banner names such as Lorée, tend to crack, and they react greatly to weather changes. They require far more maintenance and care and will lose value with every passing year. Over time, the hand-me-down course of action these instruments go through ultimately destroys them. Consequently, a plastic instrument, which will always be more durable, will prove to be the most cost efficient in the long run.

Many authorities recommend plastic oboes for school systems. Fox oboes have a better warranty and resale value than do other plastic oboes; they use a professional bore on nearly all models, a more porous plastic (which allows for better tone and projection), and a more complete key system. They are less finicky to make reeds for and have a better-tuned scale than most professional full-conservatory wood model oboes.

If the student is more advanced and is moving on to a better instrument, the best advice is to try many of them before buying. Many dealers will send out a number of instruments on trial for a few weeks at a time. Others will require a down payment to hold. Whatever the case, compare as many as you can. Try several of each brand available to you. Be sure to consider each company's track record for cracks, repairs, and warranty. Don't be taken by the shiny quality or color of the wood or the name. Every instrument is individual and should be evaluated with an open mind. Because buying an oboe is most certainly an investment, it is advisable to approach it with some trustworthy information. If you haven't done so already, this is an occasion to "adopt an oboist" within your music community for some guidance.

Giving Your Oboe a Checkup

Oboes go out of adjustment from regular use, as the leather slips under the screws tips become worn or fall away. These slips are used primarily for noise reduction. Many new oboes use Teflon-tipped screws, which require little adjustment or maintenance but do tend to be more percussive and at times bend or squash. Most of the problems incurred on the oboe are fairly simple screw adjustments. The key to adjusting is threefold: (1) identify the problem; (2) identify which keys are primary and which are secondary; and (3) identify which screw will remedy the problem.

1. Definition of principal and secondary keys.
   a. The principal keys are always larger than secondary keys.
   b. The principal keys are those that the fingers press.
   c. The secondary keys are those that are activated by the principal keys.
   d. The principal key creates the action that moves the secondary key.
2. Tightening the adjustment screw will always tighten the secondary key. Loosening the adjustment screw will always loosen the secondary key. The opposite effect happens to the principal key.
3. The oboe has only thirteen adjustment screws. All other screws are set screws, pivot screws, or rod head screws.
4. Adjustment screws.
   #1. When fingering bb^1, the c secondary key should seal
   #2. When fingering a^1, the c secondary key should seal
   #3. When fingering g^1, the bb secondary key should seal
   #4. When fingering $f\#^1$, the g# pad should should not move when the key is added
   #5. When fingering e^1, the f# resonance should seal
   #6. When fingering d^1, the f# resonance should seal
   #7. When fingering d^1, the forked-F resonance should seal
   #8. When fingering c^1, the e key and f# resonace should seal
   #9. When fingering $c\#^1$, the left Eb pad should seal when adding the Eb key
   #10. When fingering b, the $c\#^1$ should seal
   #11. When fingering bb, the b should seal
   #12. This deals with only the height of the c^2 secondary keys for tuning c^2
   #13. This deals with only the height of the half hole for the tuning of $c\#^3$

Key names and screw numbers have been identified in Figure 17.4 (p. 287). Use this illustration when dealing with repair technicians.

Test the seal of each pad in question by dragging a narrow slice of ungummed cigarette paper under the pad. It should grab slightly and equally all around the pad. In general, each pad should have approximately the same grab. Although the test can be done by feel, touch is often not the most critical method. The drag test is much more telling. Remember to turn the screw in small increments when making screw level adjustments. To help remember how far you have gone or, should you need to backtrack, it is advisable to use the "clock method," whereby the position of the screw head corresponds with the positions on a clock. It is also a good idea to play the instrument to confirm your success.

CHECKING FOR CRACKS OR LEAKS

Problems caused by leaks or cracks include the following:

- Decreased resonance or increased stuffiness
- Poor response, especially in the low register
- Faulty intonation or distorted intonation problems
- Distorted reed-making techniques

To check for cracks or leaks in the upper joint, place one finger (or a rubber stopper) on the tenon end of the top joint and close all three primary key holes with your fingers. From the reed well, suck as much air as possible out of the top joint. Suction should occur for up to ten seconds. If the suction holds for less than ten seconds, the instrument is not functioning at peak efficiency. The same procedure can be used on the lower joint. For the lower joint, it is easier to use a rubber stopper or cork to close one end.

Common causes of leakage include the following:

- Decayed or worn pads
- Pads that are not balanced in their placement in the key bed
- New cracks in the wood or old cracks with poor refinishing
- Cracked tone holes that were repaired without tone hole inserts
- A gap between the octave vent and the wood
- Poor screw adjustments
- Worn or missing leather slips from beneath the adjustment screws
- Collapsed or missing Teflon screw tips

Outline of Concepts from the Introductory to the Advanced

ELEMENTARY PRINCIPLES

RANGE

OBOE ASSEMBLY   Beginners should be able to assemble the oboe without causing injury to the bridge joints. They should have a clear understanding of how to hold the oboe when putting it together and taking it apart, as well as how to store it when it is not being played. They should also clearly understand how to handle the reed.

POSTURE   Beginners should have a grasp of hand positions, finger placement, and the posture of the torso for best production of tone.

EMBOUCHURE   While most beginners cannot spell the word, they should be able to establish an embouchure and describe how it is done. Try a three-point embouchure to start: (1) place the reed on the lower lip with the tip of the reed just touching the top lip when the mouth is closed; (2) open the mouth, keeping a round formation by saying "O" to cause the lips to curl naturally; (3) close the opening of the "O" by bringing the lips together. This is a drawstring embouchure.

BREATHING   The concept of the double-action breath (expelling air before taking in air) should be reinforced regularly. This will, in turn, create greater endurance. While beginners may find long tones difficult, they should aim for playing long tones at ten-second intervals for each note. Eventually they should be able to build their lung capacity to play a long tone beyond sixty seconds. In the beginning, however, forty-five seconds may be their best. Dynamics should be limited to *mf–f*.

KEYS   Beginners should be able to manage the B♭ and C major scales two octaves, as well as D, E♭, F, G, and A for one octave, and the chromatic scale for two octaves. While none of these require any alternate fingerings, the chromatic scale requires pivoting from low b♭ to b♮ (if the oboe has a low b♭ key) and from c¹ to c♯¹. Beginners should also be aware of which notes within the two-octave range use half hole, thumb octave key, and side octave key.

ALTERNATE FINGERINGS   At this stage, the forked F and regular F should be introduced and employed with understanding. The low b♭–b♮ and low c¹–c♯¹ pivots should be introduced for the chromatic scale.

DIFFICULT RHYTHMS

INTERMEDIATE PRINCIPLES

RANGE

BREATHING   All of the above elementary concepts should be reinforced and checked throughout their development. At this level, long tones should be easier and freer. Playing a pitch for forty-five to sixty seconds should be more approachable. Intermediates should be able to locate sensible places for breaths and to map out an effective breathing approach for the solos and études they are studying. Dynamics should be more widely explored to include *pp–ff*.

POSTURE   Intermediate students should be encouraged to practice standing. The use of a mirror should be a regular tool. At this stage they should be learning to police themselves on the basics.

ALTERNATE FINGERINGS   These should include the two F fingerings and the left F (if the oboe is so equipped), left E♭, right A♭, the employment of the double A♭/E♭, the C♯ and D trills as well as the A♭ to B♭ trill. As the range expands, the new notes (c³, c♯³, d³, e♭³, and possibly e³ and f³) should be addressed. Students should have a clear understanding of when alternate fingerings are needed and employed.

KEYS Intermediate players should be able to manage two octaves on the major scales of B♭, B, C, D, D♭, E♭, E, and F. The minor scales of B, C, D, E, and F should also be manageable at two octaves.

OTHER The following concepts should be introduced and used: mixed and compound meters, trills, some moderate ornamentation (graces, appoggiaturas, cadential trills), quintuplets, the double sharp and double flat, intonation compensation techniques, general concepts in distinguishing between good and bad reeds, general ideas about determining the level of pieces (easy to hard), and the execution of several different articulation styles (slurred legato, tongued legato, marcato, staccato, sforzando, accented). Vibrato should be introduced. Intermediate students should also understand some of the more common terms and abbreviations (accellerando, *allegro* versus *adagio, animato* versus *animando, morendo,* etc.) and should be able to decipher the subdivisions of rhythm and meters.

DIFFICULT RHYTHMS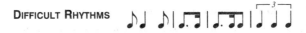

ADVANCED PRINCIPLES

RANGE

BREATHING Advanced players should be able to manage full pieces with little endurance difficulty. The double-action breath should be a natural occurrence rather than a studied practice. Some advanced players may be able to develop the practice of circular breathing. Dynamics should be mastered throughout the range from *pp* to *ff*.

KEYS All major and minor keys should be manageable. The use of half hole, the two (possibly three) octave keys, alternate fingerings, and trill fingerings should be firmly understood and well under control throughout the range up to at least g^3.

RHYTHM Subdivision of compound rhythms and meters should be competently executed.

ARTICULATIONS At least six different styles of articulation should be adopted and competently executed throughout all the ranges. Some players will be able to develop the practice of double and triple tonguing.

OTHER Ornamentation should include more than trills, appoggiaturas, and graces. Advanced players should understand the various Baroque styles of ornamentation, Italian, French, and German in particular. Relating to ornamentation is the construction of cadenzas.

Vibrato is often a point of disagreement. Some believe that it should happen or develop naturally, while others teach it as a learned attribute. Whatever the case, advanced players should be able to use vibrato as a nuance and tool for expression at any tempo and with a variety of shape for the many demands of the music.

Large leaps, especially downward leaps, should be manageable at the advanced level. This comes, in great part, with the development of a flexible embouchure. Large interval leaps require that the jaw, tongue, and lips be flexible enough to allow for the extreme variety in air speed and reed vibration between the registers.

The flexibility of the embouchure allows for finer tuning and desired changes in tone color as well as a greater field of dynamics.

The finishing of reeds allows for all of the above to occur freely. Learning to identify the problems in each reed and to correct these problems should be within the grasp of the advanced player.

CHAPTER 21

Additional Information

Selected Oboe Repertoire

The basis for grading the solo literature is Elementary = I, II; Intermediate = III, IV; Advanced = V, VI.

ELEMENTARY

Benson, Warren	Evening Piece	Boosey and Hawkes	I
	Classical Album	Boosey and Hawkes	I, II
Labate, Bruno	Miniature Concert Repertoire	Fischer	II, III
	Oboist's Repertoire Album	Fischer	II, III
	The Labate Oboe Repertoire	Witmark	II, III
Moyse, Louis	Forty Little Pieces in Progressive Order for Beginner Flutists	G. Schirmer	II, III
Murray, Dom Gregory	Oboe Album	Schott	II, III
	Oboe Solos	Belwin Mills	III
Telemann, G. P.	Heldenmusik	Peters	II, III

INTERMEDIATE

Albinoni, T.	C Major Concerto, Op. 5, No. 5	Musica Rara	IV
	D Minor Concerto, Op. 9, No. 2	International	IV
Bach, J. C. F.	Andante (arr. Johnson)	Belwin	III
Bach, J. S.	15 Grand Solos de Concert	Andraud (complete)	IV
	Famous Arias		IV
	Siciliano		IV
	Arioso		IV
Bakaleinikoff, V.	Pastorale	Belwin	III
Barlow, Wayne	The Winter's Past	Eastman School of Music	III
Bartók, B.	3 Folk Songs (arr. Szeszler)	Boosey and Hawkes, EMB	III, IV
Bertain, J.	Serenade—15 Grand Solos de Concert	Andraud	IV
Bitsch, M.	Romanza	Leduc	IV
Bleuzet, H.	Les Classiques du Hautbois	Leduc	III, IV
Boisdeffre, R.	Village Scenes	Andraud	IV
Busser, Henri	Eclog—15 Grand Solos de Concert	Andraud	IV
	Piece in B♭	Leduc	IV, V
Caine, Evelyn	Andante	Mills	III

Cimarosa, D.	Concerto (arr. Benjamin)	Boosey and Hawkes	IV, V
	Contemporary French Recital Pieces	International	IV, V
Corelli, A.	Air and Dance	Musicus	IV, V
	Concerto (arr. Barbirolli)	Oxford	IV
Demase, Jean-Michel	Rigaudon	Lemoine	IV, V
Dunhill, Thomas	Three Short Pieces	Boosey and Hawkes	IV, V
Fiocco, J. H.	Arioso (arr. Bent and O'Neill)	Schott	IV, V
Fischer, Johann	Four Suites	Hortus Musicus-McGinnis and Marx	IV
	Suite in G	Schott	IV
Francaix, J.	Flower Clock	EMT	IV, V
Franck, C.	Piece V	Leduc	III, IV
Geminiani, Francesco	Sonata in E Minor	Hortus Musicus	IV, V
Gibilaro, A.	Four Sicilian Miniatures (ed. Rothwell)	Mills	IV, V
Godard, Benjamin	Scenes Ecossaises	Hamelle	IV
Graun, B.	Concerto in C Minor	Sikorski	IV
Grovlez, G.	Sarabande et Allegro	Leduc	IV, V
Handel, G. F.	Concerto No. 1 in B♭	Boosey and Hawkes	III, IV
Hanson, Howard	Pastorale	Fischer	IV
Head, M.	Elegaic Dance	Boosey and Hawkes	III
	Gavotte	Boosey and Hawkes	III
	Presto	Boosey and Hawkes	III
	Siciliana	Emerson	IV
Holst, G.	A Fugal Concerto for Flute and Oboe	Novello	IV, V
Jongen, L.	Humoresque	Leduc	III, IV
Labate, Bruno	Concertino	Jack Spratt	IV
	Pastorale	Fischer	III
	Tarantella	Fischer	IV
	Villanella	Fischer	IV
Locatelli, P.	Aria	Edition Amsco	IV
Neilsen, C.	Romance and Humoresque—15 Grand Solos de Concert	Andraud	IV, V
Pascal, Claude	Piece	Durand	IV
Pergolesi, G.	Concerto (arr. Barbirolli)	Oxford	IV
Pierne, G.	Piece in G Minor	Cundy Bettoney	III
Purcell, H.	The Princess of Persia	Boston Music	III, IV
	Two Pieces	Rudall, Carte	III
Rachmaninoff, Serge	Vocalise Op. 34, No. 14	Edition Amsco	III
Ratez, Emil	Five Pieces for Oboe	Leduc	IV, V
Reger, Max	Romance in G	Edition Breitkopf	III
Reutter, H.	Pastorale de Noel	Leduc	III
Robbins, G.	Regates	Leduc	IV, V

Sibelius, J.	The Swan of Tuonela	Baron—English Horn and Piano	IV
Sinigaglia	12 Variations on a Theme of Schubert	Breitkopf	IV
Tcherepnine	4 Pieces for Oboe	Boosey and Hawkes	III
Telemann	Sonata in G Minor	Breitkopf	IV, V
	Sonata in A Minor	Breitkopf	IV, V
Valentine, Robert	Sonata in F Major No. 1	Schott	IV, V
Vivaldi, A.	Concerto in C Major for two oboes	Boosey and Hawkes	IV
Voormolen, A.	Pastorale	McGinnis and Marx	IV
Weinberger, Jaromir	Sonatine	Fischer	III
Whitcomb, R.	Sonata in One Movement	Interlochen Press	IV

ADVANCED

Albinoni, T.	Sonata in A Minor	Hermann Moeck-Celle	IV
	Concerto Op. 7, No. 3 in B♭ Major	Boosey and Hawkes	V, VI
	Concerto Op. 7, No. 6 in D Major	Boosey and Hawkes	V, VI
	Concerto Op. 9 in D Minor	International	V, VI
Alwyn, William	Concerto for Oboe, Strings, and Harp	Mills	VI
Andriessen, Hendrick	Ballade	Donemus, Amsterdam-Peters	V
Arnold, Malcolm	Fantasy	Faber	V, VI
	Sonatina	Mills, Faber	V, VI
Babell, J.	Sonata in C Minor	Universal	IV,V
Bach, C. P. E.	Concerto No. 1 in B♭ Major	Peters	VI
	Sonata in G Minor	McGinnis and Marx	VI
Bach, J. C.	Concerto in F Major	Schott	VI
Bach, J. S.	Andante—15 Grand Solos de Concert	Andraud	V
	Concerto in C Minor for Oboe, Violin, and Piano	Peters	VI
	Menuet—15 Grands Solos de Concert	Andraud	V
	Rondo—15 Grands Solos de Concert	Andraud	V
	Two Sonatas for Oboe and Piano in G Minor	Peters	V, VI
	Three Small Pieces (arr. Gillet)	Andraud	V
Bassi, J.	Nocturne	Rubank	V
Beck, Conrad	Sonatine	Schott	VI
Bellini, V.	Concerto		V
Benda, F.	Sonata in F Major	Edition Musicus	V
Benjamin, Arthur	Divertimento on Themes of Gluck	Boosey and Hawkes	VI
Bennett, R. R.	Concerto	Universal	IV
Bentzon, Niels Viggo	Etude Rhapsodique for English Horn and Piano	Tenney	VI
	Two Pieces for Oboe	Tenney	V

Berger, A.	Sonata da Camera	Broude Bros.	V
Berkeley, L.	Sonatine	Chester	VI
Besozzi, C.	Sonata in G Major	Chester	IV
Boni, G.	Sonata in G Major	Chester	V
Bononcini, G.	Divertimento da Camera	Hermann Moeck	V
Borris, Siegfried	Sonata No. 1 Op. 48	Sirius, Berlin–Tenney	V
Bowen, York	Sonata Op. 85—Music for Oboe Series	McGinnis and Marx	VI
Bozza, E.	Fantaisie Pastorale	Leduc	V, VI
	Suite Monodique	Leduc	VI
Breville, P. de	Sonatine	Rouart, Lerolle	VI
Britten, Benjamin	Six Metamorphoses after Ovid	Boosey and Hawkes	IV, V
	Two Insect Pieces	Faber	V
	Temporal Variations	Faber	V
Bruns, Victor	Sonata No. 25	Hofmeister–Tenney	V
Buchal, F.	Sonata for English Horn in E♭ Major	Edition Breitkopf	V
Busser, Henri	Asturias	Andraud	V
Castelnuovo-Tedesco, M.	Concerto da Camera	Mills	VI
Chedeville, N.	Sixieme Sonate	Siecle Musical, Geneva	VI
Cooke, A.	Sonata	Novello	V
Corelli, A.	La Follia Op. 5, No. 12	McGinnis and Marx	V
Corigliano, J.	Cincerto	G. Schirmer	VI
Couperin, F.	Concerto VI in B♭ Major	Schott, Musica Rara	V
Daelli, G.	Fantasie on Themes of *Rigoletto*	Universal	VI
Dallier, T.	Fantaisie and Caprice—15 Grands Solos de Concert	Andraud	V
Devienne, F.	Three Sonatas Op. 71	Musica Rara	V
Diemer, Louis	Two Pieces Op. 35	Durand	V
Dorati, A.	Five Pieces	Boosey and Hawkes	V
Dutilleux, Henri	Sonata	Leduc	VI
Dittersdorf, C.	Concerto in G Major	Breitkopf	V
Eichner, E.	Concerto for Oboe and Strings (arr. Rothwell)	Oxford	V, VI
Evans, Peter	Sonata—Music for Oboe Series	Rothwell	VI
Fasch, J.	Concerto in C Major	Simrock	V
Fiala, Joseph	Concerto No. 1 in D Major	Boosey and Hawkes	VI
Fischer, J.	Concerto in E♭ Major	Schott	V, VI
Fontayne, Lucian	Fantaisie Pastorale for English Horn	Andraud	V
Foret, Felicien	Patres et Rhymes Champetres	Andraud	V
	Sonata in G Major	Baron	VI
Foss, Lukas	Concerto	Southern Music	VI
Girnatis, Walter	Sonata	Sikorski	V

Goosens, E.	Concerto in One Movement	Leone	VI
Graun, B.	Concerto in C Minor	Sikorski	VI
Grovlez, Gabriel	Sarabande and Allegro	Leduc/Andraud	V
Giulhaud, G.	First Concertino—15 Grands Solos de Concert	Andraud	V
	Four Pieces in Two Suites	Costallat	V, VI
Gregson, G.	Sonata	Emerson	V
Handel, G. F.	Concerto No. 2 in B♭ Major	Boosey and Hawkes	V
	Concerto No. 3 in G Minor	Boosey and Hawkes	V
	Three Sonatas and Largo	Andraud	V
	Concerto in E♭ Major	Peters	V, VI
	Sonatas No. 1 and No. 2	Schott	V
	Sonata in B♭ Major	Schott	V
Haydn, J.	Concerto	Breitkopf/Peters	V, VI
Hindemith, Paul	Sonata for English Horn and Piano	Schott	V
	Sonata for Oboe and Piano	Associated	V
Hoddinott, A.	Bagatelles for Oboe and Harp	Oxford	V
Hollingsworth, Stanley	Sonata Op. 2	G. Schirmer	V
Horovitz, Joseph	Sonatina Op. 3	Mills	V
Howells, A.	Sonata	Oxford	V
Hummel, J. N.	Adagio and Theme with Variations	Eulenburg	V, VI
Ibert, Jacques	Escales	Leduc/Andraud	V
	Symphonie Concertante–arr. for oboe and piano	Andraud	VI
d'Indy, Vincent	Fantaisie Op. 31	Durand	VI
Jacob, Grodon	Concerto for Oboe and Strings	Mills	VI
	Concerto No. 2 for Oboe and Orchestra	Mills	VI
	Rhapsody for English Horn and Piano	Mills	V
Jirak, J. B.	Sonata No. 73	Independent	VI
Kalliwoda, J.	Concertina	Musica Rara	VI
	Morceau de Salon Op. 288	Nova	VI
Kirnberger, Johann Phillip	Sonata in B♭ Major	McGinnis and Marx	VI
Klughardt, A.	Concertino	Universal	V
Kramer, Fr. V.	Concerto in F Major	Boosey and Hawkes	VI
Krebs, Johann	Fantasy for Oboe and Organ or Piano	Breitkopf	V, VI
Krenek, E.	Sonatine		V
	Four Pieces	Barenreiter	VI
Krommer, J.	Concerto Op. 52	Musica Rara	V
Lapis, Santo	Three Sonatas	McGinnis and Marx	VI
Latham, William P.	Sonata	Jack Spratt	V
Lebrun, A.	Concerto No. 1	Schott	VI

	Concerto No. 4 in C Minor	Simrock	V, VI
Leclair, J.	Sonata No. 9 in B Minor	McGinnis and Marx	VI
	Concerto in C Minor Op. 7/3	Leuckart	V
Lefebvre, C.	Andante and Allegro—15 Grand Solos de Concert	Andraud	V
Loeillet, J. B.	Sonata No. 6 in E Major and G Major	Lemoine	VI
	Sonata in C Major—Music for Oboe Series	Rothwell, Chester	V
	Sonata in E Minor	Musica Rara	V
Lutoslawski	Epitaph	Chester	VI
Maasz, G. W.	Concertino	Sikorski	V
Majgue, J. M. L.	Pastorale	Andraud	V
Malipiero, R.	Sonata	Zerboni	V
Marais, M.	Les Folies d'Espagne	Barenreiter	VI
Marcello, A.	Concerto in C Minor	Peters	V, VI
Martensen, Otto	Sonata	Wm. Hansen, Copenhagen, Tenney	V
Mihalovici, Marcel	Sonatine	Andraud	VI
Milhaud, Darius	Sonatine	Durand	VI
Milwid, A.	Sinfonia Concertante	McGinnis and Marx	V
Molique, B.	Concertino	McGinnis and Marx	VI
Mozart, W. A.	Concerto in C Major	Boosey and Hawkes	VI
	Concerto in E♭ Major	Schmidt	V, VI
	Concerto in E♭ Major—15 Grand Solos de Concert	Andraud	V, VI
	Quartet—Music for Oboe Series	Rothwell	V, VI
Mueller, Gottfried	Sonata for Solo Oboe	Sikorski	VI
Mueller, Sigfried W.	Sonata in E♭ Major Op. 52	Breitkopf	V, VI
Murgier, Jacques	Concerto	Lemoine	VI
Paladilhe, E.	Solo de Concert—15 Grand Solos de Concert	Andraud	V
Pasculli, A.	Variations on a Theme of Donizetti	Musica Rara	VI
	Variations on a Theme of Verdi	Musica Rara	VI
Pedrollo, Arigo	Concertino	Peters	VI
Pepusch, J. C.	Sonata (rev. Ruyssen)	McGinnis and Marx	VI
Persichetti, V.	Parable	Elkan–Vogel	VI
Philidor, Anne Danican	Sonata in D Minor	Hortus Musicus	VI
Pilss, Karl	Sonata in E Minor	Tenney	V
Pinkham, D.	Variations for Oboe and Organ	Peters	VI
Piston, Walter	Suite	E. C. Schirmer	V
Planel, R.	Prelude and Dance	Leduc–Baron	V
Poser, Hans	Sonata No. 9	Sikorski	V
Poulenc, F.	Sonata	Chester	V, VI
Raasted, N. O.	Sonatine Op. 44	Borups, Copenhagen	V

Raphael, G.	Sonata for Oboe and Harp	Breitkopf	V, VI
Reizenstein, Franz	Three Concert Pieces	Boosey and Hawkes	V, VI
	Sonatine	Boosey and Hawkes	V, VI
Roman, J.	Partita in C Minor (arr. Rosenberg)	Carl Gehrmans, Stockholm	VI
Ropartz, Guy	Lamento	Lerolle, Rouart	V
Rosegen, Champion	Nocturne	Leduc	V
Rousse, C.	Three Pieces	Costallat	V
	1. A Travers les Champs		
	2. Dans le Chemin Creux		
	3. Sur la Grand Route		
Saint Saëns, C.	Sonata	Durand	V, VI
Sammartini, G.	Sonata in G Major—Music for Oboe Series (ed. Rothwell)	Chester	V, VI
Scarlatti, D.	Concerto No. 1 in G Major	Chester	V
Schouwman, Hans	Tweed Sonatine Op. 38	McGinnis and Marx	V
Schroeder, Hermann	Concerto	Muller, Heidelberg, Tenney	V, VI
Schumann, Robert	Three Romances	Schirmer	V, VI
Scott, Cyrill	Concerto for Oboe and Strings	McGinnis and Marx	VI
Shinohara, M.	Obsession	Leduc	VI
Smith, David Stanley	Sonata Op. 43	G. Schirmer	VI
Sowerby, Leo	Ballade for English Horn and Organ	Grey	V, VI
Stamitz, Johann	Concerto	Sikorski	V
Still, William Grant	Incantation and Dance	Fischer	V, VI
Stoelzel, Gott. Hein.	Concerto in D Major	Sikorski	V
Strauss, R.	Concerto	Boosey and Hawkes	VI
Szalowski, Antoni	Sonatine	Amphion	V, VI
Telemann, G. P.	Concerto in C Minor	McGinnis and Marx	V
	Concerto in D Minor	Boosey and Hawkes	V
	Concerto in E Minor	McGinnis and Marx	V
	Concerto in F Minor	Andraud	V
	Six Partitas	Hortus Musica	V, VI
	Sonata in A Minor	Andraud	V
	Sonata in B♭ Major	Sikorski	V
	Sonata in C Minor	Edition Breitkopf	V
	Sonata in E Minor	McGinnis and Marx	V
	Sonata No. 8 in G Minor	Breitkopf	V
	Sonata in G Minor	Leduc	V
Valentine, R.	Sonata in F Major	Schott	V
Vaughan Williams, Ralph	Concerto	Oxford	VI
Vernon, Ashley	Rhapsody for Oboe and Strings	Elkan Vogel	VI
Verroust, S.	Fourth Solo de Concert Op. 77	Andraud	V
	Souvenir of Old Quebec	Andraud	V

Vincent, Thomas	Sonata in D Major (arr. Dawes)	McGinnis and Marx	VI
Vivaldi, A.	Concerto in F Major	Ricordi	V
	Sonata in G Minor	McGinnis and Marx	V
	Sonata in C Minor	McGinnis and Marx	V, VI
Weeks, Gilbert	Pastoral Morning for Oboe and Organ	Ed. Musicus—Oboe and Strings	V
Weinzweig, John	Divertimento II for Oboe, Strings and Percussion (arr. Diamond)	Associated	VI
Wolf-Ferrari, E.	Idillio Concertino	McGinnis and Marx	V, VI

Collections

BAROQUE MUSIC FOR OBOE. ED. P. WESTALL. BOOSEY & HAWKES. III–V

Sammartini: Minuet from Sonata No. 3

Telemann: Largo from Methodical Sonata No. 5

Albinoni: Allegro from Concerto Op. 7, No. 12

Babell: Adagio from Solo No. 2

Loeillet: Vivace from Sonata No. 4

Besozzi: Andante from Solo No. 6

Geminani: Minuet gracieux

Chedeville: Les jardins

CLASSICAL ALBUM. ARR. A. WILLNER. BOOSEY & HAWKES. II–III

Purcell: March

Handel: Siciliana

Handel: Allegro

Corelli: Prelude

Marpurg: Menuet

Haydn: Adagio

Mozart: Menuet

Beethoven: Alla Marcia

Schumann: Romance

CONCERT AND CONTEST COLLECTION. ED. H. VOXMAN. RUBANK. III–IV

Haydn/Hervig: Allegro

Loeillet/Beon: Andante and Allegro

Goedicke: Gavotta Op. 80, No. 1

Haydn: Menuetto and Presto
Pierné: Pièce in G Minor
Schumann: Romance No. 1
Bach: Sinfonia from Cantata 156
Handel: Sonata No. 1 in C Minor
Mozart: Sonatina from Divertimento No. 2
Six other selections

CONTEMPORARY FRENCH RECITAL PIECES.
INTERNATIONAL. III–V
Murgier: Capriccio
Auric: Pavane
Barraud: Romance
Jolivet: Fisherman's Song
Berghmans: Impromptu
Planel: Serenade

EVERYBODY'S FAVORITE OBOE SOLOS ARR. J. ARNOLD.
AMSCO. III–VI
Telemann: Concerto in F Minor
Locatelli: Cantabile
Bach: Gavotte
Goddard: Legende pastorale Op. 138
Cui: Orientale Op. 50
Schumann: Three Romances
Handel: Three Sonatas
Mozart: Sonata after the Quartet, K. 370
Labate: Zephyrs
Thirteen other selections

FIFTEEN GRAND SOLOS DE CONCERT. REV. A. ANDRAUD.
SOUTHERN. IV–VI
Mozart: Concerto in E-flat
Dallier: Fantasie Caprice
Bertain: Serenade
Guilhaud: First Concertino
Busser: Eglog
Paladilhe: Solo de Concert
Nielsen: Romance and Humoresque
Colin: Third Solo de Concert
Lefèbvre: Andante and Allegro
Bach: Six Short Solos

MUSIC FOR OBOE SERIES. ED. E. ROTHWELL.
CHESTER. IV–VI

> Bach: Adagio
>
> Field: Nocturne
>
> Handel: Rondo and Air
>
> Loeillet: Sonata in C Major
>
> Marcello: Largo and Allegretto
>
> Mozart: Oboe Quartet
>
> Sammartini: Sonata in G Major
>
> Bowen: Sonata
>
> Elliott: Three Pieces
>
> Evans: Sonata
>
> Le Flemming: Air and Dance
>
> Nicholas: Melodie and Rhapsody
>
> Scarlatti: Concerto No. 1

OBOIST'S CONCERT ALBUM COMP. A. ANDRAUD.
SOUTHERN. III–V

> Bach: Aria and Siciliano
>
> Colin: Grande fantasie and Les echos
>
> Colin: Solo de Concert Nos. 1, 3, 4, 5, 6, 7
>
> De Boisdefere: Scènes villageoises
>
> De Grandval: Concerto
>
> De Vilbac: A Cyrian Song
>
> Flegier: Celèbre villanelle
>
> Leclair: Aria et musette
>
> Goddard: Scotch Scenes
>
> Handel: Concerto in G Minor
>
> Handel: Sonatas Nos. 1 and 2
>
> Lenom: Musette
>
> Pierné: Pièce in G Minor
>
> Soler: Souvenir de Madrid
>
> Verroust: Fourth Solo de Concert

OBOIST'S REPERTOIRE ALBUM. ED. B. LABATE.
CARL FISCHER. III–V

> Grieg: Solveig's Song
>
> Sitt: Waltz
>
> Reineke: Savoyard
>
> Schumann: Warum?
>
> Bach: Siciliano
>
> Haydn: Andante

Handel: Bourée
Rimski-Korsakov: Song of India
Labate: Musette

OBOE SOLOS 2 VOLS. ED. B. EDLEFSEN.
BELWIN MILLS. II–IV
Foster: Becky's Song
Mascagni: Intermezzo
Erickson: Polka
Borodin: Polovetsian Dance
Erickson: Prelude and Dance
Edlefsen: Spanish Dance, Slow Dance
Tchaikovsky: Swan Lake, Sleeping Beauty Waltz
Edlefsen: Sweet Nightingale
Macdowell: To a Wild Rose
Delibes: Waltz from *Coppelia*
Numerous other selections

OBOE SOLOS. 2 VOLS. ED. J. BROWN. CHESTER. III–VI
Danzi: Larghetto, Arietta, Andantino
Buchner: Orientale
Thurner: Andante in F Minor Op. 56
Poessinger: Menuettto and Trio
Rossini: Musical Moment, Andante Sostenuto
Ferlendis: Adagio from Concerto in F
Cherubini: Polonaise
Eichner: Menuetto from Sonata No. 3
Verroust: Andante Cantabile from 4th Solo de Concert
Widerkehr: Adagio from Duo Sonata
Several other works

SOLOS FOR THE OBOE PLAYER. ED. W. TUSTIN.
G. SCHIRMER. III–VI
Bach: Aria from *St. Matthew Passion*
Loeillet: Andante and Allegro
Handel: Concerto No. 8 in B-flat Major
Wagner: Dreams
Yamada: Karuka-Karuka
Fasch: Largo
Debussy: Mazurka
Schumann: Romance No. 1
Telemann: Sonata in A Minor

Glière: Song from Two Pieces
Bizet: Theme from Symphony in C
Berger: Toadinha
Laurischkus: Two Arabian Dances
Liszt: Two Songs
Rachmaninoff: Vocalise

THE REALLY *EASY OBOE BOOK.* BY R. HINCHLIFFE. FABER. I–III

March of the Ducks

Daydreaming

Holiday Trot

Mellifluous Minuet

Nocturne

Spring Song

Elizabethan Lament

Jovial Jig

Christmas Song

Twelve other short works

FREQUENT AUDITION EXCERPTS

Bartók	Concerto for Orchestra
Beethoven	Symphonies 1–9
Berlioz	*Benvenuto Cellini* Overture, *Symphonie fantastique, Romeo and Juliet* Symphony
Bizet	Symphony in C
Brahms	Symphonies 1–4, "Haydn" Variations, Violin Concerto
Debussy	*La Mer, Images, Iberia, Jeux*
Dukas	*The Sorcerer's Apprentice*
Dvořák	Symphony No. 2, *New World* Symphony (No. 9)
Hindemith	Symphonic Metamorphosis, *Mathis der Mahler* Symphony
Mahler	Symphonies 1, 3, 5
Mendelssohn	Symphonies 3, 4
Moussorgsky	*Pictures at an Exhibition*
Mozart	Symphonies 40, 41
Prokofieff	Symphonies 1, 5, *Romeo and Juliet* Suites, *Peter and the Wolf*
Ravel	*Le Tombeau de Couperin, Daphnis et Chloë,* Piano Concerto, *Ma Mere L'Oye, La valse*
Respighi	*The Birds, Fontani di Roma*
Rimsky-Korsakov	*Scherezade*

Rossini	*La scala di seta, Italian in Algiers*
Schubert	Symphonies 5, 7, 8
Shostakovitch	Symphonies 1, 5
Smetena	*Bartered Bride* Overture
Strauss	*Don Juan, Don Quixote, Til Eulenspiegel*
Stravinsky	*Le Sacre du printemps, Pulcinella* Suite, *Petrouchka, Fire-bird* Suite, Symphony in C, Symphony of Psalms, *Le Rossignol*
Tchaikovsky	Symphonies 4–6
Vaughan Williams	Symphony No. 4
Wagner	*Die Meistersinger* Overture

PART 5

Saxophone

CRAIG WHITTAKER

CHAPTER 22

Introduction

The saxophone was designed and built in the early 1840s by Adolphe Sax, a Belgian instrument maker who is famous for his work with brass and woodwind instruments. The saxophone was conceived as an instrument that would combine a brass, conical-bore body with a woodwind fingering system and single reed mouthpiece. The members of the saxophone family use the same fingerings; their parts are notated in the treble clef.

The normal saxophone range is from (written) b♭ to f³, with some professional models extending to f♯³ and professional model baritones extending down to low a♮. Thus the written ranges for the entire saxophone family are almost identical. Saxophones are transposing instruments, however, and as a group cover a large concert range.

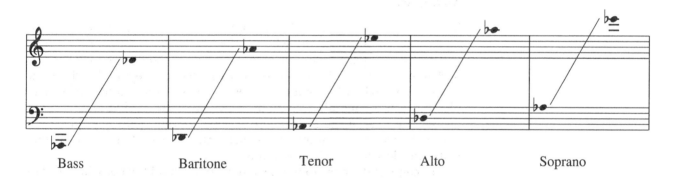

Example 22.1. Range of saxophones in concert pitch

The saxophone neck and body are constructed of brass; the mouthpiece is made of hard rubber, metal, or plastic. Most soprano saxophone models are constructed without a curve, a model known as a "straight" soprano. The alto, tenor, baritone, and bass saxophones are curved. Slight mechanical changes have not affected the basic design of the instrument.

Adolphe Sax manufactured and exported the first saxophones ever built. Patented in 1846, the saxophone gained immediate acceptance by French military bands. European composers began using the saxophone in a variety of solo and chamber music, and saxophone instruction took place in Paris and Geneva before the 1850s. Adolphe Sax eventually became the first professor of saxophone at the Paris Conservatory, teaching more than 150 students from 1857 to 1870.

The Saxophone Family

The most commonly used saxophones are the soprano, alto, tenor, and baritone. These four instruments are found in many band and jazz ensemble scores and on countless jazz recordings. The other members of the saxo-

341

phone family include the sopranino, bass, and contrabass. The latter are seldom used and rarely heard except as color instruments in the orchestra or saxophone ensemble.

Physical considerations such as facial structure should not affect a student's ability to play the saxophone. As long as there is no extreme overbite, any student should be able to begin study on this instrument. The fingerings are the same and the embouchure is essentially the same on all of the saxophones, making it relatively easy to move from one to the other. The main challenge involved with switching instruments is voicing the notes on the color saxophones. A few hours' practice on the unfamiliar instrument will probably correct any voicing problems.

Most teachers start students on the alto or tenor saxophones. Both are a good choice, since they are not very large and can produce a good tone with minimal effort. The best method of determining if the student is suited for a larger instrument is to see if he or she can reach the left hand around the palm keys without lifting the thumb off the thumb rest. A saxophonist who is producing a good tone on the alto or tenor is ready to move to the baritone if desired. Tall students will have an easier time playing the larger saxophones.

Assembly

It is best to sit while putting the instrument together. Begin by placing the mouthpiece on the neck cork with a sliding or twisting motion. A new cork will probably require some cork grease to help the mouthpiece slide on the neck more easily. A light coating of grease is all that is required and should be used only when the mouthpiece will not slide on without force. The placement of the mouthpiece on the neck affects the tuning and, to some degree, the tone of the instrument. A good starting point is to place the mouthpiece so it extends about one inch onto the neck. Small adjustments will then allow for matching a tuning pitch.

To connect the neck to the saxophone body, hold the body in your lap with the left hand around the bell. Avoid holding the instrument around rods or keys, as they bend rather easily. Check to make sure the tightening screw at the top of the body tenon is loosened. Pick up the neck with the right hand and carefully center the bottom of the neck over the top of the body. Gently slide the neck into the top of the body, placing the octave key

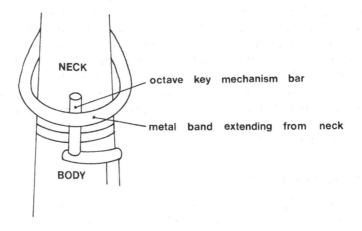

Figure 22.1. Proper neck/body alignment

mechanism rod that extends off the body at a point near the center of the metal band extending from the neck. Once the neck is in place, tighten the screw so the neck does not move from side to side. It may be necessary to place a few drops of key oil on the neck tenon once in a while. This helps the neck slide into the joint more easily. Do not use cork grease for the purpose of lubricating the neck joint. If the neck is too loose, paper may be used in the joint as a temporary solution. An instrument repair technician will be able to expand the neck joint for a tighter fit.

Place the ligature on the mouthpiece, being sure to place it correctly. Most ligatures are designed to hold the reed with the screws on the bottom, but some are designed with screws on top. You will usually find an area on the ligature that is shaped to fit the reed. With the ligature in place, slide the thick end of a soaked reed under the ligature, lining the tip of the reed up to the tip of the mouthpiece. The flat part of the reed should be wet enough to create an airtight seal against the facing of the mouthpiece. Make sure that the reed is centered on the rails of the mouthpiece, then tighten the ligature screws just enough to hold the reed firmly in place. The mouthpiece cap may be used to protect the reed and keep it moist when the instrument is not going to be played for a few minutes.

Care and Maintenance

The saxophone requires little care to keep it clean and in good playing condition. After playing, the inside of the neck and body should be swabbed dry with a soft cloth. A pull-through swab with a small weight should be used for the body, pulling the swab through the bell and out the top of the body. A small chamois neck swab should be used on the neck, being careful to use a swab that is sized for your instrument. Swabs with bristles should be avoided, as they may scratch the instrument.

The mouthpiece should be cleaned periodically with a 50/50 solution of vinegar and water and dried with a soft cloth. Be careful when cleaning the mouthpiece, as any scratches or dents will affect tone production.

Sticky pads can be cleaned with ungummed cigarette paper. Place the paper under a raised pad and press the key until the pad touches the tone hole; then gently pull the paper out. Repeat until the paper comes out clean. Avoid using pad powder or paper loaded with no-stick powder. The powder temporarily reduces sticking but will eventually build up on the pad.

Pads will eventually become worn and need replacing. Worn pads will feel dry or brittle, look dark brown or black in color, and may even split open. Pads that stay closed on the instrument when not being used are usually the first to wear out. A leak light will help determine if any pads are leaking air and should be reseated or replaced. Replace only those pads that will not hold their seal upon being reseated.

A saxophone overhaul involves replacing all pads, felts, corks, and springs that are worn or missing. An instrument that is played daily may require a complete overhaul every few years. An overhaul should be performed by an experienced woodwind repair specialist.

The exterior of the saxophone may be cleaned using a cotton swab and a soft cloth. Cotton swabs are effective at cleaning on and around tone holes and in other places a cloth will not reach. Use the cloth to clean large, open areas of the saxophone body.

To reduce wear and key noise, apply light key oil to places where brass rubs together, such as where rods meet posts that extend off the body. The plastic rollers on pinkie keys also require occasional oiling to prevent noise.

CHAPTER 23

Fundamentals of Saxophone Playing

Breathing

Breathing is often taken for granted by wind instrument musicians because it is such a natural function of the body. Playing the saxophone, or any wind instrument, involves using the muscles that affect breathing in a new way. A discussion of breathing and support is therefore an important part of saxophone pedagogy.

Learning to control the involuntary muscle known as the diaphragm is an important step toward proper breathing on a wind instrument. The diaphragm is a dome-shaped muscle located at the bottom of the chest cavity. It separates the lungs from the stomach and is attached to the ribs with muscle tissue. The diaphragm flattens out during inhalation and returns to its normal position as it relaxes and pushes air out of the lungs. This action is involuntary and takes place day in and day out. The muscles that attach the diaphragm to the ribs, however, are voluntary. We are therefore able to control these muscles and affect the shape of the diaphragm.

To gain a better understanding of how the ribs and diaphragm function, stand up straight and place your hands at the bottom of the rib cage. Your thumbs should be around toward the back, and the rest of the hand should be resting at the place where the ribs end and the stomach area begins. Slowly fill the lungs with air without lifting the shoulders and notice how the ribs and stomach area expand. Hold the expanded position briefly, then slowly let the air out. As the diaphragm resumes its normal, cupped shape, the ribs and stomach area collapse inward. This is considered normal breathing.

Proper wind instrument breathing involves supporting the air that is being released into the instrument. The only way we can achieve true physical support is to keep the diaphragm from resuming its normal position for as long as possible. By holding the ribs and stomach area out during exhalation, we can keep the diaphragm in a flattened shape and create a supported stream of air. We are thus using voluntary muscles to help control an involuntary one.

This method of breathing should first be learned away from the instrument. Practice holding the ribs out to the front and sides while slowly exhaling. Use the hands to feel the muscle action and stand in front of a mirror to see how long you are able to hold the ribs out. They will eventually collapse in, of course, but we want that to occur at the very end of the breath. Do this exercise several times each day to strengthen the rib muscles, which may become sore from being used in a new way. The saxophone may be added once you are able to hold the ribs out comfortably while exhaling.

Playing Position

The saxophone is suspended from the neck by a neck strap, although a saxophone stand is useful for supporting the baritone saxophone. The playing position depends largely on the size of the player and the instrument, but some guidelines are helpful.

The soprano saxophone is held in front, like a clarinet, but with the bell away from the body and the mouthpiece at approximately a forty-five-degree angle. A neck strap is helpful but not required to hold the soprano. The alto saxophone is held in front by most adults or children whose arms are long enough to reach the keys in this position. Smaller individuals may choose to rest the alto against the right side when seated. The tenor and baritone saxophones are best held to the right side.

Posture is important whether playing in a seated or standing position. The head should be held erect and not tilted to one side. The neck strap should be set high enough that the top teeth feel like they are being gently pushed up, thus eliminating any possibility of pressure on the lower lip or hands. The back should be straight yet relaxed and the feet spread slightly apart on the floor.

Figure 23.1 Seated posture

Neck strap comfort is important to the young and mature saxophonist alike. A variety of neck strap styles are available, some of which are quite good. The student should choose a neck strap that does not cut into the back of the neck or allow the saxophone to bounce around. A harness-style strap is popular with baritone saxophonists and individuals with back problems. Be sure the strap clips securely onto the instrument and will not slip out.

The hands should be held in a comfortable position with the wrists neither tilted nor bent. The left thumb will rest on the thumb pad next to the octave key and should be placed so it can operate the octave key with a simple rocking motion. The right thumb rest is located under the neck strap connector. The fingers of both hands should assume a gentle arch and remain relaxed. The young student should understand that the keys do not need much pressure to close and that the fingers should remain close to the keys. Good hand position is a prerequisite to developing solid fingering technique.

Embouchure

Unlike the other woodwind players, the modern saxophonist uses two kinds of embouchures: one for concert or "classical" style and one for jazz. It is best to learn the embouchure for playing classical style first and add the jazz embouchure later.

The "classical" embouchure should be controlled but not tight. The mouth should form a circle around the mouthpiece, allowing for equal pressure from all sides as if the lips were a wide rubber band. The embouchure should remain fairly still throughout the entire range, although some tightening of the muscles is often necessary for the extreme upper register. A correct embouchure will look very much the same as when the saxophonist does not have the mouthpiece in the mouth, allowing for any bite adjustment to line up the teeth.

To form the embouchure, roll the bottom lip in over the bottom teeth, place the top teeth approximately one-half inch from the tip of the mouthpiece, and seal the lips around the mouthpiece. The teeth must then be lined up to correct an overbite or underbite. This may require some prac-

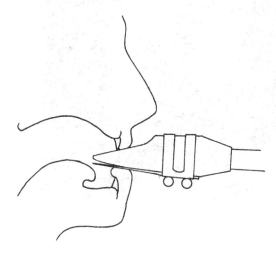

Figure 23.2. Alignment of teeth

tice, especially if the natural bite is fairly over or under. Advanced saxophone study will be difficult for anyone who experiences discomfort when lining up the teeth. When the teeth are aligned, check to make sure the neck strap is set high enough to eliminate any pressure on the bottom lip.

The throat position should be open and relaxed, as if saying the syllable "ahh." The mature saxophonist will use the throat and mouth for subtle pitch and tone color changes, but for now, an open throat will produce the best tone.

A thin rubber or plastic patch placed on top of the mouthpiece is often helpful when aligning the teeth. You may even wish to make an indentation on the patch at the half-inch mark to indicate where the top teeth should rest on the mouthpiece.

The embouchure used for jazz playing is much more flexible than the "classical" embouchure. Jazz players manipulate the jaw to affect tone and pitch and to produce accents. The jazz saxophonist also drops the lower jaw down and back to produce a breathy sound called "subtone."

Tonguing

Learning how to articulate properly is one of the most important first lessons for the saxophonist. Since the tongue is always used to start the saxophone tone, being able to initiate the tone with confidence and clarity is an essential element of saxophone tone production. The following instructions simplify saxophone tonguing and encourage early success.

First, assemble the instrument and put a soaked #2 or #2 ½ reed on the mouthpiece, placing the ligature completely on the bark of the reed. Hold the instrument in playing position with the mouthpiece close to the mouth. Take a quick breath, place the top teeth on the mouthpiece, and form an embouchure. Use the tongue to push the reed against the tip of the mouthpiece and hold the reed shut. Blow a steady and well-supported stream of air against the reed and take the tongue off the reed to produce a tone. Note that the steps mentioned above occur very quickly and should be practiced with speed as an eventual goal.

Simply stop blowing air when you wish the tone to stop. If you wish to rearticulate, touch the reed with the tongue while continuing to blow air. The air pressure should be steady and strong as when water remains pressurized with the tap turned off. (Be sure to avoid puffing the cheeks, although a slight stretch in the cheek muscles is fairly normal). Jazz saxophonists stop the tone with the tongue, whereas the classical style involves a subtle finish to the note that can only be achieved by stopping the airstream.

The first note we will learn is g^1, which is played by pressing the first, second, and third fingers of the left hand. The left thumb lies on the thumb rest below the octave key. The right hand thumb lies on the thumb rest below the neck strap clip, and the fingers of the right hand do not touch any keys. Once the hands are in place, the instrument may be adjusted so the embouchure may be formed around the mouthpiece.

The beginner's first tone may be rather loud and uncontrolled. It will not be long, however, until the student is able to produce a good tone at various dynamic levels. The main goal in the first lesson is to have the student understand how to hold the instrument, to be able to form an embouchure, and produce a tone that is initiated by the tongue. Once this has been achieved, the student is ready to practice starting and stopping the tone.

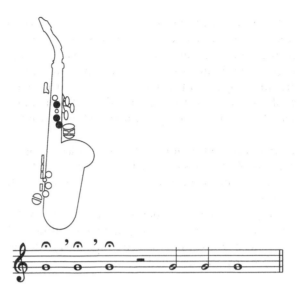

Example 23.1.

Tongue placement varies somewhat and depends on the size and shape of the mouth and teeth. Generally, the reed is touched just below its tip by the top side of the tongue. This point is usually very close to the tip of the tongue. The exact contact points are not important right now. Just be sure that the tongue is touching the reed to articulate the tone.

Remember that it is the process of removing the tongue from the reed that initiates the articulation. When the tongue is not articulating it remains very close to the reed. Some saxophonists, especially jazz players, keep the tip of the tongue behind the bottom teeth at the gum line, articulating farther back on the tongue. This method of articulation is known as "anchor tonguing," since the tip of the tongue remains anchored to the teeth. Anchor tonguing produces a more legato articulation and harder accents that are typically used in jazz. Individuals with a small mouth but large tongue tend to favor anchor tonguing over tonguing with the tip of the tongue. The anchor tongue method is easily employed after a few lessons, or when the student becomes interested in jazz.

Some common tonguing problems young students encounter are difficulty tonguing in the low or high register; a harsh attack that resembles a slapping sound or a squeak; and neglecting to use the tongue to start the tone, or using the tongue without actually touching the reed. Using a constant, properly supported airstream improves most tonguing challenges, but sometimes the following checklist needs to be reviewed:

- Be sure the reed is a #2 or 2 ½, soaked and in good condition.
- Make sure that the flat part of the reed is wet, that it is properly centered on the mouthpiece, and that the ligature is installed correctly.
- Some students use more air than is needed or hit the reed too hard and just need to be more gentle with the tongue.
- The jaw and lips should remain still during articulation.
- Review the tonguing instructions presented earlier in this section.

CHAPTER 24

Progressive Exercises

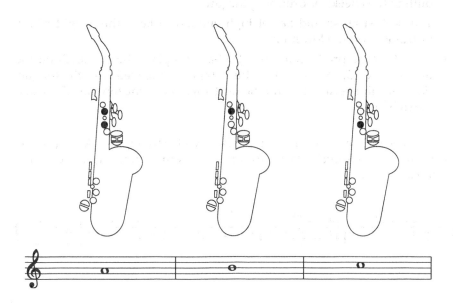

Example 24.1. New notes

Use the same fingerings with the addition of the octave key to play the upper register.

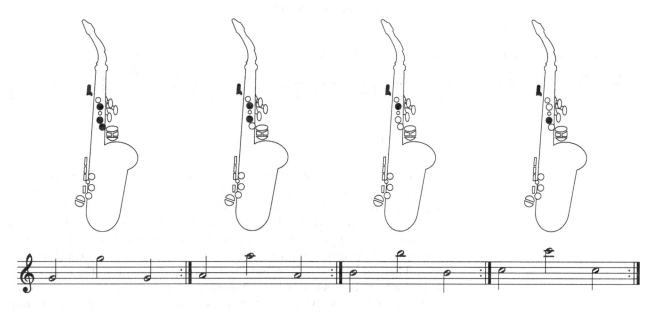

Example 24.2.

Reminders:

- The embouchure should remain still from the beginning to the end of each tone. Do not move the lips or jaw until the note is finished.
- The tongue should touch the reed lightly during articulation.
- Listen for intonation and tone quality, being especially sure to avoid puffing the cheeks or dropping the jaw.
- The neck strap should be set high enough to keep the weight of the instrument off the lower lip.
- Steps for tone production are (1) inhale, (2) place the top teeth on the mouthpiece, (3) set the embouchure, (4) close the reed with the tongue, (5) create air pressure behind the reed, (6) remove the tongue, (7) sustain a steady tone.

Practice the exercise in Example 24.3 while striving for clean, precise, yet soft (not explosive) attacks. Aim for a smooth, uninterrupted tone that is full and clear.

Example 24.3.

- Thinking "ooh" or "ahh" helps open the throat and produce a warm, resonant tone.
- Breathing in rhythm helps set the breath properly.
- Keep the top teeth on the mouthpiece and bottom lip on the reed when taking a breath. Relax the top lip and take a quick, deep breath.
- Imagine saying "tah" and "dah" while articulating to obtain both crisp and softer articulation styles.

Example 24.4.

At this point the following exercise may be used to determine if the embouchure is set properly: play the low a^1 and, using the thumb of the right hand to press the octave key, play the high a^2. If the a^2 does not sound, the embouchure is probably too loose. Push the corners of the lips in toward the mouthpiece and repeat the exercise. After the a^2 speaks, release the octave key and the a^1 should sound. There may be some extraneous sound between the a^2 and a^1, but the a^1 should come out. If the a^1 does not sound when the octave key is released, try loosening the corner muscles slightly. Finding the proper embouchure may take some experimentation, so keep working with this exercise until both a^1 and a^2 respond well with the action of the octave key.

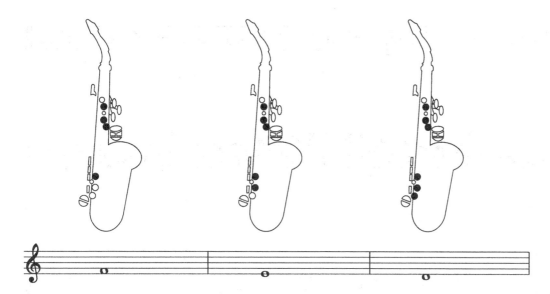

Example 24.5. New notes

Example 24.6.

- Note that the right hand fingerings are used only when the left hand fingers are pressed down.
- Do not play too loudly and avoid puffing the cheeks or dropping the jaw in the low register.
- Experiment with softer articulations such as "doo" or "dah" to help low-register notes speak without an explosive attack.

Example 24.7. New note

Example 24.8.

Example 24.9. C-major scale

Mary Had a Little Lamb

French Tune

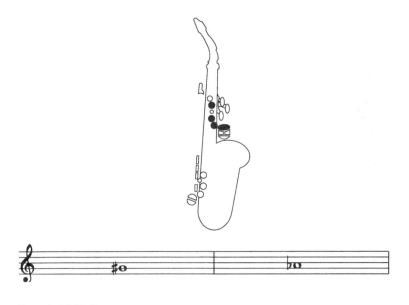

Example 24.10. New notes

Example 24.11.

Repeat each exercise until comfortable, feeling free to vary the articulations.

Exercise 24.1.

Exercise 24.2.

Exercise 24.3. A harmonic minor scale

Twinkle, Twinkle Little Star

The next note to be learned is a¹♯ or b♭¹. These notes are played using either the side B♭ key or the bis B♭. The side B♭ is located on the side of the instrument near the F key and is pressed using the index finger of the right hand. The side B♭ key is known as the first right side key. The tip of the finger needs to stay near the F key, so the side B♭ will be pressed using the area near the first bone joint of the finger. The bis B♭ key is the smaller button located between the B and A keys. Operate the bis B♭ by pressing both the B key and bis key with the index finger of the left hand. Bis b♭¹ should not be used when moving from or to b♮¹.

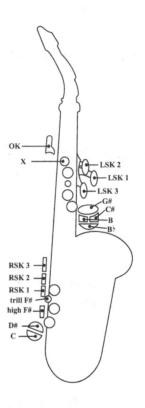

Figure 24.1. Fingering bis b♭¹

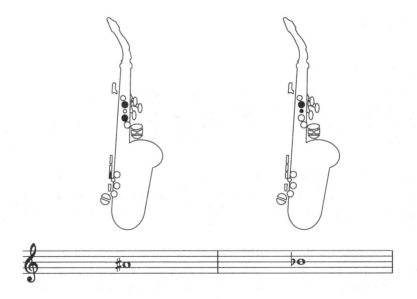

Example 24.12.

Example 24.13. F-major scale

Exercise 24.4.

The Scale Song

Deck the Halls

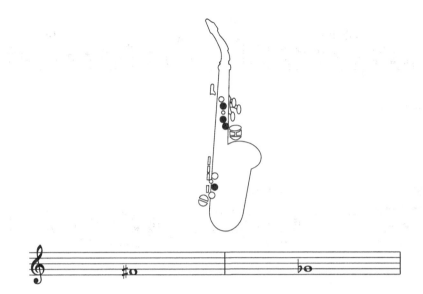

Example 24.14.

Example 24.15.

Work for a smooth tone and connection between notes in the following tune. Try to eliminate hard attacks and bumps in the musical line.

Korean Folk Song

Blue Bird

Tuning on the Saxophone

An important goal of musical training on the saxophone is to develop pitch accuracy when playing with other winds, a saxophone section, or keyboard instrument. One of the beneficial characteristics of the saxophone is its great flexibility to play many distinct pitches within a half-step span. With flexibility comes the challenge to hear and place notes in tune. Early training must involve work on intonation and pitch adjustment. This will avoid having to compensate for poor intonation later on.

Three basic rules apply to pitch flexibility on the saxophone:

1. Pitch is more easily lowered than raised.
2. Notes with longer tube lengths or closed keys have less flexibility.
3. The high register is more flexible than the low register.

As a result, lowering the overall pitch center by pulling out the mouthpiece will generally help the high register, which is often sharp, leaving the low register almost unaffected. This is important to remember when dealing with a sharp high register and flat low register, a common predicament with saxophonists.

A tuner or recently tuned piano may be used as a tool to help the saxophonist develop an awareness of pitch. The tuner should be the type that can sound pitches in addition to having a visual measurement device. Proper use of a tuner involves developing the ear rather than the eye.

The tuning exercises below are designed to help the saxophonist develop good intonation and are valuable when evaluating an instrument.

EXERCISE 1: HEARING FIFTHS

This exercise requires a tuner that automatically meters the pitch played. Begin by playing a low c^1, close your eyes, and slur to a perfect fifth above the C. When you think the g^1 is in tune, open your eyes and check the tuner meter. If it is in tune, play the g^1 and slur up to a d^2. Keep on going until you reach your top note. Repeat any intervals that are not in tune until the ear guides the throat to voice it correctly. Transpose the exercise to begin on other notes.

EXERCISE 2: HEARING "BEATLESS" INTONATION

This exercise requires either a tuner than can sound a pitch, an in-tune piano, or another saxophonist with good pitch. Play a major arpeggio while a sustained reference pitch is sounded, oftentimes the root of the arpeggio. Play slowly enough to allow time to eliminate any beats that are heard between the moving and reference pitches.

EXERCISE 3: MATCHING THE PIANO

Prepare a tape, using a tuner or piano, of any musical passages where you are having pitch problems. The reference tape may contain the melody pitches that you should match or a complete harmonic accompaniment. Either way, it is best if the tape is made under tempo so you have time to hear and make adjustments.

Use the following methods of adjustment, either one at a time or in combination:

1. Lip adjustment involves squeezing the muscles around the lips to form a "pucker" or relaxing the muscles for a looser seal. The slight pressure created by the pucker closes the reed and raises the pitch, whereas a relaxed embouchure lowers the pitch. Be careful to listen to the tone while using lip pressure or relaxation, and avoid using the jaw to correct pitch.

2. Changing the shape of the oral cavity will affect pitch in a more subtle fashion than the lip and will not affect the saxophone tone nearly as much as lip adjustment. An open throat position is created by imagining "ahh" and will lower the pitch. A closed throat and raised pitch will occur with the sound "ee." This technique is known as *voicing.*

3. Airspeed affects the pitch the least of the three methods. Faster air will raise the pitch slightly, and slower air will lower it. Be careful to listen for any undesired tone color changes when using airspeed to affect pitch.

4. When lip, throat, or airspeed is not successful at correcting a pitch, the advanced saxophonist may use fingering adjustments. These vary from instrument to instrument, and the number of options is too numerous for presentation here. For more detailed information on fingering adjustment, refer to *The Art of Saxophone Playing* by Larry Teal.

Exercise 24.5. Tuning practice

Lightly Row

C♯ is one of the most difficult notes on the saxophone because of tuning and tone considerations. Keep the throat open and relaxed to warm up the tone on all three C♯s. You will also need to lip up the pitch on c♯^{2} and bring the pitch of c♯^{3} down. Check these notes with a reliable pitch source to be sure how much adjustment is necessary. Note that adding the F, E, and D keys of the right hand will significantly lower the pitch of c♯^{3}.

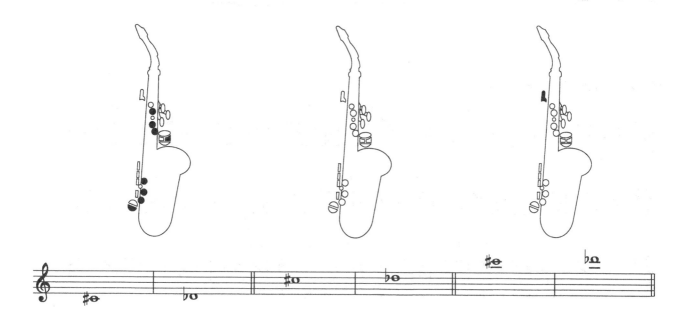

Example 24.16. New notes

Exercise. 24.6.

Johnny Has Gone for a Soldier

The tune in Exercise 24.7 should be played gently, with a supported tone and soft articulation. Avoid accenting any of the notes.

Exercise 24.7.

My Bonnie Lies Over the Ocean

Music Shall Live Alone

Example 24.17. New notes

Duet

The two-octave chromatic scale is next. Note the use of side or chromatic fingerings for A♯ or B♭, F♯ or G♭, and C in the chromatic scale.

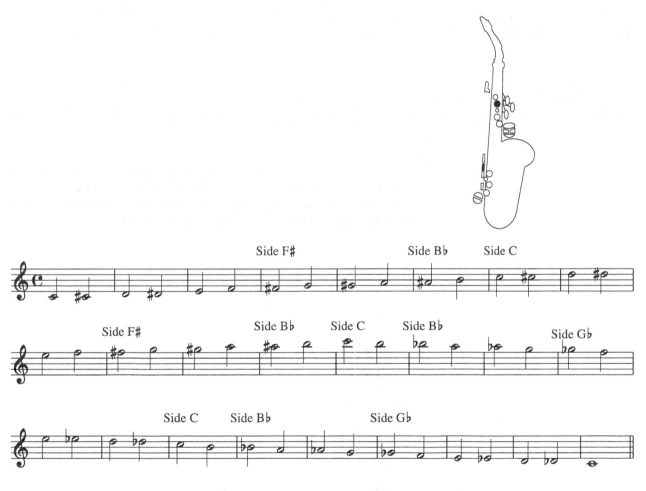

Example 24.18. Chromatic scale

Note that the bis B♭ fingering should not be used when moving from b♭¹ to b♮¹ (or vice versa).

Deck the Halls

Scarborough Fair

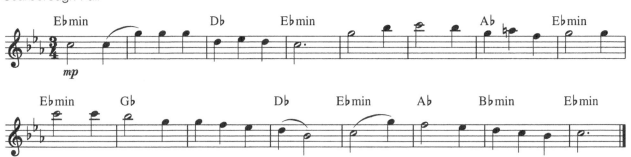

The next note to be learned is d³, which is played by pressing the left side key #1 open with the index finger of the left hand along with the octave key. The tip of the finger needs to remain close to the B key, so the D key will be pressed near the first bone joint of the finger.

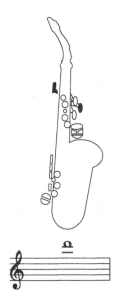

Example 24.19. New note

Exercise 24.8.

Simple Gifts

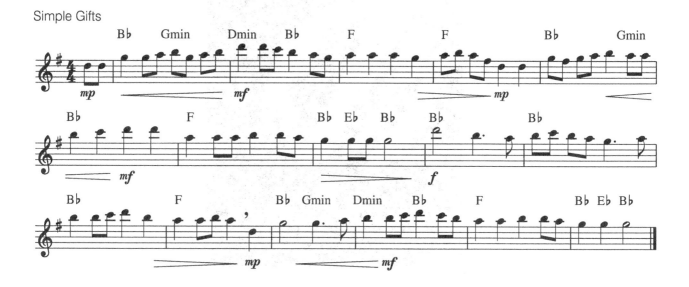

Duet

Whittaker

   The next notes to be learned are d♯³ (or e♭³) and e³. The D♯ or E♭ palm key is pressed, using the index finger of the left hand near the second bone joint. The D key will also need to be pressed, as when playing d³. The e³ is played by adding the top side key of the right hand to the d$\sharp^3$ fingering. The index finger of the right hand will need to shift position to reach the side key used to sound e^3.

Figure 24.2 Right-hand position to finger e^3

Command of the left-hand palm keys is accomplished by slow, repeated practice of these notes.

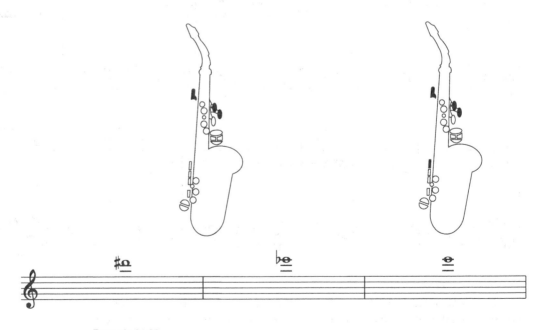

Example 24.20.

Exercise 24.9.

The next new note is f³, which is played as e³ with the addition of the third palm key. This key is pressed using the middle finger of the left hand. The fingering chart also shows the alternate f³ fingering, which is easier to use when moving from c³ to f³, as when playing an F major arpeggio. Some instruments will have a f♯³ key (located near the e¹ key), making possible the fingering for f♯³ (or g♭³) presented here.

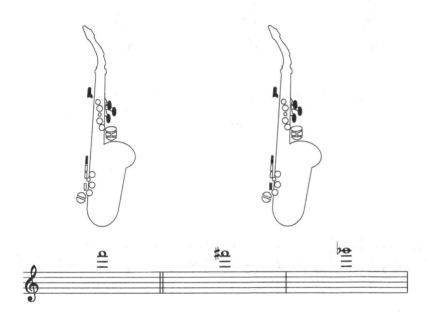

Example 24.21. New notes

Little Annie Rooney

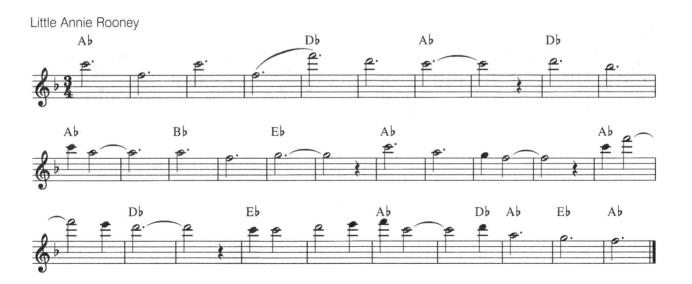

The low c♯¹, b♮, and b♭ require a strong little finger of the left hand. Practice Exercise 24.10 and the following duet until the left little finger feels strong and relaxed.

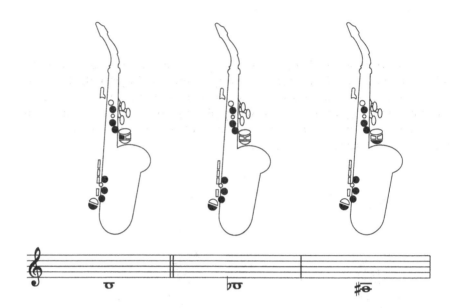

Example 24.22. New notes

Exercise 24.10.

Spring Has Come

Duet

CHAPTER 25

Additional Information

Guidelines for Choosing a Saxophone Student

The saxophone is a popular choice with beginning band students, and the instrumental teacher will probably have no difficulty finding students. The size of the student will determine at what age he or she may begin learning the saxophone, as a small person may not be able to reach all of the keys. Generally, a third or fourth grade student is capable of handling the instrument successfully.

The only other consideration when choosing which students should play saxophone is facial construction. An extreme overbite or underbite can make lining up the teeth uncomfortable or impossible. A student with either type of extreme bite should be encouraged to play an instrument other than saxophone, and should probably avoid the wind instruments.

Choosing a Saxophone

Because of the increasing cost associated with purchasing an instrument, the instrumental music teacher should become educated about the brands of saxophone that are available. It is advisable to purchase the highest-quality instrument one can, since better-quality saxophones play more in tune, have a superior tone, and stay adjusted longer than lesser-quality instruments.

The following makes of saxophone are well-known brands and are easily found in music stores throughout the United States.

Model

The Selmer Company
P. O. Box 310
Elkhart, IN 46515-0310
(219) 522-1675

Yamaha Band and Orchestral Instruments
3445 E. Paris Avenue S.E.
P.O. Box 899
Grand Rapids, MI 49512-0899
(616) 940-4900

Yanagisawa Woodwinds
G. Leblanc Corporation
7001 Leblanc Blvd.
Kenosha, WI 53141
1-(800) 558-9421

Buffet Crampon
1925 Enterprise Ct.
P. O. Box 130
Libertyville, IL 60048
(847) 816-2500

The Mouthpiece

The mouthpiece affects nearly every aspect of tone production and should be chosen with care. The saxophonist should try several different brands and sizes before making a purchase, and should buy only a mouthpiece that has been play-tested. This is not the kind of item that can be mail-ordered without being played. Young students may be able to use the mouthpiece supplied with the instrument, but it will be to their advantage to begin using a high-quality mouthpiece as soon as possible.

Hard rubber is the material of choice for alto saxophonists, while most tenor saxophonists will choose a hard rubber mouthpiece for classical and a metal mouthpiece for jazz playing. The choice of brand is somewhat dependent on the player, but most classical saxophonists tend to stay with well-known brands used by master performers and teachers.

The number placed on the mouthpiece indicates the size of the mouthpiece opening at the tip. A higher number indicates a larger opening. A number 5 is considered a medium opening, and a 10 is a very large opening. The Selmer Corporation manufactures popular mouthpieces that have letters instead of numbers to indicate size. A "C" is medium, a "D" is more open, and so on. A star (*) that follows the mouthpiece size indicates a longer facing, which will produce a louder tone because more reed vibrates. Thus a 7* mouthpiece will play more loudly than a 7. Some brands also include a chamber size indication, with "M" designating a medium chamber, "S" for small, and "L" for large. Larger chambers tend to help the saxophonist produce a darker tone.

The wide variety of brands, tip openings, facings, and chamber sizes that are available can overwhelm the student and teacher who has not had saxophone training. The only solution is to try several mouthpieces commonly used by professionals. Choose a mouthpiece that produces the desired tone and is comfortable to play.

Once a purchase has been made, you may wish to place a plastic or rubber patch on top of the mouthpiece. A patch holds the teeth in position and opens the mouth slightly, resulting in a larger oral cavity and warmer tone. A patch also reduces teeth vibration, an important consideration with young players whose teeth are still developing.

The Reed

As with the other reed instrumentalists, the saxophonist is at the mercy of the reed. Fortunately, several manufacturers produce good to excellent reeds that may be purchased at your music dealer. Some brands are manufactured for classical or "concert" use, some are manufactured for the jazz player, and others seem to be used by both classical and jazz saxophonists. Consult with your music dealer if you are unsure which are which, and do not be afraid to experiment with brands.

Reed sizes are commonly indicated by number, although some manufacturers assign "soft," "medium," and "hard" labels. The lower the number, the softer the reed and the easier it is to produce a tone. Most beginners start with a #2 reed and move up to a #2½ relatively quickly. Advanced students and professionals tend to use #3–3½, or medium-hard reeds. Reed strength choice varies from player to player, depending on the mouthpiece and facial characteristics. Contrary to popular belief, the ability to play stronger reeds is not an indication of advanced proficiency on the saxophone.

The reed can have a huge effect on the quality of the tone and ease of tone production. An old or overplayed reed will tend to produce a harsh, thin tone, and response in the low and high registers will suffer. A soft reed tends to play flat in pitch and produces an unfocused tone. A reed that is too hard will produce an airy, dull tone. The ideal reed is one that produces a full, vibrant tone with ease. Tone color is a matter of individual choice, but even dark-playing reeds can produce a sound that is alive with resonance.

Caring for the Reed

Most saxophonists are not interested in spending time adjusting reeds, as we have been spoiled by commercial reeds that play well right from the box. My experience has been that learning about the parts of the reed and where to scrape is interesting, but few saxophonists use that knowledge. For this reason, we will not discuss saxophone reed adjustment.

Saxophone reeds that work when new and receive proper care should provide weeks of service. A few guidelines will help with the crucial break-in period and with the life of the reed:

- During the break-in period of one week, limit the time playing a new reed to no more than five minutes each day. Hard tonguing and extreme low or high playing should be avoided.
- Polish the back (flat side) of the reed on a piece of paper before playing it.
- Soak the reed briefly in purified water, being sure the entire reed is wet.
- Allow the reed to air dry for a few minutes after playing it and then store it in a sealed container that allows light to reach the reed.

Following the above guidelines will help the reed remain flat and limit fiber damage due to the shock of rapid drying and rewetting.

Vibrato

Vibrato may be introduced once a student is able to produce a consistently focused tone that is clear, warm, and steady. Vibrato should be used to enhance a beautiful tone rather than to cover up an unfocused or out-of-tune sound.

Saxophone vibrato is produced using a slight chewing action of the jaw. The jaw transfers the change in pressure to the reed via the lips. The result is a slight variation in pitch, timbre, and volume. Begin practicing vibrato by pulsing at an even rate with a metronome. Start with three vibrato pulses per beat with the metronome set at 60. Play a descending F major scale in half notes, varying the number of pulses per beat and the tempo (see Exercise 25.1).

Work for a smooth vibrato that is not so wide as to affect the pitch by more than a few cents yet wide enough to be noticed from a distance. Variety of speed and width is eventually a desirable trait, but this takes time and practice. For now, work on a pleasant, regularly pulsed vibrato before moving on to changing the vibrato to suit the music.

One of the best ways to learn about the musical subtleties of vibrato is to listen to recordings of instrumentalists and vocalists. Pay attention to how and when vibrato is used and imitate the vibrato that you enjoy hearing.

VIBRATO EXERCISES

3 or 4 pulses per beat to start, then use up to 5 or 6 pulses per beat.

Exercise 25.1.

Play Exercise 25.1 several times each day until you are comfortable using anywhere from three to six pulses per beat. Be sure to use a supported tone and work for a smooth, continuous vibrato rather than a newly initiated vibrato on each note.

Exercise 25.2 helps with turning the vibrato on and off. Start with a nonvibrato tone, then rearticulate the note with vibrato. Do this on several notes, including low and high notes. Pay careful attention to the vibrato in the high register, as this can become too wide or overbearing.

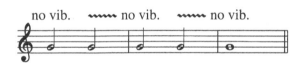

Exercise 25.2.

Exercise 25.3.

Exercise 25.3 involves playing the first five notes of a major scale. The first four notes are played without vibrato but with a crescendo that leads up to the last, which is played with vibrato. This exercise may be transposed to all keys and played in all registers. It is especially helpful for understanding how vibrato is used in a musical line. Once the vibrato becomes natural you may add it to longer note values in your music, as indicated in the tune below.

Nocturne   Mendelssohn

Saxophone Supplies

A partial list of sources for saxophone supplies and music is given below. Your local music store may also stock or be able to special-order the materials you need. It is a good idea to call each of the vendors to request a current catalogue.

Vendors

The Woodwind
19880 State Line Road
South Bend, IN 46637
(800) 348-5003

Weiner Music
216 E. Jericho Turnpike
Mineola, NY 11501
(800) 622-CORK

Dorn Publications
P.O. Box 206
Medfield, MA 02052
(800) 527-6647

Moore Music Company
615 W. Market Street
Greensboro, NC 27401
(336) 274-4636

The Saxophone Shop
2834 Central Street
Evanston, IL 60201
(708) 328-5711

Selected Methods and Materials

The following graded list gives the author, title, and publisher of each book.

EASY

NILO HOVEY. *Elementary Method for the Saxophone.* Rubank.

E. ROUSSEAU. *The Eugene Rousseau Saxophone Methods.* 2 vols. Kjos.

WEBER/COGGINS. *The Alto Saxophone Student.* Belwin.

MEDIUM

TEAL. *Daily Studies.* Etoile.

H. VOXMAN. *Selected Studies.* Rubank.

ADVANCED

MILHEL-FRANZ FERLING. *48 Famous Studies.* Southern.

BERBIGUIER/MULE. *18 Etudes.* Leduc.

WILLIAM SCHMIDT. *10 Contemporary Etudes.* Western.

The following list of solo works for saxophone contains pieces that are suitable for young saxophonists. The works are listed by composer/title/publisher.

EASY

WARREN BENSON. *Cantilena.* Boosey & Hawkes.

A. CORELLI (ARR. MULE). *Adagio.* Leduc.

A. GRETCHANINOFF. *Two Miniatures.* Leduc.

G. F. HANDEL (ARR. ROUSSEAU). *Adagio and Allegro.* Wingert-Jones.

G. F. HANDEL (ARR. MULE). *Largo.* Leduc.

J. IBERT. *Aria.* Leduc.

M. MOUSSORGSKY (ARR. GEE). *The Old Castle.* Marks.

C. A. WIRTH. *Dark Flows the River.* Studio PR.

MEDIUM

MARCEL BITSCH. *Villageoise.* Leduc.

EUGENE BOZZA. *Aria.* Leduc.

ARTHUR FRACKENPOHL. *Air for Alto.* Kendor.

PIERRE LANTIER. *Sicilienne.* Leduc.

H. PURCELL (ARR. S. RASCHER). *Two Bourrées.* Bourne.

W. G. STILL. *Romance.* Bourne.

M. WHITNEY. *Rhumba.* Bourne.

C. A. WIRTH. *Beyond These Hills.* Studio PR.

Selected and Representative Works

A. GLAZUNOV. CONCERTO FOR ALTO SAXOPHONE AND ORCHESTRA Alexander Glazunov (1865–1936) was one of Russia's great masters of counterpoint. He had composed a quartet for saxophones before writing the concerto, which was commissioned by Sigurd Rascher. This work bears a resemblance to his numerous works for stringed instruments and has been studied by advanced string students and saxophonists alike. It is one of only a few works for saxophone composed in a late Romantic style, making it ideal for performance contests. A through-composed concerto, it is not overly technical and is well suited for a mature high school student.

B. HEIDEN. SONATA FOR E♭ SAXOPHONE AND PIANO Bernhard Heiden (1910–) was born in Germany and emigrated to the United States in 1935. A student of Hindemith, his works exhibit colorful harmonic interest within neo-Classic structures. This three-movement work is a standard in the classical saxophone repertoire and is approachable by an advanced high school student. It is serious in nature and requires mature phrasing, rhythmic confidence, and strong endurance.

P. MAURICE. *TABLEAUX DE PROVENCE* FOR ALTO SAXOPHONE AND PIANO Paule Maurice (1910–67) composed this suite in five movements from images she recalled from her childhood years. This is a classic saxophone work in the French style. Each movement has its own character, with the inner three movements being rather short and not as technically challenging as the outer movements. Eugene Rousseau has recorded the inner movements as a set, and in this way they are approachable by a good high school student.

A. JOLIVET. *FANTASIE-IMPROMPTU* FOR ALTO SAXOPHONE AND PIANO André Jolivet (1905–74) employed polytonality and asymmetrical rhythms in his music, which is harmonically adventurous and spirited in nature. This slow-fast work explores dark and bright moods, with the fast section containing jazzy rhythms and effects that are fun to play. This short piece is playable by a mature high school student.

D. MILHAUD. *SCARAMOUCHE* SUITE FOR SAXOPHONE AND WIND QUINTET Darius Milhaud (1892–1974) employed Latin rhythms in many of his lighter works, and this suite is a prime example of exotic and jazzy syncopation. Originally scored for two pianos and used as theater music, Milhaud arranged the suite for wind quintet and saxophone, an instrument for which he enjoyed writing. Though technically challenging for all six instruments, it is playable by a very advanced high school student. It is also available for saxophone with piano accompaniment.

J. RUEFF. *CHANSON ET PASSEPIED* FOR ALTO SAXOPHONE AND PIANO This two-movement work was the first saxophone piece by the French composer Jeanine Rueff (b. 1922). The composer makes use of folklike melodies in the slow section and odd meter in the fast part. A delightful work, it is especially suited for an above-average high school saxophonist.

A. TCHEREPNIN. *SONATINE SPORTIVE* FOR ALTO SAXOPHONE AND PIANO Alexander Tcherepnin (1899–1976) used folk music, modes, and rhythmic polyphony in his instrumental works, which are neo-Romantic in style. The Sonatine is in three movements, each depicting a different sporting event. The music is exciting and not overly technical, making it a wonderful piece for an advanced high school student.

Troubleshooting Guide for the Saxophone

Problem	Possible Solutions
Low notes will not speak	The fingers are not pressing keys down all the way; student is not using enough air; student may be dropping jaw down or back; the G♯ adjustment not correct (likely if c♯^{1}, b♮, or b♭ are not speaking); check for leaking pads.
High notes will not speak	The student is not using enough air; the throat is too open—try singing the desired pitch first, or match another saxophonist playing the pitch; tuck the corners of the mouth in toward the mouthpiece; the student may be taking too much mouthpiece.
Fuzzy tone	The student needs a new or better reed; student may be dropping jaw down or back from the reed, creating a "subtone."
Flat in low register	The student is probably dropping the jaw away from the reed.
Unstable d^2–g♯^{2}	Check to make sure the top octave key (on the neck) is not opening by accident—for these notes, only the lower octave key should open (located on the body). Bend the top octave bar to fix. Student may also be taking too much mouthpiece or dropping the jaw.
Difficult downward slurs	Use enough supported air; have the student learn to voice the notes by singing the interval first; the throat should be more open for the lower note (think "ahh"); lightly tongue the lower note a few times, then slur; fingers may not be landing precisely.
Squeaking or squalling	The student may be accidentally bumping a side key—arch the fingers more; make sure the ligature is in good shape and tightened; try another reed.

Sharp in high register	The student is applying too much pressure on the reed—be sure the neck strap is set high enough to take pressure off the bottom lip and that equal pressure is applied by the muscles from around the entire mouthpiece.
Thin, bright tone	Try a harder reed; make sure the student is taking enough mouthpiece.
Noisy or unclear tone	Try another reed; wash the mouthpiece and swab the neck; check the mouthpiece for chips; make sure the ligature is working properly; clear saliva from the reed and mouthpiece.

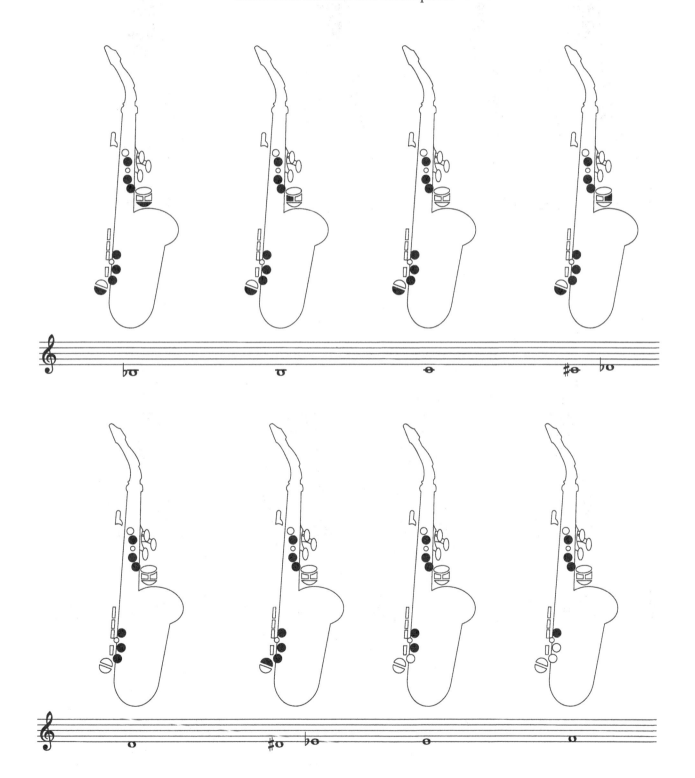

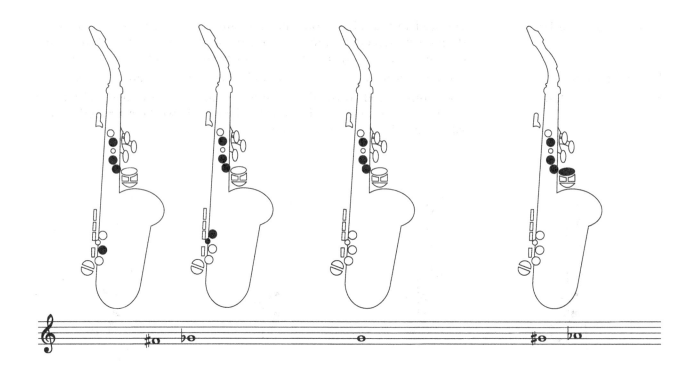

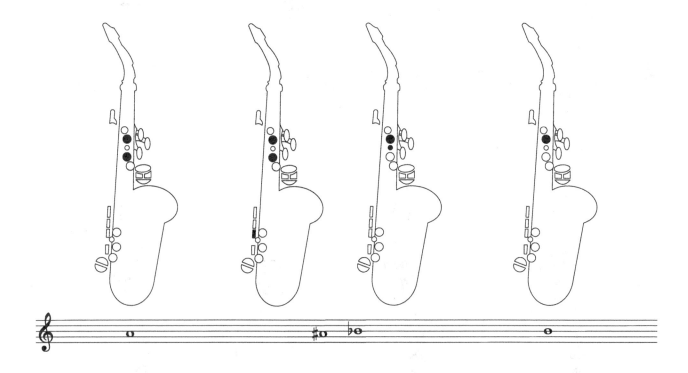

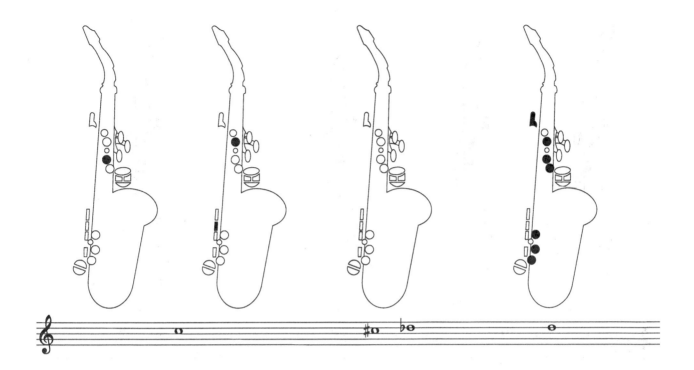

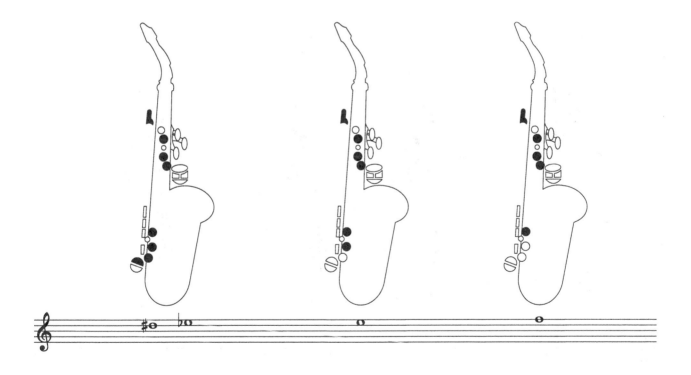

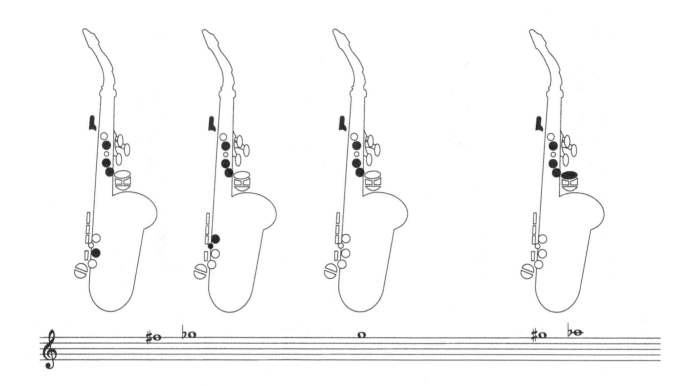

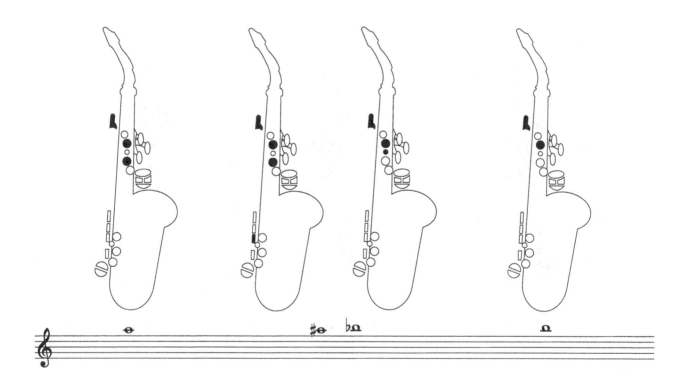

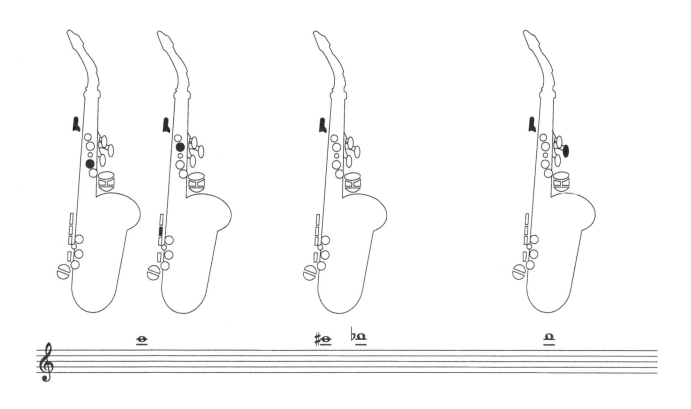

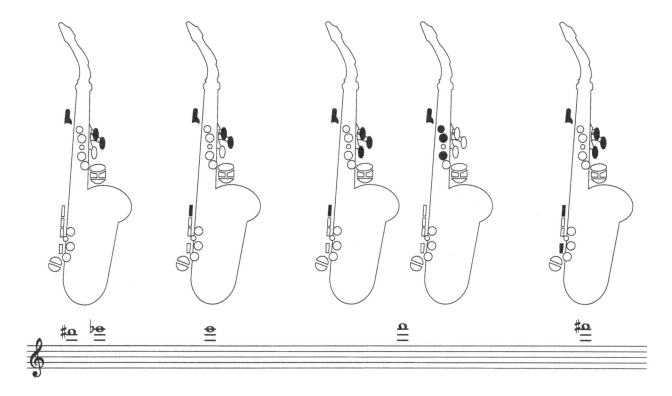

Index

Bassoon

Abdominal muscles, 12
Air pressure, 18
Air velocity, 33, 52
Almenrader, Carl, 5
Aperture, 73
Articulation, 18
Assembly, 7

Balance, 24
Bass joint, 7, 9
Bass pommer, 4, 5
Bassoon length, 3
Bassoon parts, 3
Bassoon range, 3
Bassoon Reed Making, 69
Bell, 7, 9
Bocal, 7, 10, 32, 68
Boot, 7, 8
Breathing, 12
Buffet, 6

Chamber music, 75
Characteristic vibrato, 20
Choosing a bassoon, 67
Choosing a bassoon student, 65
Conical bore, 4
Contrabassoon, 7
Cooper, Lewis Hugh, 28
Cracking notes, 43

Daily care, 10
Dexterity, 62
Diaphragm, 12
Diaphragm vibrato, 20
Dulcian, 4, 5

Ebonite, 3
Embouchure, 13
Essentials of Bassoon Technique, 28
Exercises for vibrato, 21
Exhalation, 12, 13
Extreme ranges, 61–64

Favoring pitches, 33
Fingerings, 81
Flicker keys, 53

Flicking, 47, 51–55
French bassoon, 6

Glickman, Loren, 69
Glickman-Popkin Bassoon Camp, 81

Half hole, 25, 40, 41, 42, 43, 44
Hand postions, 21, 25
Hand rest, 24, 25, 26
Hard cushion, 13
Heckel, J. A., 5
Heckel, William, 4, 5
Heckel system, 6

Index finger (left hand), 25, 40, 41, 42, 49
Inhalation, 12, 13
Internal tuning, 32, 33
International Double Reed Society, 81

Jaw, 14, 33

Knife, 69

Langwill, Lyndesay, 4
Left-hand finger spread, 28
Lips, 14, 33
Long-term maintenance, 11
Lungs, 12, 18

Mandrel, 69, 70
Methods/Study material, 74
Metronome, 21
Middle register, 52
Milde, Ludwig, 74

Neck strap, 21, 24, 26
Nye's clock oil, 11

Oropharyngeal cavity, 14, 33

Pancake key, 7
Parts of the reed, 70
Posture, 21–24
Pitch level tuning, 32

381

Plaque, 69, 70
Pliers, 69, 70
Popkin, Mark, 69
Practicing vibrato, 20
Preparatory octave, 27

Reamer, 69, 70
Recorder for learning vibrato, 21
Reeds, 70, 71, 72 , 73
Representative works, 79, 80
Resonance key, 42

Sandpaper, 70
Seat strap, 21, 22, 26
Secondary break, 49
Setup, 32
Shawm, 4
Soft cushion, 13
Supplies, 73
Support, 12

Tenor clef, 63, 74
Tenor joint, 7, 8
Tone, 19
Tongue, 14, 17, 18
Tongue placement, 15
Tonguing, 14–19
Tonguing errors, 16, 17
Toplansky, Howard, 28
Tuning, 32

U-tube, 4, 6
Upper register, 47

Vibrato, 19
Vibrato production, 19, 20

Weait, Christopher, 69
Weissenborn, Julius, 74
Whisper key, 42, 49
Wind quintet, 77

Clarinet

Abdominal muscles, 105
Air support, 131
Albert of Brussels, 93, 94
Altissimo register, 110, 131, 141–42
Anchor tonguing, 108
Arundo donax, 143

Baermann, Heinrich, 93
Barrel, 95, 140
Boehm system, 93
Breaks, 123–24, 132
Breathing, 105–06
Buffet, Louis, 93

Chalumeau register, 92, 110–11,
    116–17, 119
Chromatic fingerings, 119, 127, 136–38
Clarion, 110, 123–125
Condensation, 97
Cork grease, 94, 97

Denner, Johann Christian, 91, 92
Diaphragm, 105, 107
Double lip, 99

Eichner, Ernst, 92
Embouchure, 99, 100, 103, 106, 123–24,
    131, 140–41, 144
Etudes, 148–49

Finger coordination, 131, 144
Finger position, 101–04, 122
Fingerings, 153–56

Fux, Georg, 92

Hand position, 101–02
Hermstedt, Johann Simon, 93

Intonation, 131, 139, 140–42, 146

Klosé, 93, 148, 149

Lefevre, Jean Xavier, 93
Ligature, 96–97
Lone tone exercise, 106
Lotz, T., 93

Maintenance, 97–98
Methods, 148–49
Molter, Johann Melchior, 92
Mouthpiece, 92, 94–97, 99–100, 103,
    107, 124–25, 140, 144, 148
Müller, Iwan, 93, 94

Neck strap, 103

Oehler, Oskar, 94, 95

Posture, 100

Reed, 96–97
Reed strength, 143
Registers
    Altissimo, 110, 131, 141–42
    Chalumeau, 110–11, 116–17, 119
    Clarion, 110, 123–25

Throat tones, 110, 122
Repertoire, 149–52
Rubank, 149

Single lip, 99
Sliding, 136
Staccato, 107–09
Stadler, Anton, 93

Stamitz, Karl, 92
Swab, 97

Throat tones. *See* Registers
Tongue placement, 107–08
Tonguing, 106–09

Weight compensation, 103–05

Flute

Abdomen, 166, 167
Acoustical design, 182
Air, 167, 168, 170, 172
Air capacity, 176
Air column, 171, 178
Air pressure, 171
Air releases, 173
Air volume, 177
Airflow, 167, 169, 172
Airspeed, 169, 170
Airstream, 169, 170, 172, 173, 177, 178
Airy sound, 170
Alignment, 170
Alternate fingerings, 183
Alto flute, 180
Alveolar ridge, 171, 172
Amber, 159
Angle of the airstream, 169
Aperture, 167, 169, 170, 172
Aperture size, 169
Appreciation of value, 183
Arms, 176
Arpeggios, 167
Articulation, 171
Assembly and alignment, 161, 162
Attack, 171

Bach, 159
Balance points, 173, 174, 175
Bands, 169, 177
Baroque flute, 160
Barrel, 161, 162
Bass flute, 180
Bathing the head joint, 165
Beginners, 169
Body, 162, 163, 176, 183
Boehm, Theobald, 160, 182
Boehm's 1832 model, 160, 161
Boehm's 1847 model, 161
Brass, 161
Breath attack, 172
Breath staccato, 172
Breath support, 172
Breathing, 166, 167, 176
    abdomen, 166

chest cavity, 166
diaphragmatic muscles, 166
gasping, 166
intercostal muscles, 166
lips, 166
lungs, 166
throat, 166
Breaths, 179
Bronze springs, 182

C key, 160
C♯ key, 160
C♯ trill key, 182
Carbon fiber, 159
Care and maintenance, 163
Carpal tunnel syndrome, 173
Case, 161, 165
Cellophane tape, 164
Chest, 167
Chest cavity, 166
Chin, 174, 175, 176
Classical flute, 160
Cleaning rod, 163, 164, 165
Collar bone, 167
Color, 178
Concial body, 159
Condensation, 165
Construction material
    amber, 159
    brass, 161
    carbon fiber, 159
    gold, 159
    ivory, 159
    nickel, 159
    plastics, 159
    platinum, 159
    porcelain, 159
    silver, 159, 161
Cork grease, 161
Cork stopper, 164
Crochet hook, 164
Cross fingerings, 159
Crown, 164
Cupid's bow, 169
Curved head joint, 182

Cylindrical body, 159
Cylindrical bore, 161

D♯ rollers, 182
Denatured alcohol, 164
Depreciation of value, 183
Diaphragm, 172, 178, 179
Diaphragmatic muscle, 166
Disassembling, 161
Double tonguing, 172
Drawn tone holes, 182
Drawn tube, 161
Dynamics, 170
Dynamics and intonation, 177

Elbows, 176
Electronic tuning machines, 177
Embouchure, 167, 168, 169, 177
Embouchure-high register, 168
Embouchure-low register, 168
Embouchure-side blown, 169
Embouchure hole, 183
Embouchure plate, 183
Exhalation, 167

Faulty intonation, 178
Felts, 164
Fife, 159
Finger motion, 173
Finger pressure, 163
Fingerings, 182, 183
Fingernail polish, 164
Fingerprints, 163
Fingers, 175, 176
Flute manufacturers, 183
Flute resources, 235–40
Flutter tonguing, 173
Foot joint, 162, 163
Foot joint rod, 162
French model, 159, 182
Fundamentals of flute playing, 166

Gasping, 166
Glue, 164
Gold, 159
Gold springs, 182

Hand position, 173, 175, 182
Handel, 159
Head, 176
Head joint, 162, 163, 167, 169, 170,
    171
Head joint cork, 183
Head joint placement, 177
Head tilt, 176
Health problems, 173
Hiss, 170

History,
    Bach, 159
    conical body, 159
    cross fingerings, 159
    fife, 159
    Handel, 159
    Rameau, 159
    Renaissance flute, 159
    thirteenth-century flute, 159
    transverse flute, 159
Holding position, 169, 173

Industrial revolution, 160
Inner surface of lips, 167, 168
Intercostal muscles, 166
Intonation, 170, 178, 182
Intonation tendencies, 178
Ivory, 159

Jaw, 172, 177
Joints, 183

Key action, 182
Key clicks, 183
Key height, 183
Key noise, 183
Keys, 161

Legato articulation, 172
Lip aperture, 170
Lip formation, 169
Lip plate, 161, 167, 168, 169, 175
Lip tube, 168
Lips, 166, 167, 169, 170, 172, 173, 176,
    177
Literature and methods, 223–36
Little finger, 162
London, 160
Long tones, 167
Lubricants, 161

Members of the flute family, 180
Membranes, 168
Metronome, 179
Metal polish, 163
Mirror, 167, 169
Modeling, 169
Modified embouchure hole, 182
Moisture, 163
Movement when playing, 176
Muffled tone, 170
Munich, 160
Musical line, 178

Nasal tone, 170
Nickel, 159
Nicholson, Charles, 160

Offset G key, 182
Oiling the flute, 164
Open-hole flutes, 182
Opera singer, 167
Options, 182
Orchestras, 178
Ornament, 178
Overhaul, 164
Overinflation, 167
Overtone series, 178

Pad condition, 182
Padded covers, 161
Paint brush, 164
Palate, 171
Parabolic head joint, 159, 161
Performance examples, 194
Performance levels, 222–23
Phosphor springs, 182
Piccolo, 180, 181
Pipe cleaner, 164
Pitch, 178
Pivot screws, 164
Plastics, 159
Plateau model, 159
Platinum, 159
Pointed key arms, 182
Porcelain, 159
Position and balance, 173
Posts, 164
Posture, 167, 169, 176, 177
Pout formation, 167
Properly aligned flute, 162
Pulsations, 180

Rameau, 159
Range, 170
Register changes, 168
Renaissance flute, 159, 160
Repair, 164, 182, 183
Repertoire, 180
Resonance, 182
Response, 182
Ribbed construction, 182
Right-hand position, 162
Rockstrow thumb postion, 175
Rods, 161, 164
Romantic flute, 160
Rubber bands, 164

Scales, 167, 182
Screwdrivers, 164
Seated position, 176, 177
Selecting an instrument, 182
Seven-keyed flute, 160
Shallow tone, 170
Shoulders, 167, 176

Silver, 159, 161
Silver head joint/tubing, 182
Sluggish keys, 183
Smiling muscles, 168
Sockets, 161
Soldered tone holes, 182
Sound, 178
Special effect, 182
Split E key, 182
Spread tone, 170
Spring tension, 173
Springs, 164, 182
Staccato articulation, 172
Stainless steel springs, 182
Standing position, 176, 177
Stiffness, 177
Strike edge, 168, 170
Strike wall, 170
Student model flutes, 162
Support, 178
Swabbing, 163
Swabs, 165
Syllables used for tonguing,
    172

Taper releases, 173
Tarnish, 163, 164
Technical efficiency, 163
Teeth, 167, 171, 172
Tendinitis, 173
Tenons, 161
Tension, 17
Thin tone, 170
Thirteenth-century flute, 159
Throat, 166, 172, 173, 178, 179
Throat tension, 178
Thumbs, 173, 174, 175
Tip of the thumb, 173
Tonal color changes, 168
Tonal consistency, 182
Tone, 167, 170, 178, 179, 180
Tone control variable, 169
Tone-holes tenons, 183
Tone production, 169, 170
Tone studies, 177
Tongue, 171, 172
Tongue anchoring, 172
Tongue placement, 172
Tongue strokes, 172
Tonguing, 167, 171, 173, 180
Tools for repair, 164
Transverse flute, 159
Trills, 183
Triple tonguing, 173
Tubing, 161
Tubing thickness, 182
Tuning, 177

Unfocused tone, 170

Vocal chord noises, 167
Vibrato, 167, 178, 179
Vibrato exercises, 179, 180

Vibrato problems, 180
Vibrato speeds, 179

Wind noise, 170
Wrists, 174

Oboe

Adjustment
    primary key, 246–47
    reeds, 300–10
    screws, 246–48
    secondary keys, 246–47
Alternate fingerings
    forked F, 281–83
    left E♭, 284–85
    left F, 281–83
    right A♭, 284–85
Articulation, 269–70
Assembly, 244–45

Baroque oboe, 244
Books
    methods, 315–17
    Reed Making, 317–18
    reference, 317–18
breathing, 259–65
    double action, 261–62
Brod, 243–44

Care and maintenance, 246–48, 321–22
Chamber music, 314–15
Charts, 287–99, 304–05
Concepts in playing
    advanced, 324–25
    elementary, 322–23
    intermediate, 323–24
Conservatoire Systeme Six, 244

Embouchure, 266–69
English horn, 244

Ferlendis, 244
Fingerings
    alternate, 281–85
    charts, 287–99
    half-hole, 271–75
    octave keys, 276–80, 290–92, 296–99
    pivoting, 281
    third octave, 290–92
    trills, 293–99

Gullickson, 260

Half hole, 271–75
Hotteterre, 244

Left E♭, 284–85
Left F, 281–83
Light, J., 268–70
Loree, 244

Mack, J., 260
Maintenance
    oboe, 246–48, 321–22
    reed, 245–46, 305–06
Method books, 315–17

Niblock, 284, 317

Oboe d'amore, 244
Octave keys, 276–80, 289–92,
    296–99

Philador, 243
Pivoting, 281
Posture
    body, 250–57
    hand, 248–50
    resting, 251
    sitting, 255–57
    standing, 252–54
Primary keys, 246–47

Range, 276, 322–24
Reeds
    care, 245–46
    crowing, 300, 304–05
    making, 300–10
    suppliers, 306–10
    tools, 304
    troubleshooting, 304–05
    tuning, 286
Reference, 317–18
Repertory, 311–14, 326–38

Screws, 246–48
Secondary keys, 246–247
Shawm, 243

Still, R., 260
Swabs, 246

Triebert, 243–44
Trills, 293–99

Troubleshooting, 304–05
Tuning, 285–87

Zurna, 243

Saxophone

Alto saxophone, 341, 345
Anchor tongue, 348
Assembly, 342

Baritone saxophone, 341, 345
Bass saxophone, 341, 342
Breathing, 344

Chromatic fingerings, 361
Cork grease, 342

Diaphragm, 344

Embouchure, 346

Hand position, 346
Heiden, B., 373

Glazunov, A., 373

Intonation, 358

Jazz, 346, 347, 369
Jolivet, A., 374

Key noise, 343

Ligature, 343
Lungs, 344

Maintenance, 343
Maurice, P., 373
Milhaud, D., 374
Mouthpiece, 342, 347, 350, 369, 374, 375

Neck, 342
Neck strap, 345, 346, 350

Pads, 343
Pitch flexibility, 357
Position, 345
Posture, 345

Ranges, 341
Reed care, 370
Reeds, 348, 369
Rueff, J., 374

Sax, Adolphe, 341
Saxophone family, 341
Soprano saxophone, 341, 345
Sopranino saxophone, 342
Stop-tonguing, 348
Subtone, 347
Swab, 343

Tcherpnin, A., 374
Teal, Larry, 358
Tenor saxophone, 341, 345
Throat position, 347
Tone, 350, 370
Tonguing, 347, 348
Troubleshooting, 374
Tuner, use of, 357, 358
Tuning, 357

Vibrato, 370
Voicing, 358, 374